ANXIETY

Psychological Perspectives
on Panic and Agoraphobia

ANXIETY

Psychological Perspectives on Panic and Agoraphobia

Richard S. Hallam

Department of Audiology, Royal National Throat, Nose and Ear Hospital
and
Institute of Laryngology and Otology, University of London
London, England

With a foreword by Theodore R. Sarbin

1985

ACADEMIC PRESS

(Harcourt Brace Jovanovich, Publishers)

London   Orlando   San Diego   New York
Toronto   Montreal   Sydney   Tokyo

ACADEMIC PRESS INC. (LONDON) LTD.
24–28 Oval Road
LONDON NW1 7DX

United States Edition published by
ACADEMIC PRESS, INC.
Orlando, Florida 32887

British Library Cataloguing in Publication Data

Hallam, Richard S.
    Anxiety : psychological perspectives on
    panic and agoraphobia.
    1. Anxiety----Physiological aspects
    I. Title
    616.85'22307   RC531

ISBN 0-12-319620-5

Library of Congress Cataloging in Publication Data

Hallam, Richard S.
    Anxiety, psychological perspectives on panic and
agoraphobia.

    Bibliography: p.
    Includes index.
    1. Anxiety. 2. Panic. 3. Mental illness--Diagnosis.
4. Agoraphobia. I. Title.
RC531.H26 1985   616.85'22   84-18613
ISBN 0-12-319620-5 (alk. paper)

Contents

5. Panic-Anxiety and Somatic Complaints

6. Panic-Anxiety and Alcohol Dependence

7. Depersonalisation

PART II   PSYCHOLOGICAL THEORY AND PANIC-ANXIETY

8. Introduction to Part II

9. Rational Approaches: Appraisal, Verbal Mediation, Labelling and Attribution

10. Learning Models and Central Mechanisms

Foreword

This book is a welcome addition to a growing literature that treats perplexing and sometimes disabling conduct from a psychological rather than a biomedical perspective. It is one of an increasing number of treatises that boldly assume that psychological events may be studied in their own right without reducing the phenomena to biological or mentalistic categories. Among other topics, Hallam critically reviews the clinical and experimental work on self-reported anxiety, panic and agoraphobia. He demonstrates with considerable force the disutility of the traditional practice of assigning such phenomena to a world of disordered minds.

Anxiety has been employed as a key concept in many psychoanalytic and psychological theories. Before its use as a theoretical construct, anxiety was a lay construct, a metaphor invented to communicate about vaguely perceived and poorly understood sensory experience. This lay construct, or metaphor, was metonymically transformed by certain theorists seeking a universal intervening variable to account for puzzling conduct. That is to say, the theorists transfigured anxiety to a *cause* from its original use as a metaphor for *effects* of interpersonal actions and physiological responses. As a staple of biomedical research and practice, anxiety is a reified metaphor. One of the results of the uncritical use of the reified metaphor was the creation of such unproductive diagnostic categories as anxiety neurosis, anxiety hysteria and anxiety state. Hallam's review of research and practice makes abundantly clear that this metaphor-to-myth transformation has little utility, either as a heuristic for research or as a model for therapy.

Many lessons are to be learned from this book, not the least of which

ix

is the demonstration that the lay construct, anxiety, is multireferential. When a clinician asks a client for referents for such complaints as, 'I am anxious' (or 'panicky' or 'agoraphobic'), the client's response is drawn from a limitless pool of vague and ambiguous descriptors. Examples of the interpretations offered by clients include such diverse referents as 'I had the feeling I was about to die', 'I was suffocating, gasping for air', 'My legs became rubbery', 'I was about to faint', 'My brain was racing ahead of my thought', and so on.

From Hallam's detailed analysis of the multireferential nature of anxiety complaints, one could formulate the following rule for praxis: When a client employs 'anxiety' or a similar descriptor in his or her self-report, regard it as metaphoric utterance, not as a statement that demands causal analysis. The metaphoric utterance, that is, the complaint, is a social construction whose building blocks include the client's beliefs, linguistic skills, purposes and concurrent existential or identity problems.

Another lesson to be learned from this book is the continuity of anxiety complaints as reported in clinical settings with those of persons who do not come to the attention of professional helpers. Such continuity is an argument against the identification of anxiety complaints as a psychiatric disorder. For example, the fear of strange places may be universal and not restricted to a clinical population if the definition of strange places is broad enough.

The author holds that the client, like the rest of us, constructs his or her world from perceptions, beliefs, imaginings and rememberings. Thus anxiety is a construction, and it is communicated to others (and to the self) with the aid of metaphoric and metonymic translations. This constructivist view is fast displacing the entrenched biomedical view that treats human beings as passive reactors to stimuli according to still-to-be discovered mechanistic laws. Metaphors drawn from physics, geology and technology, so tightly woven into the texture of the mechanistic world view, have lost the power to stimulate meaningful research and theory about the complexities of human action. As a result, social scientists are turning to humanistic disciplines for their working metaphors, among them, game playing, narrative, drama and rhetoric.

The use of such descriptive metaphors reflects a world view that is in sharp contrast to the mechanistic world view that has dominated scientific thought, including that of psychology and psychiatry, for so long. Contextualism is the name assigned to this alternative world view, and its root metaphor is the historical act. Among other things, this root metaphor entails that the actors who participate in the creation of historical acts are agents. They engage in intentional actions not only to solve problems of a practical nature, but also to maintain or enhance their identities. Toward this end, they construct their worlds. Some constructions provide the backdrop for personal drama, one outcome of which may be the self-report of anxiety. Another element of the contextualist metaphysic is that change and novelty, rather than invariance, are to be expected.

Hallam's critical review of the scientific literature on anxiety and emotion supports the conclusion that the failure of modern science to formulate a general theory of anxiety is traceable to the slavish (and often unrecognized) adherence to the biomedical model. The users of this model seek causality within the organism, either in the somatic networks or in the assumed mind-space. It is not an inappropriate strategy, given their stance that the objects of their attention are regarded as passive, not as active agents. The supporters of the biomedical model have failed to achieve a consistently workable theory as a basis for therapy because human beings are, in fact, agents. Thus, a clinician who reads this book and elects to apply its wisdom would not address a person's complaint of anxiety with the question, What is the cause of the anxiety? but rather with questions of this sort: What are the antecedent and concurrent interpersonal conditions that influence a person as agent to turn his or her attention to vaguely defined internal events, to choose the sick role or to describe perplexing happenings with particular metaphors or metonymies? What are his or her concerns about death and dying, being abandoned or loss of face? What are the person's power relations and how does the sick role influence his or her relative power? How does the person's self-narrative fit into the self-narratives of significant others?

In my own experience, I have found it useful to look upon complaints of anxiety as a form of attention deployment, not unlike the attention deployment of the classical hypochondriac. The broad focus on bodily symptoms, besides providing the basis for adopting the sick role, effectively supports efforts in the context of significant social relationships not to spell out certain imagined or perceived flaws in one's character. The question that guides the search for understanding is, What are the client's reasons for turning attention to complaints of anxiety? In this respect, the clinician might entertain the hypothesis of self-deception and its implications for discovering and formulating reasons for the client's attention deployment to events described as anxiety.

The foregoing remarks are but a sample of the clinical and theoretical notions generated in my reading of Hallam's treatise. A bountiful harvest of insights awaits both the practicing clinician and the laboratory scientist engaged in solving the mystery of anxiety. The rich yield is due in no small measure to the author's ability simultaneously to reflect his experience as clinician and as scientist. As clinician–scientist, he illuminates many puzzling observations and opens the way for a better understanding of human problems.

THEODORE R. SARBIN
UNIVERSITY OF CALIFORNIA

Preface

This book has two main objectives. The first is to describe a dimension of psychological distress I have called panic-anxiety. This takes up the first part of the book, which surveys literature that is primarily descriptive and psychiatric. The second objective is pursued in the second part of the book, in which I examine a large number of theories of anxiety to see what they might have to offer in explaining the panic-anxiety cluster of complaints. I am therefore concerned to apply psychological theory to a real-world problem, that is, to what people who seek professional help loosely describe as panic, anxiety and fears of public situations.

The theoretical and experimental literature on anxiety is so vast that I have had to be disciplined and in no small measure prejudiced in favour of a particular theoretical perspective. I have attempted as far as possible to treat anxiety as a *lay construct*, that is, as a social construction and not a scientific concept. For this reason, I have endeavoured to refer to *reports* of anxiety or to *complaints* of anxiety in order to avoid the common tendency to reify anxiety as an entity which exists independently of the social origins of the term. Accordingly, I believe that the relevant question to ask is not, What is anxiety? but, What are the antecedents of reports (or complaints) of anxiety?

It is intended that this book should provide a coherent perspective on a common form of psychological distress, of value to therapists, researchers and students of abnormal psychology. In many ways, the problems for which people seek help do not define 'natural' areas of scientific research, and so it is difficult to combine theoretical and practical interests in one book. The complaints with which I am particularly concerned—*panic* and *fears of public places*—can be analysed to reveal scientific questions which have a significance much wider than the explanation of particular complaints made to professionals working in a clinical context. Apart from its obvious social significance, a clinical area is therefore simply a point of departure for scientific investigation. My intention, then, is to use this clinical area as an illustration of how such problems might be tackled from a theoretical perspective which is essentially psychological.

The theoretical position I have adopted owes much to the views of Sarbin (1964, 1968), Mandler (1975) and Averill (1980a,b). In taking anxiety to be a lay construct, I assume that the 'What is?' questions rightly belong to the sociology of knowledge. Of course, the applied psychologist also has substantive issues to consider. For example, How can this individual be helped to report calmness rather than anxiety? or, How can that individual be helped to travel freely on public transport? I suggest that the most positive contribution a social constructivist position has to offer is to dissuade researchers from regarding these real-life problems as reflecting an underlying *emotion* of anxiety, or, even less helpful, an anxiety disorder.

Biological and medical research on anxiety is also considered in this light. Reductive biological and pathological hypotheses are rejected, but an attempt is made to integrate the biological aspects at a higher level of analysis. For this reason, the book differs from others which tend to confine themselves to a description and explanation of postulated disorders or syndromes. Because the emphasis of this book is essentially conceptual, there is relatively little discussion of assessment and therapy, apart from a general critique of current approaches.

Most experiences described as fear or anxiety in an everyday context have an identifiable source or object. When these experiences are reported as unbearably intense or lead to the avoidance of various situations, they are generally referred to as *phobias*. In the past 20 years there has been a considerable advance in the technology of reducing and eliminating unwanted phobias. The new methods of imaginal and real-life confrontation are successful in the majority of cases when anxiety is reported in connection with specific eliciting stimuli. The same success cannot be claimed for methods of dealing with complaints of anxiety that appear to be unrelated to identifiable circumstances. In one form of these complaints, a person may suddenly feel overwhelmed by unpleasant sensations which are usually described as a panic attack. Panic and other complaints of anxiety which are perceived as irrational form the principal interest of this book. A second major concern is the problem of fears of public places, often referred to as agoraphobia. Typically, the person who complains of these fears is unable to leave the home unaccompanied, although travel by car, a 'safe' environment, is usually possible. Although agoraphobia is tied to situations, the fear is not reported to be *about* these situations but is usually expressed as a fear of experiencing a panic attack *in* these situations. As I will argue, fears of public situations appear to be associated with panic and complaints of anxiety of a nonspecific kind.

As noted above, my restricted attention to certain types of psychological distress should not be taken to indicate a narrow theoretical focus. Whatever the deficiencies of anxiety as a theoretical construct, I have not lost sight of the fact that suffering expressed as anxiety is real and demands our continued investigation. An attempt to produce a conceptual integration in this area may pay greater dividends than an earnest search for a therapeutic panacea.

Among those whose help I acknowledge here, I am indebted most of all to Mary Boyle for carefully reading the manuscript and offering constructive criticism and encouragement. I have enjoyed and benefited from discussions with many friends and colleagues amongst whom I would particularly like to mention Mike Bender, Alison Cooper, Edna Foa, Simon Jakes, Roger Marsden, Kieron O'Connor and last, but not least, Jack Rachman. Mike Bender and Sophie May have provided welcome diversions from the task of writing. Finally, my thanks go to the anonymous individuals who allowed me to record the intimate details of their experience of panic.

1

General Introduction

REIFICATION OF ANXIETY

What are the antecedents of reports of anxiety and how should they be investigated? In the clinical literature we usually find a straightforward answer to this question—anxiety is the perceived effect of a pathological disorder. The research implications of the disorder model are not so much stated as implied. The implication is that somewhere in the neurophysiology of the brain or the putative structures of the psychological apparatus are to be found the correlates of disorder. In essence, anxiety is granted a timeless, objective standing. With advancing technology and improved understanding of the workings of the brain, the problem of anxiety disorders, it is believed, will one day be solved.

I wish to elaborate, instead, Sarbin's view that anxiety has been reified (Sarbin, 1964); that is, it cannot be explained away as a phenomenon that expresses the natural workings of a universal and timeless human psychology or the derangement thereof by pathological processes. Reification refers to a process whereby empirical phenomena that are the products of social and historical practices are abstracted from that context and treated as realities independent of their social origins (Sampson, 1981). It is not claimed that reifications misrepresent existing social reality. However, they portray that reality in terms of basic and inevitable characteristics of individual functioning.

In two largely unheeded articles, Sarbin (1964, 1968) advanced the thesis that the concept of anxiety came about as a result of certain historical mistakes occasioned by the literal interpretation of metaphors. Metaphors are used as a means of communication, often to bridge gaps in our

1

understanding by employing the linguistic device of describing something as if it was something else. Thus, 'butterflies in the stomach' refers
to gastric sensations. It is evident that communication about many
human attributes presents difficulties. In the case of gastric sensations,
the antecedent conditions are internal to the body and public referents
are lacking. Further, if the antecedents of an attribute are unknown,
whether they be internal or external, the conceptual gap is likely to be
filled by an explanation that invokes new entities of a metaphorical kind.
Sarbin (1964) noted that the etymological derivation of *anxiety* is from
Old French *anguisse,* which referred to a painful choking sensation in the
throat, an apt metaphor taken from events whose major features are of a
public nature. *Anguish* appeared in Middle English along with many
other ecclesiastical terms which referred to the inward and spiritual
aspect of faith. Anguish came to denote spiritual suffering. As a religious term reflecting the invisible and immaterial spirit which was
assumed to reside in the empty spaces of the body, anguish came to be
regarded as *internal.* Descartes, in the seventeenth century, contributed
to the transformation of soul into mind, by making use of a religious
idiom to describe human attributes such as thinking and willing. His
religious metaphor eventually became the 'mind', which Ryle (1949) so
incisively analysed as the 'ghost in the machine'.

I will attempt to avoid the scientific traps—which are the consequence
of reification—by concentrating my attention on the *behaviour* of reporting or complaining about anxiety. Most discussions of anxiety in the
clinical and experimental literature use the concept in the lay sense, so I
will confine myself to the lay construct. I assume that the behaviour of
reporting anxiety has antecedents in the internal and external environment which can be analysed using scientific methods (see Chapter 14).
The antecedents are assumed to include events that can be defined at
the biological, psychological and sociological levels of analysis. All levels
of analysis are necessary to develop an adequate model of the antecedents of reports of anxiety, but at the present time there are simply no
scientific theories that can achieve this integration. This is not a failure of
theorists of anxiety, but a feature of the current state of the biological
and social sciences.

I assume that anxiety is a *multireferential* lay construct. In other words,
a report of anxiety does not have a unique set of referents. We should
not, therefore, expect a high correlation between verbal reports of anxiety and other measures of behaviour or physiology. Moreover, if it is
assumed that the antecedents of reports of anxiety include *patterns* of
internal and external events, the search for a specific biological correlate
of reports of anxiety can, at best, yield partial answers. Further, if the

antecedents also include behaviours which are functionally equivalent, but mediated by different neurophysiological processes, the quest for a unique biology of anxiety is put further in doubt. These points are stressed, not because research into the biological antecedents of reports of anxiety has little to offer, but because it is often wrongly conceived.

These remarks about the lay construct apply also to the so-called anxiety disorders observed in a clinical context. It is common practice for clinical researchers to group subjects for research on the basis of super-ficial similarities in behaviour and clinical labels. This tendency is found amongst psychologists trained in a behavioural tradition, just as it is amongst any other group of researchers. As Wolpe, one of the founders of the behaviour therapy movement, pointed out, a variety of condition-ing experiences may lead to the same manifestation in behaviour (Wolpe, 1981). That is, complaints described in a similar way may have quite different causal antecedents.

CLASSIFICATION OF LAY CONSTRUCTS

As Sarbin has demonstrated, a linguistic and conceptual analysis of lay constructs has a valuable place in scientific endeavour. Certain con-ceptual issues often need to be clarified before sensible causal questions can be asked. Unfortunately, the disorder model has been so influential (influencing lay concepts as well as scientific concepts) that there have been few attempts to relate complaints of anxiety to other aspects of social cognition, that is, to attributions of causality and implicit beliefs about the nature of social reality. A different book would need to be written to explore these issues in any detail.

In developing the concept of panic-anxiety, I have simply relied on statistical analyses of subjects' responses to standardised enquiries about the kinds of distress they experience. This approach has been taken because there is little else to consider in the way of empirical data. For the most part, the studies on which I draw are factor analyses of questionnaires and psychiatric ratings. Inevitably, the choice of items reflects current psychiatric theories, although the results of analyses have not always supported the conventional wisdom. The relationship between the lay construction of psychological distress and the 'official' or institutional categories is extremely complex but almost certainly in-teractive. I have briefly touched on this issue in Chapter 14.

As far as possible, I have avoided the terms *patient, symptom* or *syn-drome* because of their close connection with a disorder model. Instead, I have generally substituted the more neutral terms of *distress, complaint* or *problem*, reported by persons, subjects or clients.[1] Switching to a new vocabulary never comes easily, and so the reader is asked to forgive any awkwardness of expression. It is of course true that many clients describe themselves as suffering from symptoms and ask for a diagnosis. In many respects, the disorder model *is* the lay construction of distress. It is not claimed that this construction of reality is 'mistaken'. However, it is not the only way in which distress can be construed, and I suspect that the disorder model frequently obscures the existence of events that, on examination, will be found to antecede reports of distress. In fact, clients' use of the terms *symptom* and *illness* does not usually imply a firm belief in an underlying pathology. It is noteworthy that the newer psychological therapies require clients to keep a detailed diary of the events that precede and follow their symptoms, a practice which often changes the way in which the problem is construed. Of course, in some intervention techniques, there is a deliberate attempt to change the client's understanding of the nature of the problem. The 'disorder' that afflicts an individual can therefore be seen as a labelling process that is a constituent part of the problem.

---

[1]In the following text, I often use terms such as *anxiety disorder, agoraphobia* and *anxiety neurosis*. This is done for convenience and should not be interpreted as a tacit acceptance of the disorder model.

PART I

Psychiatric Research and
Panic-Anxiety

2

Introduction to Part I

This book has been divided into two parts: the first deals with research on complaints of anxiety and related problems, the second with
psychological theory. I have invented a descriptive label, *panic-anxiety*,
to tie together the themes of Part I. Panic-anxiety is not a diagnostic
concept, and my justification for introducing the term is presented in
Chapter 3. It refers to a cluster of complaints which feature acute episodes of distress (usually described as panic) and to reports that daily
life is affected by anxiety, tension and somatic distress of various kinds.
Public situations, in which distress is experienced more acutely, are
commonly avoided. Chapter 4 consists of the edited transcripts of three
interviews with clients who display this cluster of complaints.

I have not assumed that panic-anxiety complaints correspond in a
one-to-one fashion with psychological or physiological processes. Multidimensional causation is assumed, by which I mean to imply also that
boundaries between complaints do not represent a rigid separation of
underlying causal processes. Just as a complaint which manifests itself
in a given way may indicate different causal antecedents, so ostensibly
different complaints may have common antecedents. With this concept
in mind, I have tried to trace the potential links between the panic-
anxiety cluster of complaints and dependence on alcohol in Chapter 6
and depersonalisation in Chapter 7. The relationship between panic-
anxiety and somatic complaints is more complex, and I have attempted
in Chapter 5 to clarify this area.

PANIC-ANXIETY AND THE MEDICAL MODEL

As it is my intention to review literature of a mainly psychiatric nature, the concept of panic-anxiety needs to be related to contemporary psychiatric classifications of neurotic disorders. However, as a dimension of description derived from factor analysis of lists of complaints, panic-anxiety cannot be equated with a psychiatrist's conception of disorder. Psychiatric classification has a variety of conceptual bases and does not simply aim to provide a descriptive framework for the complaints that clients present. Psychiatric taxonomies are, in fact, multiaxial schemes from which it is very difficult to deduce their precise conceptual bases. Besides grouping together psychiatric symptoms into syndromes, some methods of classification stress the mode of onset, the course of a disorder or response to therapy.

I will regard factor analytic techniques as a useful means of ordering the mass of observations that make up descriptions of complaint. However, the predominantly *psychiatric* nature of the available data must be recognised. Not only are the complaints defined in psychiatric terms, but also many of the studies have been performed on psychiatric subjects. It is by no means clear how people would ordinarily choose to describe their emotional distress; but the influence of psychiatric terminology is strong, and many terms such as *anxiety* and *depression* belong to both psychiatric and lay discourse.

It is not intended that the concept of panic-anxiety should imply a discontinuity between the causes of normal and abnormal behaviour. The cluster of complaints is the end point of a complex interaction between psychological and social factors occurring over many years. Panic-anxiety is, however, an important starting point for research because it is what the client actually reports as distressing him or her.

Psychiatric description of a disorder usually carries an implication of underlying dysfunction. Roth and Mountjoy (1982) denied a continuity between complaints of emotional distress in the community and clinic. At some point, normal anxiety becomes a neurotic illness, but the basis of this distinction is not made clear. In fact, the concept of psychiatric illness seems to rest more on professional practice than on any demonstration of underlying dysfunction. However, the contrasts that are commonly drawn in psychiatry between the form and content of a disorder and between personality and symptoms suggest the strength of the analogy with physical illness and therefore of a distinction between functional and dysfunctional states of the individual.

It is important to determine whether there is, in fact, any real difference between the nature of the determinants of normal behaviour, such as everyday reports of anxiety, and anxiety described as severe and disabling; that is, whether new psychological or biological processes need to be invoked. Panic may be alarming and incomprehensible, but this is not itself a criterion for underlying abnormality. I will assume that theories of normal anxiety can be used equally well to explain abnormal anxiety. In other words, even though biological dysfunctions or physical illness may contribute (in association with other factors) to the causes of panic-anxiety, they are not assumed to be in any sense *necessary* factors in causation (see Chapter 5).

The term *disorder* or *illness,* as used in psychiatry, seems to be another way of stating that a person is distressed or causing distress. It is rare that anything beyond this meaning is conveyed about the underlying causes of complaint. In other words, categories of mental illness appear to be descriptive, and the illnesses or disorders which are asumed to underlie them are not hypothetical constructs whose existence could, in principle, be demonstrated by experimental means. Anxiety disorder is not a disorder of any known, or potentially discoverable, structure or process. However, the mental illness concept is commonly represented as abstract or formal. A *formal* observation should derive meaning from its relation to a wider set of concepts or assumptions, but most diagnostic manuals simply stipulate that certain conditions have to be fulfilled for the diagnosis to apply, for example, that four out of a possible eight symptoms must be present. This is not equivalent to operationalising a concept (e.g. length) by choosing an international unit. Instead, the operation defines the concept, a concept which is not, in any case, closely tied to a network of theoretical assumptions. The object, it appears, is simply to *classify* for professional purposes (e.g. for the selection of treatments, standardisation of training) and not for scientific purposes.

The *content* of a formal observation is usually framed in commonsense concepts; for example, it might be alleged that panic is a content observation which permits the formal observation of anxiety disorder to be made. To illustrate with respect to psychotic illness, it has been argued that an underlying disorder (form) is universal but that specific manifestations (content) vary. Murphy (1976) studied several societies and found that they all had concepts similar to the Western ideas of mind and body and that a minority of persons fell into a class of persons whose minds were thought to be deranged. This derangement (insanity, craziness, etc.) was expressed in patterns of behaviour which were found to be formally similar in different societies. For example, the behaviours deviated from social norms, were unintegrated, and the beliefs expressed were nonsensical or inappropriate.

Although there are no fundamental objections to applying formal Western concepts in a non-Western context (Malpass, 1977), the illness/disorder concept appears to add nothing of theoretical value over and above the criteria described by Murphy. The universality of the mental illness concept was, however, implied when she wrote 'nor does the amount of mental illness seem to vary greatly within or across the division of Western and non-Western areas', or when she stated that, although there may be no explicit concept of neurosis, this does not mean that 'manifestations of such phenomena are absent' (Murphy, 1976, p. 1027). At the present time, the concept of neurosis is too vague and ill-defined to claim that it is a formal description of behaviour with any theoretical import.

The panic-anxiety cluster of complaints should therefore be regarded as culturally conditioned phenomena. Formal descriptions of certain components could probably be developed and applied in a non-Western setting; for example, a cross-cultural distinction between a familiar home-base and a more threatening 'untamed' external environment might be made. Concepts of physiological arousal and escape/avoidance behaviours might also be universally applicable.

HOW PREVALENT ARE ANXIETY COMPLAINTS?

The prevalence figures for psychiatrically defined problems are presented here to give a general idea of the numbers of people who are sufficiently distressed to seek help. A few community surveys have also been conducted, and so it is also possible to estimate numbers reporting fear and anxiety whether or not they have sought help.

Anxiety was found to be the fifth most common diagnosis made by general practitioners in two careful studies in the United States (Schweitzer & Adams, 1979). The diagnosis accounted for 3% of patient visits, but, compared to physical complaints, emotional problems take up a disproportionate amount of the physician's time. Estimates range from 20 to 70%. It is estimated that about 4 to 5% of the population is treated for anxiety complaints each year (Schweitzer & Adams, 1979).

In a population survey of New Haven, Connecticut, Weissman (1983) reported that the current prevalence rate of any anxiety diagnosis was between 4 and 5%. Complaints of generalised anxiety were most common, followed by phobias and panic. Only about a quarter of those subjects who warranted a diagnostic label had received professional help for an emotional problem in the previous year. However, the group with an anxiety diagnosis utilised nonpsychiatric health facilities with greater frequency than any other designated psychiatric group. They were also heavy users of minor tranquillisers.

In another community survey, currently underway in three different sites, the 6-month prevalence rates for panic were 0.6–1.0%, and for agoraphobia, 2.7–5.8% (Weissman, 1983). An almost universal finding is that women are several times more likely than men to complain of anxiety or receive an anxiety diagnosis.

In a study of the fears and phobias of a random sample of women in Calgary, Canada, Costello (1982) found that around 13% reported separation (agoraphobic) fears in the previous year. however, no woman in his sample of 449 was said to have incapacitating fears of this type.

Just as the predominant research perspective on complaints of anxiety is based on a disorder model, the main therapeutic approach is medication, although this is slightly less popular than it once was. In 1972, over 70 million prescriptions were written for the two most commonly prescribed antianxiety drugs in the United States at a cost of $200 million (in 1972 U.S. dollars) (Rickels, 1979). Lader (1981) found that 1 in 10 adult British males and 1 in 5 adult British females receive prescriptions for the benzodiazepine class of tranquilliser during the course of a year. Chronic users are said to number at least half a million.

People who express distress (which clearly has psychological antecedents) in the form of bodily complaints commonly think that they are physically ill and seek help inappropriately from general physicians. It seems timely to switch the emphasis to a psychological and sociological perspective on complaints of anxiety. This may open the way, through education and understanding, to a change in the lay construction of anxiety and eventually to an end of 'the age of anxiety'.

3

Psychiatric Research and Panic-Anxiety

DIMENSIONAL CLASSIFICATION

Studies which are specifically concerned with anxiety complaints are reviewed later. At this point, consideration is given to factor analyses of the broad spectrum of psychiatric symptoms. The most extensive investigations of this type have been carried out with the Hopkins Symptom Checklist (HSCL) and with extended versions of this scale (HSCL-90 and SCL-90). These scales have been administered to community samples and hospital patients, and the results will be considered representative for our purposes.

Derogatis and his colleagues have identified the following five major areas of complaint and replicated their findings in numerous studies (Lipman, Rickels, Covi, Derogatis & Uhlenhuth, 1968; Derogatis, Lipman, Covi & Rickels, 1972; Derogatis, Lipman, Rickels, Uhlenhuth & Covi, 1974; Derogitis, Yevzeroff & Wittelsberger, 1975).

1. *Somatisation* reflects distress arising from perceived dysfunctions in the cardiovascular, gastrointestinal and respiratory systems; also included are pain, headache and other somatic complaints.
2. *Obsessive–compulsive* reflects unwanted and repetitive impulses and actions and certain cognitive difficulties.
3. *Interpersonal* reflects inadequacy, inferiority and discomfort during interpersonal interaction.
4. *Depression* reflects dysphoric mood, withdrawal of interest in life and hopelessness.

TABLE 3.1

Phobic-Anxiety Factor Items: Hopkins Symptom Checklist[a]

Being afraid of traveling in buses, subways and trains
Being afraid of open spaces or of being on the street
Being afraid of going out of the house alone
Feeling uneasy in crowds, such as when shopping
Having spells of terror or panic
Becoming suddenly scared for no reason
Being afraid of fainting in public
Avoiding certain things, places or activities because they are
    frightening

[a]Adapted from Derogatis and Cleary (1977) and Lipman, Covi and Shapiro (1979).

5. *Anxiety* reflects phobic avoidance, nervousness, tension and epi-
    sodes of intense anxiety which appear to be unrelated to external
    circumstances.

The five complaint dimensions have been identified *within* diagnostic groups (e.g. patients diagnosed as suffering from anxiety and depressive disorders) and in community samples. In the expanded versions of the HSCL, anger/hostility and paranoid ideation are additional orthogonal dimensions (Lipman, Covi & Shapiro, 1979; Derogatis & Cleary, 1977). Somatisation is the dimension perceived most similarly by doctors and patients and is the most stable factor with consistent definition across the social classes (Derogatis, Lipman, Covi & Rickels, 1971). Minor variations in factor structure have been found; two anxiety factors rather than one were found in data from the lowest social class in this last-mentioned study.

In the expanded versions of the HSCL, it was in fact expected that, corresponding to the psychiatric diagnoses of generalised anxiety and phobic anxiety, two anxiety factors rather than one would be extracted. Lipman et al. (1979) administered the HSCL-90 to outpatients reporting anxiety and depression but found only one phobic anxiety factor. It is perhaps surprising that amongst outpatients with various complaints, a general (nonphobic) anxiety dimension was not extracted. Derogatis and Cleary (1977), using a heterogeneous sample of outpatients, obtained more support for two dimensions but certain items that had been predicted to load the the anxiety factor (especially panic and irrational fears) loaded the phobic anxiety factor instead. This factor, which may be equated with a restricted definition of panic-anxiety, contains the items shown in Table 3.1.

THE PANIC-ANXIETY DIMENSION
AND PSYCHIATRIC DIAGNOSIS

The panic-anxiety dimension does not characterise a *category* of individuals, although a suitable scale could be used to operationally define subjects who scored above a cutoff point. However, I implicitly assume that certain diagnostic groups (e.g. agoraphobic clients) would score high on this dimension. If this assumption were not made, it would be pointless to review the psychiatric literature in order to support the panic-anxiety concept. Various studies have shown that the same complaint dimensions can be extracted from different psychiatric groups (and also nonpsychiatric subjects). It may be inferred from this that complaint dimensions overlap considerably within individuals. That is, an individual may predominantly report anxiety but also report unease in interpersonal situations or a depressed mood. For research purposes, therefore, it would be desirable to form groups of subjects on the basis of multidimensional criteria.

Psychiatrists and clinical psychologists have generally employed *diagnostic* criteria to select their subjects for research investigations, and it is this research we must consider. The diagnoses which appear to be most relevant to the panic-anxiety concept are anxiety neurosis, agoraphobic syndrome, panic disorder, generalised anxiety disorder and, in earlier times, neurasthenia and neurocirculatory asthenia.

Sheehan, Ballenger, and Jacobsen (1980) subsumed a similar collection of diagnoses under the term *endogenous anxiety*. Their views are linked with those of Klein (1964, 1981) who believed that episodes of panic occurring in a sudden and unpredictable manner are the central feature of a new clinical entity termed *panic disorder*. The reference to panic in the label panic-anxiety also signifies the importance I attach to unexpected episodes of altered sensation, usually of an unpleasant nature, in the development of this cluster of complaints. However, I do not make the assumption that panic is endogenous or even a distinct psychophysiological state. The label panic-anxiety is also intended to focus attention on the anticipatory fear of episodes of panic, which is also an element of Klein's theoretical views.

The concept of panic-anxiety merges complaints which are usually separated into the agoraphobic syndrome and generalised anxiety disorder (anxiety neurosis). Apart from a difference in purpose, the justification for doing so rests on the fact that there is little statistical evidence to support two separate (descriptive) dimensions of anxiety complaint. Of course, within the panic-anxiety dimension an argument could be made for extracting a number of lower-order factors (e.g. somatic complaints versus psychic complaints). However, the level at which an investigator wishes to study clusters of complaints is a matter of choice. For example, the higher-order factor of neuroticism, which includes most forms of emotional distress, is a legitimate area of study. At the level of analysis chosen for this review, the agoraphobic cluster is considered a variant of the panic-anxiety cluster.

It has been argued that the agoraphobic syndrome should not be considered along with more general affective disturbances such as generalised anxiety (Mathews, Gelder & Johnston, 1981; Thorpe & Burns, 1983, p. 5). Mathews et al. (p. 10) stated that clients who fulfill the criteria of the agoraphobic syndrome when first seen do not subsequently develop general affective disturbances when contacted years later, that is, it remains relatively the same condition. This observation, if substantiated, can be interpreted to mean that variants of the panic-anxiety cluster remain true to form over the years. This is not at odds with the concept of panic-anxiety.

Mathews and his colleagues chose to study the agoraphobic syndrome because factor analytic studies have produced a cluster of agoraphobic complaints (see e.g. Dixon, De Monchaux & Sandler, 1957; Marks, 1967; Hallam & Hafner, 1978). However, these studies tell us little about the relationship between the agoraphobic cluster and other forms of affective distress or other psychological problems. It is only by including nonphobic items and nonphobic subjects that the boundaries of the cluster can be explored. It is not very surprising that subjects who describe themselves as agoraphobic or who are diagnosed as such, produce data which yield an agoraphobia factor when analysed.

Arrindell (1980, p. 240) asserted that most agoraphobic clients respond well to therapy and, for this reason, believed that agoraphobia is a clinical entity of theoretical and practical significance. This is not a satisfactory justification for retaining the agoraphobia concept because response to therapy might be determined by factors which have little to do with underlying causal processes or descriptive dimensions. A classification based on response to therapy is an alternative to what has been suggested, not an argument against it. In any case, therapy is only partially effective, and to that extent unsatisfactory as a basis for classification. Moreover, it has not yet been shown that the same behaviour therapy methods, suitably adapted, would not also be reasonably effective with clients who report less situationally specific anxieties.

PSYCHIATRIC CLASSIFICATION OF PHOBIC AND ANXIETY COMPLAINTS

Historical Beginnings

The term *phobia* did not come into the psychiatric literature until the middle of the nineteenth century and was not used consistently until many years later (Errera, 1962). There were various references to phobias and aversions in the late eighteenth and early nineteenth centuries including fears of falling and dizziness in public places. Benedikt (1870) explained dizziness in terms of an eye muscle dysfunction which produces imbalance of optical axes and lack of visual equilibrium. A number of writers also noted the fact that complaints would disappear for periods of time. In 1871, Westphal published a classic monograph, *Die Agoraphobie*, in which he described three male patients who were unable to walk in streets without fear (or dreading that they would experience fear). Companionship, or even a walking stick, would comfort them. His patients varied in terms of the precise locations which elicited fear, and Westphal also noted that one patient worried about becoming insane. Westphal's description of the 'syndrome' and his terminology were rapidly accepted (see Errera, 1962).

The history of the classification of anxiety complaints is remarkable for the number of diagnostic labels that have been produced. Early descriptions were modelled on medical diseases with somatic feelings receiving most emphasis. A 'syndrome' in which cardiac and respiratory 'symptoms' predominated was described by DaCosta in 1871 who saw more than 300 cases in a Union army hospital during the American Civil War. He was also able to find incomplete descriptions of similar complaints from military hospital records of the preceding two centuries. He emphasised that although his newly discovered syndrome had been recognised by military surgeons evaluating soldiers unable to take the field, it was not caused by military life, since most soldiers had developed it before joining the army. Many civilians also exhibited the 'disorder'. However, it was attributed to a functional disorder of the heart and not to emotional factors. The diagnosis (DaCosta's syndrome) was taken up by physicians and military surgeons and was described during subsequent wars. In World War I there were 60,000 cases of 'disordered action of the heart' (Nemiah, 1974).

In parallel with medical terminology, psychiatric classification was being developed with broad categories encompassing a hotchpotch of symptoms. Beard, in 1880, made complaints of weakness and fatigue the basis of his new term *neurasthenia* (nervous exhaustion), which included complaints of anxiety. Freud, in 1894, wrote a paper called 'The Justification for Detaching from Neurasthenia a Particular Syndrome: The Anxiety Neurosis', in which he described a group of complaints which have much in common with contemporary anxiety diagnoses. Unfortunately, he appended an exotic theory of causation in terms of the absence, or impairment, of the experience of the sexual orgasm, which may have distracted attention from his empirical observations. Summarising from his own words, these were the presence, in anxiety neurosis, of the following features:

1. *General irritability*, such as sensitivity to noise.
2. *Anxious expectation*, which fades off into normal anxiousness. This expectation, considered to be the nuclear complaint, is one of danger from a variety of sources, such as disease (in which case the term *hypochondriasis* applies).
3. *Anxiety attacks*, a feeling of anxiety. (a) Anxiety attacks can occur without any associated idea or be associated with the nearest interpretation, such as sudden death, stroke or approaching insanity. (b) Anxiety attacks can also be combined with paraesthesias (tingling sensations). (c) Anxiety attacks can be combined with a disturbance of any one, or more, of bodily functions such as respiration, the heart's action, vasomotor innervation or glandular activity. For example, patients complain of heart spasms, difficulty in breathing, drenching sweats, and so forth. In their descriptions, the feeling of anxiety often recedes into the background or is described quite vaguely as a feeling of illness, of distress, and so on.
4. *Variance in symptoms.* The degree to which elements listed in point 3 are combined varies extraordinarily, and almost every accompanying symptom can alone constitute the attack just as well as the report of anxiety itself. Freud mentioned complaints focussed on the heart's action, respiration, sweating, tremor, shuddering, ravenous hunger, giddiness, diarrhoea, locomotor vertigo (a disorientation of the body in space), vasomotor congestion and paraesthesia.
5. *Awakening in fright*, a variety of anxiety attack which can produce sleeplessness.
6. *Vertigo*, usually described as giddiness. Vertigo can occur in attacks with or without the report of anxiety. It also produces dizziness—a feeling that the ground is rocking, the legs are giving way, that one cannot keep upright because one's legs are as heavy as lead and are shaking and wobbling. This dizziness never leads to a fall.
7. *Development of two types of phobias.* The types of phobias that typically develop are (a) one type relating to common dangers (animals,

thunderstorms, darkness, etc.), which are exaggerations of normal aversions; (b) the other type is agoraphobia, often but not always, developing after an attack of vertigo. Sometimes, attacks of giddiness do not lead to agoraphobia but only to some giddiness in certain places, while alone, in narrow streets, and so forth. However, locomotion often becomes impossible when anxiety is reported in combination with an attack of vertigo.

8. *Additional complaints,* including nausea, biliousness, diarrhoea and an urgent need to micturate.

Freud also noted that there is a striking fluctuation in the complaints, and their disappearance in toto for long periods may be followed by a sudden reappearance. In many cases he admitted that there was no recognisable cause, although he thought that the presence of similar complaints in relatives pointed to hereditary factors. Freud's description of anxiety neurosis was not readily accepted, and the term was not widely used in the medical and psychiatric literature until several decades later. His observations were, however, interesting and detailed and suggestive of testable hypotheses. Unfortunately, since that time, psychiatric research has mainly been directed at presumed biological causes. This direction was reinforced by the discovery of antianxiety drugs and efforts to evaluate their efficacy. In terms of a description of panic-anxiety complaints not a great deal has since been added to Freud's observations.

Contemporary Taxonomies

DSM III Classification

The DSM III classification (American Psychiatric Association, 1980) divides the anxiety disorders that concern us into two main divisions: *phobic disorders* and *anxiety states. Agoraphobia* is defined as a severe and pervasive phobic disorder; this means there is a persistent, irrational fear of specific situations, which are avoided if at all possible. The anxiety states are divided into *panic disorder* and *generalised anxiety disorder,* which have much in common, but the former is distinguished by episodes of intense apprehension, fear or terror, and often associated with a fear of impending doom. These *panic attacks* usually last minutes rather than hours. A subgroup of agoraphobics are also said to experience panic attacks; panic disorders and agoraphobia with panic attacks are very similar. Depersonalisation, which has often been mentioned in association with anxiety states and agoraphobia, is not included with the anxiety disorders in DSM III.

This taxonomy has been developed for practising psychiatrists, and its value for research purposes is questionable because, for example, the categories obviously overlap in terms of their defining criteria. The categories have not been developed on the basis of statistical analyses of complaints, and the defining criteria have various theoretical justifications. The DSM III classification distinguishes anxiety disorders from somatoform disorders, whereas the somatic element of complaining seems to be an important feature of the agoraphobic cluster of complaints (see e.g. Arrindell, 1980).

Roth and Mountjoy's Classification

Roth and Mountjoy (1982) represent an influential British school which questions the separation of anxiety and depressive disorders that DSM III implies. The psychiatric consensus appears to be that the configurations of anxiety and depressive complaints can be distinguished, although overlap is considerable (Klerman, 1980). Klerman pointed out that persons diagnosed as depressed rate themselves as more severely impaired than persons diagnosed as anxious, and so their ratings on scales of anxious mood are often higher. Roth and Mountjoy (1982) reserved a diagnostic category for *anxiety/depression*, a mixed state which recognises that the two clusters of complaint commonly coexist.

However, in a series of statistical studies, Roth obtained a clear contrast between various features of complaints of anxiety and depression. In particular, the anxiety cluster is characterised by a sudden rather than an insidious onset, episodes of panic, phobias, and emotional and physiological lability. Roth and Mountjoy's reasons for the belief that anxiety and depressive complaints are causally distinct are (1) that the pattern of complaint is unlikely to change over the years, (2) that the features which predict outcome are different, (3) that recovery from depressed mood is significantly more likely to occur, (4) that psychotropic medication has differential effects on the two types of complaint, and (5) that the evidence for a hereditary predisposition to anxiety is much stronger than it is in the case of neurotic depression (see Roth & Mountjoy, 1982, for supporting evidence).

The classification which Roth and Mountjoy suggested for anxiety complaints consists of six categories. *Anxiety/depression* has already been mentioned. *Anxiety psychosis* is said to be a rare state precipitated by trauma. *Agoraphobia* and *social phobia* are distinguished from *simple anxiety neurosis*, which seems to be a residual category for nonphobic complaints. *Primary depersonalisation* is regarded as a separate syndrome.

Roth and Mountjoy's classification (like DSM III) does not deal adequately with the association between complaints of anxiety and somatic distress. Their definition of social phobia also blurs the distinction which can be made between a fear of public embarrassment (shame) and anxiety reported in interpersonal situations. For example, a fear of choking in public is not usually based on social timidity but on a fear of suffocation or embarrassment. These kinds of fear are commonly observed in persons who would be classified as agoraphobic or as having simple anxiety in Roth and Mountjoy's scheme.

THE RELATIONSHIP BETWEEN DEPRESSIVE AND ANXIETY COMPLAINTS

As commonly reported complaints, anxiety and depression might be expected to occur together by chance with a high frequency. However, this is unlikely to be a true account of their relationship if, as seems likely, they have a multifactorial causation and share common determinants. Thus, the two complaints need not be considered as separate disorders with different aetiologies. Behaviour related to anxiety complaints may have effects which produce depressive mood and vice versa. It may be inferred that the real constraints and loss of satisfaction imposed by avoidance of public places are likely to lead to some depressive mood, or at least to an increased vulnerability to natural disappointments. These assumptions are consistent with observations made by Noyes, Clancy, Hoenk and Slymen (1980) on individuals diagnosed as anxiety neurotics, who were contacted several years after their initial diagnostic assessment. They found that episodes of depressive mood, reactive to events, were more commonly experienced by these subjects than by members of a comparison group of surgical patients.

It has been observed that agoraphobic clients report more depressive mood than other phobic subjects. Successful modification of their problems by behavioural methods usually brings about a significant improvement in mood (Mathews, Johnston, Lancashire, Munby, Shaw & Gelder, 1976; Emmelkamp & Wessels, 1975; Munby & Johnston, 1980; Goldstein, 1982). However, after successful therapy, a significant minority of agoraphobic clients report severe but short-lived exacerbations of phobic avoidance (Munby & Johnston, 1980), and these episodes could be related to depressed mood. It is possible, then, that anxiety complaints sometimes lead to depressed mood and that depressed mood can lead to an exacerbation of anxiety complaints.

The frequent diagnosis of depression in agoraphobic clients is interpreted by Bowen and Kohout (1979) as evidence that agoraphobia is a form of affective disorder. In their series of agoraphobic subjects, the incidence of affective disorder was high in first-degree relatives. Munjack and Moss (1981) replicated this finding but, paradoxically, found no evidence of more depressed mood, past or present, in agoraphobic compared to other phobic subjects.

The fact that many agoraphobic clients referred to psychiatrists are diagnosed as depressed might simply indicate that depressed mood is a common trigger for seeking help even though the main problems lie elsewhere.

The common co-occurence of anxiety and depressive complaints should not distract attention from the fact that they can occur separately, that is, they are not *necessarily* associated.

STATISTICAL INVESTIGATIONS OF ANXIETY COMPLAINTS

The studies reviewed below have used various forms of factor analysis. Factor structure is likely to be influenced by sample characteristics, the range of items included, the method of analysis and the number of factors extracted. I have assumed that the first two influences mentioned are likely to be of most significance and have therefore organised the review in terms of the range of items (a variety of complaints vs. fears only) and subject source (subjects with miscellaneous diagnoses vs. phobic subjects vs. community samples). It must, however, be recognised that factor analytic studies commonly have technical weaknesses, such as insufficient sample size, and so the conclusions reached below must be regarded as tentative.

Many Complaints Sampled: Psychiatric Subjects with Various Diagnoses

The first systematic statistical investigations were carried out by Roth and his colleagues. Roth (1959) labelled his new form of neurotic illness the *phobic-anxiety-depersonalisation (PAD) syndrome* because its consistent features were depersonalisation and phobic anxiety. Roth and his colleagues carried out a principal-components analysis of a set of ratings of predefined clinical features obtained during the course of a psychiatric interview with 275 neurotic patients (Roth, Garside & Gurney, 1965). The selection of ratings was, of course, partly influenced by the diagnostic concept he was proposing. Roth (1959) described *depersonalisation* as a state in which there was a loss of spontaneity in movement, thought and feeling, and a subjective experience of automaton-like behaviour. *Phobic anxiety* was described by Roth as a fearful aversion to leaving familiar surroundings and to entering public places. He noted that waiting or sitting still in such settings was prone to evoke a sense of impending disaster, acute agitation and flight. He also noted fears of collapsing before others, loss of control, making a scene and looking helpless, foolish or ridiculous.

His principal-components analysis produced a PAD dimension which contrasted with a component loaded by a cluster of problems of a more general kind indicating long-standing psychological difficulties. For example, this principal component was loaded by items suggesting a life-long disposition to report anxiety and also by unstable mood and a paranoid interpretation of social events. In contrast to the life-long nature of these features, the PAD component was loaded by items indicating a sudden onset and precipitation by events of a more severe kind. Other items included situational phobias, panic attacks, severe depersonalisation and dizziness attacks.

Of the 275 subjects, 172 were defined as PAD patients on the basis of component scores. In 103 of these subjects, phobic avoidance of public situations was the most prominent complaint when problems were first reported. These subjects would now be described as agoraphobic by most clinicians. Of the remainder, half were dominated by depersonalisation or derealization as the leading complaint, and in the other half both patterns were equally prominent. It is interesting to note that the subjects in the mainly phobic (agoraphobic) subgroup were older, more often married and were more likely to experience panic attacks and feel depressed.

A study similar to Roth's used a 700-item standardised interview which was developed for slightly different purposes (Fleiss, Gurland & Cooper, 1971). Interviews were conducted with 500 consecutive admissions to psychiatric hospitals, one-half of the patients to a New York hospital and one-half to a London hospital. From their analysis the authors obtained a phobic-anxiety pattern which was at least partially independent of a depression pattern (25 different symptom clusters were extracted from the data). The phobic-anxiety pattern included all the items that might have been expected from previous clinical descriptions, for example, avoidance of various public situations and common forms of somatic distress such as palpitations, dizziness, trembling, hot and cold sensations and difficulty in getting breath. It did not include depersonalisation and derealisation, which formed a separate factor. Items measuring more general complaints of nervousness and tension were associated with the depression pattern and thus reinforced Roth's finding that unstable mood contrasted with phobic-anxiety.

Fears Sampled: Psychiatric Subjects with Various Diagnoses

Fear questionnaires have been administered to groups of psychiatric subjects in several studies (e.g. Rothstein, Holmes & Boblett, 1972; Bates, 1971; Lawlis, 1971). Although the major fear dimensions are reproducible in these studies (see below), the fears which typically load on the panic-anxiety dimension, such as 'large open spaces', 'being left alone', and 'small enclosed places', have not been found to cluster with any regularity, if at all (Hallam, 1978).

Many Complaints Sampled: Phobic Subjects

Several studies have analysed data obtained from subjects identified as phobic or agoraphobic (e.g. Marks, 1970). Marks obtained two principal components from data collected from 900 women members of an association for agoraphobics. One component included common forms of somatic distress such as exhaustion, dizziness, fear of fainting, headache, trembling, palpitations, tension and depersonalisation. The other component was loaded by various public situations. The complaints typical of the panic-anxiety cluster were therefore distributed on two components rather than one.

Hallam and Hafner (1978) analysed a similar set of data obtained from clients with various phobias who were attending a hospital clinic. A cluster of fears of public situations formed one factor, but this cluster was not obtained when the clients diagnosed as agoraphobic were removed from the analysis. An anxiety complaint factor was also extracted, defined mainly by breathing difficulties and dizziness, and the diagnosed agoraphobics obtained higher scores on this factor.

The relationship between phobic and nonphobic items in the panic-anxiety factor was clarified in a study by Arrindell (1980). His subjects were 703 members of a phobics society in Holland. In addition to a fear survey, several questionnaires were administered that tapped mood, other distressing complaints and difficulties, and anxiety reported in social situations. The main fear factors extracted, apart from agoraphobic-type fears, were fears of social situations, injury/illness/death,

TABLE 3.2

Higher-Order Factor Analysis of Fear Factor Scores
and Questionnaire Measures of Distress[a]

Measure	Factor		
	I	II	III
SCL-90 Total score	0.78		0.55
Neuroticism scale	0.70		
Zung depression scale	0.69		
SCL-90 Social inadequacy	0.83		
SCL-90 Somatisation	0.55		0.56
SCL-90 Agoraphobia			0.83
SCL-90 Hostility	0.49		
Social anxiety	0.59	0.41	
Social avoidance	-		
FSS Social fears	0.68	0.52	
FSS Agoraphobia			0.87
FSS Injury, death, illness		0.69	
FSS Sexual and aggressive		0.69	
FSS Harmless animals		0.65	
FSS Total score		0.82	0.47

[a]Reprinted with permission from *Behaviour Research and Therapy*, Volume 18, W. A. Arrindell, Dimensional structure and psychopathology correlates of the fear survey schedule (FSS-III) in a phobic population: A factorial definition of agoraphobia. Copyright © 1980, Pergamon Press Ltd.

harmless animals and sexual/aggressive display. These findings are consistent with the results of other factor analyses of fear survey data (Hersen, 1973). A factor analysis of the fear scale scores (FSS) and the additional measures of psychological complaint was also performed. This analysis yielded three conceptually clear factors accounting for 63% of the variance (see Table 3.2). Fears of public places clustered with the somatisation scale of the HSCL. This was the smallest of the three factors, accounting for 9% of the variance. The cluster of complaints which make up this factor are listed in Table 3.3. The largest factor was loaded by global distress, depression and social inadequacy. The remaining specific phobia scales made up the second factor.

The results of Arrindell's study are consistent with Roth's finding that an agoraphobic/somatic complaint dimension contrasts with a dimension of general maladjustment. It is also significant in establishing that agoraphobic fears form a cluster which is distinct from other, more specific fears; for example, fears of public situations cannot easily be explained as reflecting a general trait of fearfulness.

TABLE 3.3
Factorial Definition of Panic-Anxiety[a]

Somatic complaints	Situation fears
Headaches	Being in open spaces or on the street
Faintness or dizziness	Going out of the house alone
Pains in heart or chest	Being in enclosed places
Pains in lower back	Being in a strange place
Nausea or upset stomach	Being in high places
Soreness of muscles	Being in crowded places such as shops,
Trouble getting breath	cinemas and churches
Hot or cold spells	Traveling on buses, subways or trains
Numbness or tingling in	Being in an elevator
parts of the body	Crossing streets
Heavy feelings in arms or	Eating or drinking in public
legs	Being alone
A lump in the throat	Fainting or collapsing in public
Heart pounding or racing	
Trouble falling asleep	
Weakness in parts of the	
body	
Sleep that is restless or	
disturbed	
Fear that something se-	
rious is wrong with the	
body	

[a]Adapted from Arrindell, 1980.

All the subjects in this study defined themselves as phobic. This constraint on subject selection may have influenced the factor structure that was obtained.

Fears Sampled: Community Samples

Results of studies conducted on members of the general community (e.g. university students) have not consistently produced evidence for a cluster of fears of public situations (Hallam, 1978). An exception is Torgerson's (1979) study, which used a sample of twins.

Summary

The statistical studies are reasonably consistent in demonstrating the existence of a factor loaded by items measuring fears of public situations and various forms of somatic distress. It seems safe to identify this factor with the *phobic-anxiety* factor described by Derogatis and his colleagues (1972, 1974, 1975; Lipman et al., 1968) mentioned earlier, especially in the light of Arrindell's (1980) findings. His factor analysis of the SCL-90, FSSs derived from a fear questionnaire, and other measures establishes this point (see Table 3.2). Some discrepancies between the results of different studies are only to be expected given that factoring techniques vary, subjects are drawn from different populations and the reported sample sizes are rather small for the number of items included in analyses. The type and range of items also varies to some extent.

CLINICAL OBSERVATIONS ON PANIC-ANXIETY COMPLAINTS

The cluster of panic-anxiety complaints has been ably described by many authors writing from a clinical perspective (Terhune, 1949; Marks, 1970; Feighner et al., 1972; Klein, 1981; Chambless & Goldstein, 1980). Most of the salient features are contained in the autobiographical accounts provided in Chapter 4. As panic-anxiety is itself multidimensional when viewed from different perspectives, it should not be converted it into a firm category of problems.

The problems that have been labelled as panic-anxiety appear to begin following an episode of altered sensation or feeling, sometimes reported as a panic-attack. Only rarely can any rational explanation of the attack be provided. The person so afflicted usually anticipates that the unpleasant sensations will recur. Anxiety is most commonly first reported in crowded shops, during bus or train travel or while crossing the road. Unpleasant sensations are subsequently reported in an ever-increasing number of situations, although the extent to which environmental triggers are identified and to which reports are focussed on them varies considerably. In some cases, the complaints are so generalised that the individual says that he or she feels constantly anxious, has ruminative thoughts and suffers a variety of somatic disturbances much of the time. The somatic sensations may be combined with feelings of unreality, depersonalisation (see Chapter 7), and lack of concentration. Confidence may ebb away and a depressed mood is often reported.

Thorpe and Burns (1983, p. 25) questioned members of an agoraphobics society about their worst fears and sensations and documented the effects of the problem on their lives. Nearly all subjects could specify a fear of what might happen during a panic attack, the most common being fainting or collapsing. Fears of death, insanity and illness were also associated with panic. The feared sensations fluctuated from day to day and from situation to situation. In general, panic was less likely to be reported in familiar, reassuring and undemanding situations, but exceptions did occur. Factors which made the agoraphobic feel worse were physical and temporal constraints (e.g. queuing, making appointments, being unable to make a rapid escape) domestic stress and other problems (Thorpe & Burns, 1983 p. 26).

During states described as panic there may be extreme weakness of the limbs and/or other unpleasant sensations such as a strong desire to urinate, a feeling of paralysis and an inability to breathe freely.

A fact which should be mentioned here is the excess of women in the clinical statistics. In one review of nine studies of agoraphobia, six reported a proportion of women in excess of 87% (Burns & Thorpe, 1977). I have speculated about the reasons for this sex bias in Chapters 6 and 12. Women are also more likely to complain of anxiety to their general practitioners (Schweitzer & Adams, 1979).

Events Associated with the Onset of Complaint

There is little evidence of a satisfactory nature about events which precede the initial complaint. This is not surprising because the first attacks are often perceived as spontaneous. By the time that the individual is interviewed by a clinician, several years may have elapsed. In spite of the retrospective and unreliable nature of the data, it is striking that a number of common themes are present in clinical reports (e.g. see Ambrosino, 1973; Buglass, Clarke, Henderson, Kreitman & Presley, 1977; Thorpe & Burns, 1983; Roberts, 1964; Roth, 1959; Sim & Houghton, 1966; Solyom, Solyom, LaPierre, Pecknold & Morton, 1974). These are

1. some kind of shock or calamity,
2. the death of close relatives or friends,
3. physical illness in the subject or a relative,
4. childbirth.

Some writers have also mentioned a change in consciousness or sudden loss of consciousness, for example, associated with fainting, anaesthesia or psychedelic drug use.

One study examined the frequency of 12 different stressors in a group of patients said to demonstrate the PAD syndrome (Roth et al., 1965). Compared to psychiatric patients without this cluster of complaints, the former were more likely to have suffered from actual or threatened physical illness, an operation or other disturbance of consciousness, childbirth or a calamitous circumstance. Stressors of a social nature or change of abode more commonly preceded other problems. The stress of break-up or threat to marriage was reported equally often in both groups.

Although the alleged precipitants are certainly unpleasant, they do not seem to be sufficiently aversive or threatening as to constitute the basis of a pervasive and incapacitating 'anxiety'. It is necessary to postulate additional interacting factors to justify this outcome (see Part II).

THE DEVELOPMENT OF PANIC-ANXIETY COMPLAINTS

The development of panic-anxiety complaints has not been monitored prospectively, and so it is necessary to rely on retrospective accounts. For some individuals, the initial complaint appears to be a magnification of a prior tendency to report anxiety (Noyes et al., 1980). Although many subjects describe an initial episode, it is not known how typical this is. Avoidance of various situations can follow immediately or develop gradually later.

Avoidance of public situations may persist for decades. In a survey of a nationwide club for agoraphobics, the average duration of complaint was 13 years (Marks & Herst, 1970). One researcher followed up 47 phobic subjects (including some agoraphobics) diagnosed between 1937 and 1940, of which 19 were contacted 20 years later (Errera & Coleman, 1963). Only one was free of phobic complaints. In a shorter follow-up of agoraphobics, only 23% had lost their fears despite intervening psychiatric treatment (Roberts, 1964).

Persons who receive the diagnosis of anxiety neurosis are also unlikely to lose their complaints (Wheeler, White, Reed & Cohen, 1950; Noyes & Clancy, 1976; Noyes et al., 1980). Complaints of severe anxiety are more likely to persist than depressed mood (Kerr, Roth, Schapira & Gurney, 1972; Schapira, Roth, Kerr & Gurney, 1972).

Noyes and Clancy (1976) followed up 82% of a sample of patients in a medical clinic who satisfied criteria for the diagnosis of anxiety neurosis. Anxiety was still being reported as distressing in 50% of the sample when interviewed 5 years later; 24% had mild complaints or none at all. In a later study at a university clinic (Noyes et al., 1980), 87% of patients diagnosed with anxiety neurosis still met strict operational criteria when contacted 4–9 years later. Only 12% of the original group had a complete absence of complaint, but of the remainder, most could carry on their lives without actual impairment of their work, marriage, family life and social activities. Less than 6% were unable to work because of complaints of anxiety. Consistent with earlier observations, it was often found that the problem disappeared for considerable periods of time. Some subjects (mainly women) developed fears of travel, crowds and enclosed places.

For comparative purposes, Noyes and his colleagues followed up a group of surgical patients matched for age and sex. Rather surprisingly, 21% met the criteria for anxiety neurosis. The group as a whole was similar in terms of marital status, employment status and annual income, but the anxiety group was rated as more impaired in a number of areas and rated themselves as more dissatisfied with working, marital, sexual and social areas of their life. They had also received more hospital treatment for physical illness and suffered more stress disorders (e.g. peptic ulcer and hypertension). The group given an anxiety diagnosis more commonly reported brief periods of depressed mood.

To sum up, the panic-anxiety cluster of complaints is associated with persisting impairment and dissatisfaction in many areas of life, although most can carry on normal social activities. A severe restriction of activities is, of course, found in those individuals (mainly women) who avoid public places and stay at home.

4

Personal Accounts of Panic

INTRODUCTION

These vivid descriptions are taken from interviews with clients who had recently completed a course of psychological therapy. Particularly noteworthy is the suddenness, unexpectedness and inexplicable nature of the panic episodes and the failure of doctors to provide information and reassurance. The development of fears of insanity and the effects on social and family life are well illustrated.

A'S ACCOUNT

Subject A is married, age 28.

The first day it hit me, really hit me, was the day I took my youngest child to the nursery. She was just 3, and when I dropped her off I thought 'Oh God, at last I'm on my own, the last one's at school'. So I set off for the shops, and I had not got very far, about a hundred yards up the road, when I started to feel sort of dizzy. I thought 'What's happening'? You know, I always had the fear of a heart attack and experienced palpitations before, indoors and outdoors, but nothing to the extent of this. So I thought I'd keep walking and I'd be alright. I carried on walking but the further I got, the worse it got; my legs started to go; I felt in every part of me there was something wrong; I couldn't breathe; I was constantly swallowing; my throat seemed to close up and I felt like screaming out 'Somebody help'. There was a small kiosk place there that sold tea, so I thought I'd have a cup of tea and see how I felt. I started to drink the tea but I couldn't swallow it. I was absolutely *panic-stricken*. I had tremors in my arms and legs. I saw a person who was familiar to me, although I didn't actually know her, and I thought it was a good idea to walk along with her because I knew she had to go along to the school to pick up the children the same time as I did. I managed to reach her and asked her if she wouldn't mind if I walked along with her. She said, 'No, alright; what's the matter?' and I told her I had just come over a bit queer. And that was that.

I kept getting these panics for a couple of days, and whenever I went out to see if it would happen again, it did. So I went to the doctor and he gave me some pills; I don't know what they were.

Q. Had you ever been to the doctor before with nervous troubles?

I had been, like years before, I've always been a bit nervy. It wasn't strange going to the doctor and getting pills; I think they were phenobarbitone he gave me at first.

Q. What did you complain of?

Oh, I didn't tell him much. I just said I was depressed, not feeling very good. I didn't tell him anything about what happened in the street because I thought he was going to laugh at me. If I said to him I felt as if I was having a heart attack, you're diagnosing your own case. So I thought I couldn't say that.

Q. Did he ask you about yourself?

No, no.

Q. How long did he see you for before he gave you the pills?

He gave them to me straight away. This kept going on by a process of elimination. I had Valium, Librium; the last pill I had was called Serenace, a little green thing. And I got really bad with that pill—one night even suicidal. He said they were to keep me level. I did tell him about these depressions, and also afterwards about this fear of going out, but he just gave me pills. Sort of 'try them for a fortnight, and if they don't agree with you come back'. That's how I was going on, a fortnight or a month at a time. I had hundreds of pills, different colours. There were so many my husband had to put them all down the toilet. My doctor never asked me anything else—he wasn't interested. He was *not* interested in how I felt. He was just interested in giving me a bottle of pills and getting rid of me. This went on for about 18 months.

I used to go short distances out of the house, but after getting these attacks in the shops I used to get them in the post office. Supermarkets used to terrify me. I'd go in like a bull in a china shop, grab everything off the shelves, things sometimes I didn't even need, and I'd get to the queue; and if there were a couple of people standing there I used to drop the basket and just go out. I couldn't even wait those few minutes. I was alright as long as I was rushing around—I wasn't looking at anything you know—just going mad picking up anything. As soon as I got outside I thought 'Thank God that's over'. But if I had to wait I'd feel dizzy, I thought I was going to be sick, I couldn't breathe and my chest, well, it seemed everyone could hear it. The palpitations made me think it was my heart.

I went to the surgery one day when I was really bad, when I couldn't even go as far as the dustbin. I used to stop at the front door and leave the rubbish and think about it, wondering if someone would find me dead by the dustbin, because all the time I thought I was going to collapse. Anyway, my usual doctor wasn't there and to this other doctor I explained everything; that I couldn't go out, that I was getting worse, and that the pills were doing me no good at all. He said he'd send me to a psychiatrist! Well, I could see myself in a padded cell in H——. I thought I was going that way but you don't let on. You think to yourself that perhaps the next lot of pills are going to do the trick; you think every lot of pills you take is the answer—that you're going to be cured. But then I started thinking they were not curing me and thought there must be something wrong—perhaps I had a tumour.

Q. Couldn't you discuss this with your family or friends?

I used to tell my husband but he said 'Pull yourself together, it's all in the mind'. There were times when I didn't tell him anything. He often worked away from home, and he always said I was having an attack when he was going away. So, of course, I never used to say anything. I was in tears, just useless when he was away, in the home as well.

When this first started, I was playing Bingo and I just got up, dropped everything and walked out in panic. My mother was with me, and she dashed out because I hadn't told her anything and she wanted to know what was the matter. I just said I was feeling hot. Then gradually afterwards I did tell her, but the family didn't really want to know. They all said to me 'You'll get over it', or 'Pull yourself together'. You wanted to say 'Look, I'm scared, I'm scared of going on buses'. And really and truly I would have loved someone to ask me to go down to the West End. I was absolutely petrified at the thought of going, but if somebody had said to me in such a way as not to make me appear a fool, I would have gone.

My husband was most concerned because it was upsetting the children. Because I didn't go out, the children didn't go out, and I wouldn't let them out because I imagined all sorts of things happening to them. I was in such a low state that I used to take it out on them. I never got violent, but I used to be shouting at them all the time, saying 'Don't do this' and 'don't do that'. I wouldn't let them out, and I wouldn't let them do anything indoors either. The eldest girl got very emotional at one time. Of course my husband turned on me and said I must do something about it. But to give him his due he did try to help. He would often phone up from somewhere and ask me to come over. And I'd say— well, the *excuses*—'Brenda is running a temperature', 'It's too cold', or 'I've got this terrible pain'—anything that came into my mind, not to go. And he used to come all the way over to pick me up and go back again.

Q. What did he think your problem was?

He knew it was agoraphobia because we've got an agoraphobic in the family. I didn't think I was completely agoraphobic because I understood agoraphobics to be entirely housebound. I'd never actually talked to this relative in the family who's been housebound for 10 years because it's a disease you cannot talk about. I thought these fears about dying were not agoraphobia because I used to get attacks indoors. Also, I couldn't go in a lift, and that's claustrophobia. I thought you couldn't have the two, agoraphobia and claustrophobia, because you'd be in such a turmoil, which I was. Anyway, my husband was trying to jolt me, which didn't help because it made me draw back more. He was trying these drastic steps, and he'd not got the knowledge anyway. He never sort of sympathised with me. More often than not I did try for his sake and the kids' sake—get myself all built up and say 'Today is the day I'm going out'. And I'd get to the door—and then go back and make myself a cup of tea, still with my coat on. Then I'd try again, come back, and think 'I just can't do it' and take my coat off. I must have put my coat on four or five times. This was going on for over 18 months when this other doctor said I should see a psychiatrist. I thought I was mad already, and this was a gentle way of getting me to hospital! He explained to me, though he didn't know the treatment, that there was a new thing going on. He said the alternative was a hypnotist in Harley Street, but he said try the clinic first. And that's how I got there.

Q. Did he try to reassure you that you were not mad?

No. I said everybody thinks I'm going mad—it's just a saying—and he sort of laughed. They don't say anything these doctors, anyway. They just do a bit of writing and you sit there and wonder.

B'S ACCOUNT

Subject B is married, age 38.

Q. When did you first notice any anxiety?

Well, as I told you, I had no feeling about anything, and as far as I was concerned I was quite normal. Then, driving along this road I knew well, one Sunday morning, for no apparent reason I noticed I was high up. There and then I felt as if a shudder went right through me. I ignored it and didn't give it another thought—did a day's work. Fortunately, it's a one-way route and you come back a different way. Two weeks after, going on this same road, the same thing happened; in fact, before I actually got to the elevation, as if I was aware of it, and as soon as I got onto it proper, it was even worse than the first time. So I was saying to myself 'What is this?' I didn't mention it to anyone thinking it would go away. Eventually, a couple of weeks later, I was starting to clean the windows, which is something I do anyway, but as I'm living on the fourth floor it's far down. I glanced down as usual and I started shaking again. Fear—I became fearful. It went on from there.

Q. How long did that last?

As long as I was cleaning the windows.

Q. Did you stay up there?

Yes, I stuck it out. I held my head straight up and I didn't look down. I was aware of danger which normally I wouldn't. After that, things which weren't apparent to me started to become a problem. Climbing ladders started to become apparent to me—you know, dangerous, and I started to avoid it—withdraw, which even at that time, I thought it was a passing phase. It was something—well, I didn't know what to think really. It never happened to me before, and I never heard anyone say that things like that happened to them.

Q. What did you try to do?

I didn't do anything—in fact I was trying to conceal it, hoping that it would go away. Not even my wife was aware of it. But in going out motoring I would find myself going slower and slower, and all this started to add up. I was thinking to myself 'Something is wrong, what can it be?' So every time I had a bit of time to myself I'd start to go over all these incidents to pick out something and I couldn't. As it went on, the worse it got, until in the end, even crossing the road was dangerous as far as I was concerned. The vehicles were quite a distance away from me, but to me they were bearing down—everything was bearing down. I became fearful even of a dog barking.

Q. Were you shaky as well?

Well, the shakiness would come actually on a ladder. My feet would start to give, and my hands—I wasn't sure if my hands would hold me up. I started to have doubts of my own self. I decided I couldn't carry on like this so I went to my family doctor.

Q. After how many months?

Ten months. After all this time I was really undergoing real agony.

Q. What were you hoping to get from your doctor?

I was hoping to get—I don't know—something to put me back where I was.

Q. A medicine?

Yes, some sort of medicine because I'd never heard of all these tranquillisers. I never gave them a thought. I knew I needed professional help. I tried everything myself—all sorts of tonics. I was thinking my body was run down. I was taking vitamin tablets, tonics—everything you can get without a prescription.

Q. Did these have any effect?

Not the slightest. In the end I was even putting on weight.

Q. Did you do anything else to help with the problem?

Well, if I was doing a job at work and I wasn't happy with the way I was feeling, I'd sit down and think there's only one way to beat this— face up to it. So instead of backing away I'd try to put myself in the forefront, but as soon as I actually got to the job the same old feeling came to me. I just couldn't beat it—I'd tried everything.

Q. Did it affect your social life?

Well, at the time I was still socialising. What I did realise was that if I had a bit of a drink—some alcohol—then I'd forget the whole thing— the feelings disappeared. I even said to my doctor once, 'No matter how shaky I feel, if I should have a drink, I'm alright. Why's that so?' She explained that alcohol was a sedative, but still it didn't make sense to me. In actual fact when I went there I thought I'd be getting something similar to alcohol but then I wouldn't be breaking the law—drink and drive sort of thing. I wanted something official. Anyway she prescribed the tablets, but all they did was ease that tension; as I said, I used to sit and think about what's happened to me—and it was as if my chest was welling up, full of wind, as if it was bursting. This is what the tablets did for me—helped that to go away. Anyway, I kept on taking the tablets, and they weren't doing me much good at all. My doctor said the only thing to do was send me to the hospital.

Q. So you came to see the consultant here.

I explained everything to her, and she was trying to pinpoint what actually happened—what causes it. She was of the opinion—because when this happened I had just returned from holiday home—mother had died and I went to visit the grave, which in a way was playing on my mind. When she died I wasn't in a position to go home and attend the funeral; but because it happened so long ago—13 years—I couldn't see the connection. But that's what she believed. I wouldn't doubt it at the same time, because whenever anyone mentions that, it's something

I really feel about inside. Maybe that's what caused it—I don't know. Even today I haven't a clue what eventually triggered this off. But although I'm feeling 90% better, that fear is still there that it should occur again.

Q. Did you think you had a physical illness?

No. I'm absolutely sure I wasn't medically ill. I didn't lose my strength, I had no pain. I knew for sure that it was something to do with mental illness.

Q. Did you have any previous experience of mental illness?

No. Never. None of my relatives either. That's what made it harder to accept. If I could think back that I had an aunt who—so I could say it wasn't my fault, it was ordained for me or something. I was always sorry for people with mental troubles, because I heard once you got it— that's it! There's no doctor who would cure it. When I reflected on this, that made it all the worse. I thought that was the end. All that I was doing was a waste of time—one day I'd just go over the top and end up in an asylum. That was at the back of my mind and made me more fearful.

Q. What treatment did you get?

Little red tablets and Valium. I noticed a difference in the first week. I'd tend to forget what happened before because always thinking back to what happened to me—that made the shakes start. I noticed I was managing better. After 4 months, the normal things like crossing a road, boarding a bus, they all went, but it left two things—open spaces and the heights.

Q. What were the main things you were unable to do?

Well, I was almost unable to do anything without fear, simple things like going out to catch a bus. I would be standing at the bus stop and, if after 5 minutes I couldn't see it, all sorts of things started to happen— getting impatient and restless. Couldn't stand in one place, you know, pacing up and down. All these things are very hard to explain, but the feeling is unpleasant. Something was going to burst; that's what it was like.

Q. What was the worst situation for you?

The worst situation I found myself in was one Sunday when I was driving to C——. Then it was as if I found myself with no escape—it wasn't as if I was on a ladder and could climb down. I had a friend in C—— who insisted on me to come, and it got to a stage when I couldn't duck out of it any longer. So I decided to take the journey. All the family was there. I was fearful before I left home, but then I said, always try to brave it and overcome it—do or die sort of thing. I was alright until I was on the motorway proper. Looking in the mirror, there was a bloke behind urging me on. Instead of speeding I looked at the speedometer and saw I was doing less than I would on a normal road. I said to myself, you can't turn around in the road, and there was no exit for some miles. I felt wobbly, as if unbalanced, but at the same time I knew it wasn't my body. I was sitting erect. The only thing I wanted to do was come off the road. Somehow, I don't know how, I managed to soldier on 'til I got to an exit, and I turned round and came back home.

Q. How about heights? How did that affect you?

Well, just looking through a window on the fourth floor gave me the shakes. I wouldn't go out on the balcony—it was as if the flooring was going to give way. Everything was magnified a hundred times—fear, fear, fear. But I wasn't afraid before. When I was home I climbed trees with the wind blowing the limbs and you're up there.

Q. Was your social life affected?

Actually at one time friends didn't exist because I wasn't visiting anybody. Ever since I started on the tablets I couldn't drink—everyone knew that you had a couple of drinks, but then all of a sudden you don't drink anymore; and because I didn't want to explain, I kept away. But because you don't explain what you're going through, they get it all wrong. Because they didn't get the full facts, you couldn't say they didn't sympathise.

Q. When you first saw me, after the first session, what did you think I was trying to do?

Well, I think you were trying to give me back some confidence. I didn't believe in my limbs. I didn't believe they could hold me up anymore. The first time we went on that roof it was as if something was pulling me over; you're not thinking straight no matter how you try. I couldn't go near the edge at all let alone look over. After the roof we came to the conclusion it wasn't really suitable because it was too high, so we looked for another wall which wasn't that high, although to me it looked a mile up. It was no good standing in one place because I wanted to move about to see if my limbs would hold me up; so, in a way, finding that wall was the key to the whole lot.

Q. When did you start to think that this would actually work?

At the beginning I thought it was hopeless. My limbs were weak and tired, and to be honest I thought it was a waste of time. At the same time I would always try it. And to my surprise, and I have to say surprise, it gradually started me to get less tension.

Q. And the main fear was that your legs wouldn't hold you?

They wouldn't hold me because of the fear. As soon as the fear enters your mind your limbs become weak and helpless. My legs were shaking, and after a while they went numb. Then I always had to hop down quickly. Gradually with a bit of will power and encouragement I achieved the right result.

Q. What effect did that have on the other fears?

It helped enormously. Every time I reached an obstacle in everyday life, my mind flashed back to that wall, remembering at the beginning that I couldn't do it and doing it eventually anyway. So I think that changed my whole outlook. I was on drugs at the time, but I still think that did more for me than anything else.

Q. At that time you expressed some worry about the drugs, didn't you?

At the beginning the drugs had a dramatic effect, but, well, I don't know if everyone is the same, but I wanted to come off them to see what would happen. I reduced them to see what effect it would have, although I didn't succeed in coming off them altogether. I started with eight reds and two yellows and after 4 months I was down to two reds and one yellow, so in that period the change was dramatic.

Q. Why did you want to reduce them?

To see if it was the tablets doing what *I* was doing. I didn't want to think I was getting alright but it was only the tablets. Now I've come off them altogether but my eyes weren't focussing properly, so I had to go back on the red one for a while. As of now I haven't taken any. I'm just hoping I'll keep like that, but whether that will be I just can't say.

C'S ACCOUNT

Subject C is single, age 23.

Q. How did your problem begin?

I first noticed it about 8 years ago. I was crossing the road and, when I got to the middle part, with nothing around me, I suddenly panicked. I wasn't quite sure what I'd panicked at because I'd never felt it before—just that I was aware of all the space around me, nothing I could touch. I went sort of clammy and nervous, I could feel my heart beating, and I had to run to the other side of the road and hold onto a lamppost.

Q. Did you feel you might collapse, then?

Well, my legs felt . . . I didn't quite know what I was expecting to happen. My legs felt shaky, and it just seemed I wanted to be next to something or hold onto something. I didn't like the space all around me.

Q. And nothing precipitated this?—cars coming?

No, I've never been afraid of crossing the road. It was just the space around me.

Q. Had you ever been worried about space around you before?

Not before that, no.

Q. Did you recover?

Yes, I got over it quite quickly and wondered what had happened. I thought it was some silly little panic. I didn't understand it, and it didn't happen again for a few months. I just forgot about it.

Q. And what happened later?

Well the same thing happened. I was crossing an open space with nothing around me, and I just felt I had to run to the nearest object, touch it, or at least stand against it. It often happened crossing roads, crossing parks, anywhere where there was a space.

Q. So this got worse then?

Yes, it got worse. Sometimes there would be a period of a few months when it didn't happen at all, and then it could happen every day for a while. It got really bad almost a year ago, when I first went to see a doctor about it. It was so bad then I just couldn't go out of the front door.

Q. Did anything happen to you a year ago that might have made your fears worse?

No, I don't think so, no emotional upset. My life was quite normal.

Q. Have your feelings and sensations stayed the same over the years?

Well, there's the feeling 'it's not quite real', a sense of unreality. I don't feel as if I'm really there at times. I wonder if I'm dreaming—that I'm just imagining everything that's going on around me. It's quite difficult to explain the feeling.

Q. Does that happen when you're in an open space, or at other times as well?

Well, usually in an open space, but it does happen at other times, when I'm feeling bad, as though I'm going to have a panic attack.

Q. And this is a feeling of things not being real? Have you ever experienced anything like that before?

No, not really. Well, I've thought for years, ever since I was about 11 years old, that I've wondered quite what reality was, and that I've been interested in what reality is, and Am I really here? What's beyond the universe? and things like that; mind/body questions that there's obviously no answer to. It seems that when I feel panicky I think of those things. When I was 13 I first took LSD, and then I started thinking about reality and things like infinity, you know, What *is* infinity? What's beyond it? All sorts of crazy things like that, that people do think about on LSD. That's when I first started having those feelings about reality.

Q. Did you ever get frightened by those feelings when you were on LSD?

Yes, I was frightened not only because it was so strange and I hadn't felt anything like that before, although at the time it felt quite normal. But afterwards I thought what weird feelings, looking at something for hours, wondering whether it really existed or not. I think the only thing that frightened me when I was feeling that, was that I still knew I had to appear normal to everybody else. I was worried it would show, people could tell I was not quite right.

Q. Did you ever get into a panic during an LSD trip?

I did once or twice—not about open spaces. It was just a bad trip—everything seemed to be horrible, everything collapsing in on me. I'd just sit there and shake, but it wore off.

Q. What are the worst situations for you now?

The worst is standing in a queue, when I know I *have* to stand in a queue and I know I can't move, if there's space all around me. If I'm queuing for a bus, I don't know when the bus is going to arrive, and I've just got to stand there. Sometimes, I can't do that and I miss the bus. I go and sit down.

Q. Did things get better after you saw the doctor?

For the first month after seeing him, things got worse. I was put on various tablets that didn't seem to help and made me feel worse. The Valium helped a lot, but another one, Ativan, made me feel a hundred times worse. I just felt I was going crazy. I took that for a week and then stopped.

Q. When you went to the doctor, how did you explain what was the matter with you?

Well, I was so bad when I went along to the doctor, with such a bad panic attack, that the first thing I did was burst into tears. I felt really stupid about it, but he was really very good. Well, I said 'I just can't walk across open spaces, I can't go out. I don't know what's the matter with me, and it's getting ridiculous'. And he could see I was shaking and in a terrible state. He really understood. He gave me a note for work so that I was off for a few days. I was worried what he had put on the note, but he just put debility. He got me an appointment at the hospital, in fact almost the next day.

Q. How did the anxiety affect your life?

Well, it limited all the things I could do. I couldn't go shopping on my own. I couldn't go to the library, and it was very difficult to go to work. I had to take Valium in the morning, a huge dose before things got better.

I hated the Tubes. I did miss a few days at work, which was why I went to the doctor, because I realised things were so bad.

I couldn't walk down steps, at least not in the middle of them. I had to hold onto the wall or a bannister and go very slowly. I used to dread walking down steps in public places when people were behind me and wanting me to speed up. And if I looked down the flight of steps, I felt dizzy, and I thought I was going to fall down. My legs would get shaky, and I'd be clinging onto the bannister. When I was really bad I couldn't walk down the three steps from my flat to the pavement. There was nothing to hold onto there anyway. It was easier to turn round and actually crawl down them backwards, so that I couldn't see I was going down. I was looking up even when I was going down.

Q. What did you think, yourself, was wrong with you?

I don't know, that's what's so annoying. I just didn't know why I should feel like that.

Q. Had you heard of anyone else with similar problems?

Yes, of course, my mother. My mother has suffered for about 30 years.

Q. How was she diagnosed?

Well, she's had it so long. It was just called agoraphobia. She's been on Valium for 20 or 30 years, and she's never really had treatment for it.

Q. What did you understand to be the cause of agoraphobia?

I don't know—but with my mother it was different. I've always thought of her as a rather nervous, jumpy person, anyway—very sensitive. It was more annoying when I found that I was getting these things because I'd always thought that I was so normal and stable—hard in a way—that I just thought I wouldn't be susceptible to all these silly, nervy, little phobias and panic attacks. I just didn't see myself as that sort of person, which is why, when I feel OK, I get really annoyed with myself. I think 'how stupid', why can't I pull myself out of it.

Q. Have you ever had any worries that you were going crazy?

Well, I suppose that feeling comes with the depersonalisation. I feel that I'm not really there, and I do think 'Am I crazy? Am I going to do something stupid? If this doesn't all exist anyway, what stops me from doing something stupid?'

Q. What do you mean by 'something stupid'?

Well, I don't know because I've never actually done anything. I just don't know what I'm afraid of doing, but I'm afraid that if I really believe, if I have such a strong feeling that it's *not* reality, I'm *not* really there, then it doesn't matter what I do or say, because it's not really happening.

Q. Are you concerned about what other people think about you in a state of panic?

I try not to let it show. If I've got a newspaper, I stick my head in it, lean against a wall or sit down.

Q. Have you ever been in embarrassing circumstances as a result of it?

No, not really, I've managed to control it well enough.

Q. Did you ever think there was anything medically wrong with you?

No, I wished it could have been in a way. If it was simple as that, say a case of not eating something I was allergic to. There didn't seem to be any pattern to the panic attacks at all that went with anything I did, apart from drinking alcohol, of course. If I drank a lot in the evening, the next morning it would be really bad. The feeling of not quite being there. I know it always comes on when I have a lot to drink.

Q. Actually when you're drinking?

Oh no, everything's fine then, of course. Alcohol relaxes me, and I feel perfectly OK.

Q. Coming back to your mother, did you notice as a child that she was afraid of certain things or that she was panicky?

Yes, if my father wanted to go out for a meal or to the theatre or cinema, she couldn't go. If she forced herself to go, she would always sit right next to the entrance. That's something I don't panic about. It didn't affect us as children very much, but we knew that she was upset and that it did restrict her a lot.

Q. What about other members of your family. Do they have similar symptoms?

My brother, yes. I found out quite accidentally- He's had a few of the same feelings, not as bad as my mother or I do, but walking across the office or the canteen at work, he has panic attacks and feelings he's not quite there. His legs go shaky, and he feels his heart beating. His idea of getting over it is to give into it. He finds it helpful to completely accept the feeling and let it overtake him and then it just seems to wear off on its own—which I could never do. I always try to control it; bring myself back to normal.

My sister, too. That was a surprise. She just happened to be talking to us one day. She didn't know anything about how I was suffering, or my brother. She mentioned that a few years ago she had the same feeling. Just walking along the road and suddenly felt that she was very exposed, out in the open. Her legs went shaky, she could hear her heart beating, she went very clammy and she had to dash into a shop and sit down. She didn't quite know what the feeling was, but she only had it a few times.

5

Panic-Anxiety and Somatic Complaints

SOME CONCEPTUAL ISSUES

As we have seen in the previous chapters, panic-anxiety includes both psychological and somatic complaints, The latter type refers to bodily discomfort, unusual sensations or a concern about having a physical disorder, In this chapter I will examine some different meanings of the terms *somatic* and *psychological* in this context and explore the relationship between panic-anxiety and patterns of somatic complaint. Finally, I discuss several somatogenic hypotheses of the origins of panic-anxiety.

The terms *somatic* and *psychological* raise a number of vexing questions which cut across the study of emotion in general. The two terms are opposed on various grounds though primarily on the basis of *description, attribution of causality* and *scientific conceptions of causality*. These three aspects will be considered separately, although in practice they are interrelated.

Somatic and *Psychological* as Lay, or Descriptive, Terms

Broadly speaking, distress is expressed either as complaints that mental activities have been affected (e.g. thinking, willing, feeling) or that bodily activities and somatic sensation are disordered (e.g. breathing, digesting, aches and pains). In this context, *mental* and *bodily* are lay terms of a rather ill-defined nature. However, somatic complaining can simply be regarded descriptively, in the sense that the body (as commonly understood) is the focus of distress. Whether somatic complaining is associated with publicly observable changes in the body is a different matter and an empirical question. In some cases a public event is clearly implied (e.g. 'I have a broken leg'), in others it is ambiguous (e.g. 'My heart stopped still'), and in others it may not be necessary to know (e.g. 'I have a headache'). To confuse matters further, somatic words or phrases can be used metaphorically to indicate psychological states; *pain in the neck* and *headache* illustrate the general problem. For purpose of empirical study, somatic complaints can be treated in essentially the same way as psychological complaints, that is, as self-reports of distress. Their relationship with beliefs about the source of distress, or with publicly observable events, can then be investigated empirically.

Lay Attribution of Causality

The *source* of a person's troubles is part of the total conception of distress. In panic-anxiety, unpleasant sensations are commonly attributed to organic disease, and medical advice is sought. The outcome of this advice may be that the nature of the causal attribution is revised, illustrating the fact that somatic complaints are not necessarily tied to beliefs about bodily dysfunction. In fact, complaints, whether somatic or psychological, may be attributed to a variety of factors, internal or external, controllable or uncontrollable. These causal beliefs of the sufferer should be distinguished from the scientist's view, which is inferred in a different manner from observations of behaviour, self-report and physiological processes. How the lay and scientific conceptions relate to each other is of interest in its own right (see Chapter 14).

Psychological and Somatic Causation: A Scientific View

An analysis of the causal relationship between events defined in psychological and in physical terms poses a number of problems which remain largely unsolved. I will therefore just sketch out a working model as the basis for subsequent discussion.

I will take it that the events which mediate psychological events are located in the body and are therefore somatic events. This does not imply a physiological reductionism because somatic events can be considered at different levels of analysis. For example, neurons can be studied at the physico-chemical level (e.g. the conditions necessary for neural transmission), at a physiological system level (e.g. systems of neuronal pathways) and at a functional level. By functional is meant the higher-order property of neurons to organise behavioural responses. The acquisition of functional properties requires interaction with the environment, and so it would be meaningless to reduce psychological (functional) explanations to somatic processes. In other words, functional properties are conceptually inseparable from patterns of environmental events. This is so whether or not the functional properties are heavily constrained by biological properties of neural tissue or strongly determined by innate organising principles. Needless to say, the functional properties could not develop without an adequate physiological substrate. Apart from processes that maintain this substrate, somatic influences on the functional properties of neural tissue can be categorised broadly as direct and indirect. The direct effects include hormonal influences and reflexive sensory adjustments. The indirect effects depend on an information analysis of sensory events. Accordingly, the body has been regarded as an internal environment in which changes detected by body receptors are centrally processed along with other information from the internal and external environments. The general organisation of sensory pathways and the nature of central processing appear to be similar for internal and external sensory events (Brener, 1977; Pennebaker, 1982). The direct and indirect somatic influences cannot be regarded as independent in practice. For example, long chain behaviour/hormonal interactions have been suggested by Leshner (1978).

Many writers on emotion have assumed that there are specialised central neurophysiological structures which mediate reports of anxiety and the behaviours that frequently accompany them. I will reject this notion in its extreme form, that is, that there is an automatic and inexorable link between activity in a set of specialised neurophysiological structures, and a pattern of behaviour and experience which, in everyday speech, is referred to as anxiety. Once more, the concept of levels can be employed here. Even though functional subsystems of behaviour, or physiological systems can be identified, it seems theoretically unprofitable, and also inaccurate, to bracket these off as *the* biological basis of 'anxiety'. Complaints of anxiety appear to involve a complex *chain* of central, peripheral and environmental events (Lazarus, 1966). Furthermore, in order to comprehend the *verbal report* of anxiety, a higher level of central processing seems to be required, taking account of information from a variety of sources (Bandura, 1978).

One type of chaining in subjects who report severe and persisting

anxiety may involve a positive feedback process. It has long been assumed that there can be a vicious cycle (fear of fear) between the antecedents of reports of anxiety. This phenomenon may take a variety of
forms. Stated generally, the consequences of a response include the
causal antecedents of the self-same response, leading to a spiralling
effect. The following hypothetical example illustrates the principle. A
peripheral response such as muscular tremor leads to an aversive consequence (e.g. dropping a teacup), which begins to be anticipated on
future occasions. Part of the learned anticipatory reaction includes the
self-same response (tremor) which originally signalled the aversive consequence, and a positive feedback loop is set up (see Evans, 1972; Hallam, 1976a, for case examples).

In this example, somatic events have the effect that they do because of
the meaning that is assigned to them. The causal effect is indirect and
dependent on prior learning. Other examples could be provided such as
the perception of unfamiliar sensations in the context of suspected disease. Another indirect influence may arise from actual physiological
dysfunctions which can be said to mimic peripheral sensory effects associated with reports of anxiety. Diseases such as thyrotoxicosis, hypo-
glycaemia and phaeocryocytoma may have this effect.

How might somatic processes cause panic-anxiety complaints in a
more direct manner? In other words, how might somatic processes
which are not directly involved in mediating the functional antecedents
of reports of anxiety act as contributary causal factors? One possibility
mentioned earlier is that behaviour may have environmental consequences that elicit neurochemical changes in the body. These in turn
may directly influence the processes mediating the central processing of
information. Another example might be an epileptic focus in critical
cortical areas. It is clear that a strict separation of psychological and
somatic causes of anxiety is untenable. This is not to say that the psychological can be reduced to the somatic or that the somatic component is an
unnecessary part of a psychological explanation. Any reductive solution
to the problem of explanation is likely to be of restricted power and
scope.

Common Misconceptions

Emotion concepts such as anxiety are sometimes used in an explanatory way. People are said to behave in certain ways *because* they are
anxious. Although statements of this kind have common currency, they
have little scientific merit. Somatic complaints are sometimes explained

as the somatic equivalent of anxiety. This assumption may be made because the complaint is elicited in situations that normally give rise to reports of anxiety. However, anxiety has little value as an explanatory concept, and the argument begs the question about the actual antecedents of somatic complaint.

The influence of dualism is another source of confusion in discussions of causal interaction. Psychological and somatic (organic) causation are opposed as two separate spheres of determination so that the question becomes how the mind can influence the body, and vice versa. This dualistic conception can be replaced, as suggested above, by a distinction between the structural and functional properties of neural tissue. This is a logical distinction between levels of explanation and not a substantial distinction between physical as opposed to mental causes of behaviour. For example, in the case where the brain has a deficient oxygen supply, the consequences can be described at the cellular level or as the disruption of the processing of information (which directly depends on cellular processes).

Tyrer (1976, p. 96) provided an example of theory construction which is implicitly dualistic. He conceived of *expressed* anxiety as the result of two determinants: (1) bodily feelings and (2) *perceived* anxiety, which is relatively 'pure' anxiety unaffected by bodily feelings. As both terms are mentalistic, the significance of the statements must be inferred from his earlier assertions about the relationship between bodily feelings and physiology. He assumed that some physiological parameters are consciously perceivable (e.g. heart-rate) whereas others are not (e.g. blood pressure and skin blood flow). He therefore adopted a kind of psychophysiological parallelism in which the mental is equated with pure anxiety and the physical with perception of bodily states.

According to the working model outlined above, somatic and psychological complaints are both mediated by an interaction between central and peripheral physiological processes. The perceived source of the feeling is not paralleled by separate causal domains (psychological and somatic) in different spatiotemporal locations.

PANIC-ANXIETY AND PATTERNS OF SOMATIC COMPLAINT

A wide range of somatic complaints are included in the panic-anxiety cluster. Examples are dizziness, an inability to swallow, pain in the chest, difficulty in breathing, sickness in the stomach, heart-thumping, an urge to urinate and many more. Under the present heading I will examine the evidence for the existence of different clusters of somatic complaint and attempt to clarify their relationship with panic-anxiety.

Somatisation

Somatisation has already been mentioned as a pattern of complaint which clusters separately in factor analyses of psychiatric symptoms (see Chapter 3). The American Psychiatric Association's DSM III classification (1980) describes somatisation disorder as a preoccupation with multiple symptoms for which medical attention is repeatedly sought. Usually there is a conflict between the patient's and the physician's attribution of causality, the physician believing the complaint to be related to situational or psychological factors. The sufferer will usually see himself or herself as the victim of an involuntary affliction and medical advice is sought despite reassurance that nothing is medically wrong.

A somatisation factor has regularly been obtained from analyses of psychiatric symptom checklists (Lipman et al., 1979), although this pattern might not correspond with the psychiatric conception of somatisation disorder. The complaints loading on the factor include heart-pounding, hot and cold spells, pains in the lower back, numbness or tingling in parts of the body, pain in the chest, nausea, dizziness and headaches. Although somatisation is distinct from the phobic-anxiety factor, there is a close similarity between some of the items; for example, compare 'faintness' with 'feeling afraid that you will faint in public'.

At a more general level of description, somatic complaints load on the general factor of neuroticism or general maladjustment, which has been derived from analyses of data collected from the general population (see e.g. Eysenck & Eysenck, 1964). Factor analysis of the Minnesota Multiphasic Personality Inventory (MMPI) also tends to produce one general factor of maladjustment in which hypochondriasis and hysteria scale scores are included (Butcher & Pancheri, 1976). As a general rule, in more highly selected clinical samples, the general maladjustment factor fractionates into dimensions which resemble familiar psychiatric syndromes. However, even in community samples, a factor of somatic complaints has been extracted as the third largest factor of the MMPI (Kassebaum, Couch & Slater, 1959; Wiggins, 1969). This factor is commonly found in clinical samples as well (Eichman, 1961; Fisher, 1964). It seems then that the somatic and psychological expression of distress are correlated to some degree but that a dimension of somatic complaint is a strong contender as a third orthogonal dimension of description after general maladjustment and introversion/extroversion.

The evidence appears to suggest, therefore, that somatisation can be differentiated from the somatic complaints found in panic-anxiety. The former pattern is more likely to show greater diversity (particularly in complaints of a sensory-motor type), whereas in the latter, discomfort is referred mainly to the viscera. The two patterns do not appear to define groups of subjects because somatisation is obtained in samples given anxiety (and other) diagnoses (see Chapter 3).

It is not known what other physical or psychological characteristics might be differentially associated with the two patterns. One possibility is features of actual ill health because it is known that there is an association between all forms of psychological distress and physical disease (Eastwood & Trevelyan, 1972). For example, vestibular disorders can produce intermittent spells of dizziness, nausea and headache which are similar to items mentioned earlier. The reader is referred to Lipowski (1975), Roy (1982) and Fenton (1982) for discussions of the interaction between physical dysfunction and the expression of complaint.

Illness Fears

There are many other possible differentiating features of the two somatic patterns. There may, in fact, be no abnormal sensation or symptom as such but simply the interpretation of quite normal bodily sensations as abnormal. This tendency is usually associated with fears of developing an illness or the belief that a disease process is present despite medical evidence to the contrary. The nature of illness fears was clarified by Pilowsky (1967) who devised a questionnaire based on attitude statements which differentiated hypochondriacal from other psychiatric subjects. A factor analysis produced three main dimensions of complaint, which he labelled *bodily preoccupation, fear of disease* and *firm conviction of pathology*. Similar clusters of attitudes were obtained by Bianchi (1973) in a sample of psychiatric inpatients and by Pilowsky and Spence (1976) in subjects with intractable pain. Of the three factors, disease phobia appears to have most in common with panic-anxiety, and the other two factors may be more relevant to somatisation.

In Bianchi's (1973) study, ratings of anxiety and disease phobia loaded the same factor. In a group of inpatients who had a strong fear of disease, almost one-third were described as agoraphobic whereas no subject with other somatic complaints was described as such (Bianchi, 1971). The presence of illness fears amongst agoraphobics is mentioned by many authors (e.g. Buglass et al., 1977) and is evident in the autobiographical reports (Chapter 4).

It is beyond the scope of this chapter to cover the many other aspects of somatic complaint that have been researched. These include aspects of the natural history, personality and cultural factors. In particular, the converse of a tendency to report bodily symptoms such as fatigue appears to be a state of superior mental and physical fitness, rather than the straightforward absence of complaint (Barron, 1953; Delhees & Cattell, 1971; Hallam & Rachman, 1980). It is not so clear that this is true of anxiety complaints where calmness or self-confidence may lie at the opposite pole of the panic-anxiety dimension.

PANIC-ANXIETY: SOMATOGENIC HYPOTHESES OF CAUSATION

This section reviews hypotheses suggesting that somatic dysfunction of one kind or another has a primary causal role in bringing about panic-anxiety complaints. These hypotheses assume that the main direction of causation in the psychophysiological connection is peripheral/central. Many causes have been investigated, including chemicals in the blood, autonomic nervous system reactivity, sensitivity of receptors to hormonal stimulation, balance disorders and prolapse of the mitral valve of the heart.

Two points of criticism are worth noting at the outset. The first is that researchers do not always make clear whether the somatic dysfunction is a necessary, sufficient or merely contributary factor in causation. Even if only contributary, somatic dysfunctions cannot be lightly dismissed. The second point concerns exactly what behaviours or complaints are being attributed to somatic dysfunction. For example, panic attacks have been singled out for explanation, but definitions of this phenomenon vary from study to study. It is not yet known whether panic attacks can be observed reliably or how much they depend on a preferred style of reporting intense distress.

Manipulation of Peripheral Process by Hormones and Pharmacological Agents

The concept of fear of fear depends crucially on the postulation of peripheral/central feedback loops. Experimental studies have taken advantage of the fact that peripheral physiological states can be manipulated pharmacologically with minimal direct effect on the central nervous system. By blocking or facilitating peripheral physiological activity, the role of peripheral sensory feedback can be investigated. Interest in this method was stimulated by theoretical controversy over the primacy of peripheral or central events in the perception of emotion (the James-Cannon controversy). The early discovery of sympathetic nervous activity during emotional states led naturally to investigations of the effects of infusion of the sympathomimetic hormones, adrenalin and noradrenalin, which are themselves secreted as a result of neural stimulation of the adrenal medulla during emotional arousal. Although these hormones can act as central neurotransmitters, they do not, as exogenous hormones, cross the blood/brain barrier (Leshner, 1978), and therefore they do not have a direct central effect. The principal peripheral effect of adrenalin is on cardiac output, circulation and carbohydrate metabolism, whereas noradrenalin mainly modifies blood pressure.

Breggin (1964) reviewed the literature on the effects of infusions of adrenalin and concluded, like Misch (1935), that the association between sympathomimetic symptoms and reports of anxiety is learned. That is, the perception of sympathetically mediated visceral activity as anxiety has to be acquired. This conclusion was supported by two kinds of evidence. First, infusion of adrenalin is most likely to produce self-reported anxiety by subjects who have a history of anxiety complaints. Other subjects tend to report only 'cold' emotion, that is, noticeable sensory effects which do not have any affective intensity. Second, anxiety is more likely to be reported when the experimental setting is threatening.

These two generalisations were explained by Breggin as instances of the 'reinforcement of anxiety' which was dependent on previously learned associations. (The threatening aspects of having an injection could not account for reported anxiety because placebo injections had little or no emotional effect.) The concept of reinforcement of anxiety does not in itself specify a positive feedback process, and the sometimes dramatic effects of infusions are rather difficult to explain simply by a potentiation or extension of the number of cues for the report of anxiety. Furthermore, some subjects described sensations which could not have been directly mediated by sympathetic arousal. This may imply additional central processing of afferent sensory feedback.

Subsequent work has substantiated and extended the general finding that infusion of adrenalin can elicit reports of anxiety in certain subjects under certain conditions. It has been reported that digital vascular responses to adrenalin (in subjects who have previously complained of anxiety) are predictive of reports of anxiety to infusion (Vlachakis, 1974, quoted by Pitts and Allen, 1979). However, an adequate psychophysiological account of the effects of infusion in subjects who habitually complain of anxiety is still needed.

Pitts and his colleagues (Pitts & McClure, 1967; Pitts & Allen, 1979) have broadened the biochemical story by including the effects of adrenalin on carbohydrate metabolism. One effect of adrenalin is to initiate anaerobic metabolism of carbohydrates, which results in a marked elevation of sodium lactate concentrations in muscle and other tissue. It is argued that this effect is invariable and that reports of anxiety secondary to infusions of adrenalin cannot occur in the absence of increased lactate production. Therefore, lactate is thought by Pitts and Allen to be a crucial link in the causal chain. In support, it has been shown that the normal rise in blood lactate after exercise is excessive in subjects complaining of anxiety (see e.g. Jones & Mellersh, 1946). Exercise can also trigger complaint in these subjects. Moreover, infusion of sodium lactate (but not placebo) usually elicits reports of anxiety in habitual complainers; only rarely does this happen in control subjects (Pitts & McClure, 1967). Unlike a placebo, lactate produces parasthesias (tingling sensations) in most subjects and so control subjects are not immune to the effects of injection. However, they do not report panic or anxiety as well. These findings have been replicated by other workers (e.g. Kelly, Mitchell-Higgs & Sherman, 1971).

Ackerman and Sachar (1974) reviewed the lactate hypothesis of anxiety and found it wanting on theoretical, methodological and logical grounds. In essence, they pointed out that the biochemical conditions which have been put forward to account for the effect of lactate may be found in the absence of reports of anxiety and, conversely, that reports of anxiety may be present in their absence. No necessary or sufficient causes have been established.

Nevertheless, there remains the empirical observation that infusion of lactate in predisposed subjects can elicit acute distress. A case for the *specific* role of lactate ions has been argued by Pitts and Allen (1979), whereas Grosz (1973) believed that any perturbation of biophysical homeostasis is likely to elicit reports of anxiety in predisposed subjects. Grosz and Farmer (1972) infused *normal* subjects with bicarbonate or lactate ions and found few differences in their subjective effects. It remains to be seen, if Grosz was correct, whether certain types of biophysical perturbation are more likely than others to elicit reports of anxiety in *predisposed* subjects.

Ackerman and Sachar (1974) explained the effects of sodium lactate in the same way that earlier writers had interpreted the effects of infused adrenalin. In patients for whom complaints of anxiety have previously occurred in association with difficulty in breathing, rapid pulse, sweating, and so forth, the somatic sensations arising out of these responses may become phobic stimuli for the subject. Any situation which elicits these responses (e.g. one involving physical exercise) will, at the same time, produce sensory feedback to which anxiety has been conditioned. Ackerman and Sachar rightly pointed out that their explanation leaves the question about the original cause of reports of anxiety unanswered.

A study by Bonn, Harrison and Rees (1971) supports the assumption of a learned association between the effects of lactate and reports of anxiety. In the first place, 12 out of 20 of their subjects who complained of anxiety did *not* experience distress after the infusion, but some of them said that they would have done so had it not been for the presence of the doctor. This argues for a central mediation of the effect. Second, Bonn et al. successfully used repeated infusion of lactate over a 3-week period as a therapeutic procedure. Their patients reported significantly fewer complaints of anxiety at termination of therapy and 6 weeks later. No experimental controls were employed, but, even so, the decline in complaints of anxiety is more readily explained by the extinction of an acquired, centrally mediated response to peripheral sensation than by a somatogenic hypothesis.

The Use of Beta-Blocking Agents to Investigate the Somatogenic Hypothesis

Adrenalin has different effects on different types of blood vessels, causing vasoconstriction in skin and vasodilatation in muscle. It is now known that there are two adrenergic receptor systems, called alpha and beta, associated with the innervation of different organs of the body. Adrenalin has both alpha and beta effects, while noradrenalin has almost pure alpha effects. Propranolol is a drug which reduces the effect of adrenalin by blocking the beta receptor site. Propranolol and related drugs have little detectable effect on centrally mediated psychological functions (Tyrer, 1976), and so it may be assumed that changes in peripheral activity, such as decreased visceral activity or motor tremor, are responsible for the subjective and behavioural effects of administration of the drug.

Early reports suggested that propranolol had a specific effect on *somatic* anxiety complaints (Granville-Grossman & Turner, 1966; Suzman, 1971). In particular, muscular weakness and tremor, fatigue, breathlessness and palpitations were reduced. Propranolol seemed to be less effective in modifying the psychological aspects of complaints (Tyrer & Lader, 1974). Attempts were then made to understand peripheral/central interactions by experimental administration of beta-blocking agents.

Tyrer (1976) demonstrated that beta-blockade reduced pulse-rate and body tremor in psychiatric patients who reported anxiety. He divided his subjects into two groups: one that attributed their distress to a somatic source, such as a disease or the bodily feeling itself; and another that made psychological attributions, for example, attributing anxiety to stressful life events. The two groups did not differ in their scores on self-reported somatic or psychological anxiety *complaints*, and so attribution of source did not appear to relate to descriptions of the complaint as mental or bodily. Tyrer found that only in the somatic attribution group did chemically manipulated changes in heart-rate and body tremor correlate with changes in anxiety complaint. This supported his argument that some subjects were distressed by sensory feedback from *actual* physiological changes. However, the results must be viewed cautiously because Tyrer did not adequately specify his criteria for assessing psychological and somatic attributions. In fact, reference to these studies often confuse somatic complaining with somatic attribution. As noted earlier, items in psychiatric symptom checklists are not worded to elicit these distinctions, and Schalling, Cronholm and Asberg (1975) even disputed, on the basis of a cluster analysis of anxiety complaints, that *somatic* and *psychological* are meaningful dimensions of description. A further criticism of Tyrer's study is that the correlations between verbal reports of distress and physiological measures may reflect, to an unknown degree, the psychological effects of pulse-rate measurement and temporal effects not due to drug action. Subjects who have fears of illness and attribute their complaints to cardiac disease are likely to be more sensitive to the significance of the measurement procedures, and this factor may have given rise to a spurious correlation.

The effects of beta-blockade on the physiological response to real-life and laboratory stressors is another avenue of investigation. It is known that changes in heart-rate and other responses are associated with short-term fluctuations in levels of plasma catecholamines (McCubbin, Richardson, Langer, Kizer & Obrist, 1983). Recent technical advances have made it possible to automate collection of blood samples and to make rapid assays of plasma catecholamines (Dimsdale & Moss, 1980). As fluctuating levels can be monitored from minute to minute, physiological events and self-reports can be correlated with some precision. Adrenalin secretion is associated with threatening and stressful situations, noradrenalin with assertion and physical exercise (Carruthers, 1981; Dimsdale & Moss, 1980). This is broadly consistent with the careful studies of Frankenhauser (1975) who measured levels of catecholamine in the urine.

The effect of beta-blockade on the cardiac response to natural stressors is considerable. Carruthers (1981) reported that oxprenolol reduced the mean maximum heart-rate of public speakers from 140 to 82. The level of plasma catecholamines did not change. However, in groups of mountain climbers and airline passengers, the drug also lessened the rise in plasma adrenalin. Carruthers believed that the high heart-rates observed during emotional stress are mediated by beta receptors and hence are suppressed by beta-blocking compounds. Suppression may also eliminate interoceptive stimuli which have acquired a cueing function for reports of anxiety, and this is consistent with the smaller rises in adrenalin secretion in the beta-blocked groups mentioned above.

Oxprenolol improved the technical performance of string musicians as judged by other professional musicians (James, Pearson, Griffiths & Newbury, 1977). This improvement was reflected in self-assessed performance, suggesting that self-monitoring may interact with drug effects to improve the general quality of performance. In a similar study by Neftel et al. (1982) a professional violin teacher judged beta-blocked subjects as less hindered by stage fright, but a sonographic analysis did not support this assessment in terms of technical improvement. Excretion of catecholamines was greater under beta-blockade, which is difficult to reconcile with diminished stage fright and the opposite effects on adrenalin release noted above in Carruther's studies.

In sum, there is support for the idea that suppression of peripheral physiological activity by beta blockade can have beneficial effects, but the precise nature of the peripheral/central interaction is not fully understood.

Researchers have asked whether the tendency to complain of anxiety is associated with increased catecholamine production, with slow removal of catecholamine from receptor sites or with beta receptor site sensitivity (Mathews, Ho, Francis, Taylor & Weinman, 1982). It is difficult, however, to draw inferences from the evidence because any abnormality of peripheral function could have sensory consequences which are perceived as threatening, thereby eliciting a centrally mediated release of adrenalin. One reviewer concluded that hyperactivity at beta-adrenergic receptor sites is responsible for the visceral sensations experienced during episodes of panic (Stampler, 1982), but this hyperactivity is attributed to unknown central or peripheral mechanisms. A somatogenic hypothesis is not, therefore, necessarily indicated.

A small proportion of subjects who complain of anxiety become emotionally distressed when injected with a beta-adrenergic agonist (iso-proterenol hydrochloride) (Frohlich, Tarazi & Dunstan, 1969; Easton & Sherman, 1976). This distressed state can be reversed by intravenous injection of propranolol, and long-term treatment with this drug is apparently effective. Control subjects do not respond with dramatic signs of distress. Although it is claimed that this group of subjects with mainly somatic complaints is suffering from beta-receptor hypersensitivity, the further assumption that the cause of their complaints has been discovered can be criticised on grounds similar to those which apply to the lactate hypothesis. For example, Frohlich reported on one subject who had beta-adrenergic hyperactivity without somatic complaints.

Panic-Anxiety and the Hyperventilation Syndrome

Hyperventilation is a state in which the ventilatory effort exceeds metabolic needs. Apart from organic and physiological causes, it may be produced by faulty breathing habits such as rapid, shallow, irregular breathing or deep, sighing respirations (Christie, 1935). However, it can also occur without visibly increased respiration rate. It produces an alteration of the pH of the arterial blood because too much CO_2 is blown off during respiration. However, the diagnosis is usually established by the symptomatic response to a controlled trial of hyperventilation rather than by determination of blood gases.

In a comprehensive review, Magarian (1982) described the various biochemical and physiological consequences of hyperventilation and their associated symptomatic manifestations. Adverse physiological effects include impaired cellular energy resources, reduced availability of oxygen for use by tissue and cerebral vasoconstriction. Magarian equated DaCosta's syndrome, the effort syndrome, and neurocirculatory asthenia with the hyperventilation syndrome, and he also noted that the symptoms are identical to those described for anxiety neurosis. These include fatigue, weakness, headache, dizziness, sleep disturbance, sweating, poor concentration, numbness and tingling, difficulty in breathing, gastrointestinal discomfort, muscular tremor and cramps, anxiety, irritability and depersonalisation. Up to 10% of patients presenting to general physicians are said to complain of signs and symptoms relating to hyperventilation (Magarian, 1982). Lazarus and Kostan (1969) described frequent phobias in these individuals relating to disease, death, insanity and being left alone. Magarian therefore makes a very strong claim in identifying what I have called panic-anxiety with an underlying physiological mechanism. Certain aspects of the hyperventilation syndrome certainly help to explain the inexplicable and unpredictable nature of panic episodes. For example, the subject may be unaware of his or her breathing pattern, and Lum (1976, 1981) believed that faulty breathing habits, simply acquired as a result of family and cultural influences, contribute to chronically low levels of PA CO_2. Then minor stressors, exercise or other factors which further increase respiration rate are sufficient to produce unexpected and inexplicable symptoms. Lum argued that, whereas a stressor may be the initial triggering event, the subject may feel additionally threatened if the symptomatic effects of hyperventilation are unrecognised by a physician. The maintenance of the syndrome in a chronic or recurrent state is therefore explained by additional psychological factors.

We are not, therefore, dealing with a purely peripheral explanation of the effects of hyperventilation. Lum pointed out that hyperventilation is a normal response to stress or, indeed, any mood change. It produces psychological distress only when it is excessive, inappropriate or persists after the stressor has been withdrawn. Second, unequivocal evidence of low PA CO_2 is lacking in almost half of the subjects he has assessed. Third, chronic respiratory alkalosis alone does not produce symptoms because residence at high altitudes requires chronic hyperventilation to compensate for the rarefied atmosphere. The *level* of PA CO_2 may not be so important as fluctuation in level due to erratic breathing (Lum, 1981). We must consider, therefore, the psychological factors which affect breathing and which lead to the perception of somatic sensations as threatening. Lum believed that the frequent failure of doctors to recognise signs of hyperventilation and the baffling nature of the symptoms conspire to heighten the subjects' sense of helplessness and fear of the incurable nature of their problems. We may conclude, therefore, that an integrated psychophysiological explanation is required to explain the syndrome. A link with the research on the effects of beta-adrenergic blockade is contained in the observation that hyperventilation is a component of the response to this form of stimulation and that beta-blocking drugs decrease the ventilatory response to catecholamines and also to CO_2 (see Magarian, 1982).

CONCLUSION: THE SOMATOGENIC HYPOTHESIS

Judging by the ready supply of explanations of panic-anxiety in terms of peripheral abnormalities, we may conclude either (1) that this is a reflection of a desire amongst medically trained researchers to discover a biomedical cause or (2) that peripheral dysfunctions *of many different kinds* might be associated with panic-anxiety. There is probably some truth in both of these conclusions. Most of the abnormalities associated with panic-anxiety can also be found in the absence of anxiety. For example, Crowe, Pauls, Slyman and Noyes (1979) observed that a prolapse of the mitral valve of the heart was present in 66% of their sample of subjects complaining of anxiety. *Mitral valve prolapse (MVP) syndrome* is said to include symptoms which are typical of anxiety neurosis, but because MVP is found in about 10% of the population, it is at best only a contributory cause of reports of anxiety. This conclusion is not without significance. It can be generalised to the proposition that *any* peripheral dysfunction that produces sensory feedback which is aversive or likely to be perceived as theatening, can be an important contributory cause of panic-anxiety. An obvious example is vestibular dysfunction, which can produce episodes of vertigo, imbalance, nausea and headache. These individuals commonly develop complaints of anxiety and agoraphobia (Pratt & McKenzie, 1958). The extent to which individuals with vestibular dysfunction can identify the separate sources of their sensations and make correct attributions is quite variable. Some subjects, who may not have been correctly diagnosed, make incorrect attributions or remain unaware of the multiple causation of their problems. As already pointed out, centrally mediated humoral and autonomic effects are difficult to disentangle from the effects of dysfunctions which are intrinsically peripheral. The separate contributions of psychological predisposition, semantic elaboration of peripheral cues, positive feedback processes, interoceptive conditioning and stimulus generalisation need to be investigated.

6

Panic-Anxiety and Alcohol Dependence

INTRODUCTION

One consequence of the use of the medical model in psychiatry is the partitioning of problem behaviours into categories which take on a life of their own as disorders. The tendency is then to look for separate causal mechanisms for each disorder. This may inhibit the discovery of conceptual and empirical connections between apparently separate problem areas. The principal assumption of the psychological model is that abnormal behaviour can be explained in terms of the processes underlying normal behaviour. What seems to be required is a multidimensional causal model in which apparently different problem behaviours are observed to share common antecedents and underlying processes, while at the same time the specificity of problem behaviour is accounted for. It is in this spirit that a link between panic-anxiety and alcohol dependence is sought.

An association between the use of alcohol and a tendency to complain of anxiety would, of course, come as no great surprise. However, research during the past decade suggests that there is more to such a relationship than the fact that alcohol can have a calming effect. It is possible that panic-anxiety and alcohol dependence have common antecedents and overlapping features.

The empirical data I discuss in this chapter relate mostly to categories of psychiatric disorder, for example, anxiety neurosis, alcohol dependence and agoraphobia. This weakens the general argument, but, unfortunately, there is little relevant research which has used a dimensional approach to measurement. The psychiatric statistics are probably influenced by a tendency to diagnose women as showing a mood disturbance and men as drinking to excess, regardless of the actual behaviour presented to the psychiatrist (Mullaney & Trippett, 1979).

Alcohol is, of course, drunk for a variety of motives, of which the relief of distress is only one. There is also some disagreement among researchers about the subjective and physiological effects of ethanol. The sedative effects are well known, but the effect depends on dosage (Peyser, 1982). In a reinterpretation of the literature on animal experimentation, Hodgson, Stockwell and Rankin (1979) argued that the evidence justifies the conclusion that alcohol *does* inhibit fear and frustration.

With regard to humans, tension reduction is one of the most commonly reported reasons for problem drinking. Although prolonged drinking can bring about dysphoria (i.e. depressed mood and tremulousness), the short-term effect is one of reduced heart-rate and hand tremor (Stockwell, Hodgson & Rankin, 1982). Alcohol-dependent subjects in the latter study judged that continued drinking would be less aversive than stopping drinking, and so the motivation for drinking may be a prevention of mood deterioration rather than calmness per se. There is, then, considerable evidence that a tension-reduction hypothesis can account for at least one form of drinking (see also Kilpatrick, Sutker & Smith, 1976).

My initial aim is to review some studies indicating that the diagnostic categories of anxiety neurosis/agoraphobia are statistically associated with the diagnosis of alcohol dependence. Two possible reasons for the association are suggested. The first is that use of alcohol is simply a means of reducing anxiety complaints. The second is that agoraphobia and alcohol dependence are sex-related expressions of some common antecedent conditions.

ASSOCIATION BETWEEN THE DIAGNOSES OF ALCOHOL DEPENDENCE AND PHOBIC ANXIETY

Epidemiological Data

Evidence has accumulated that the overlap between the psychiatric diagnostic categories of alcohol dependence and anxiety neurosis/agoraphobia is quite large and unlikely to be explained simply as the coincidence of two 'disorders' with a fairly high base rate of occurrence. Woodruff, Guze and Clayton (1972) found that 25% of anxiety neurotics were heavy drinkers and 15% were physically dependent. In the sample as a whole, drinking was more common in males, phobic avoidance in females. Quitkin, Rifkin, Kaplan and Klein (1972) reported 10 subjects with phobic anxiety who were also dependent on sedative drugs including alcohol. They estimated that chemical dependence was present in 5 to 10% of phobic patients. In a study of 500 consecutive psychiatric outpatients, alcoholism was a common additional or secondary diagnosis in males with anxiety neurosis (Cloninger, Martin, Clayton & Guze, 1981).

The prevalence of phobic anxiety in alcohol-dependent persons was studied by Mullaney and Trippett (1979). They reported that one-third of their subjects had disabling phobias (agoraphobia or social phobia) and that one-third were borderline phobic. This surprisingly high proportion was confirmed in a second British study in which, using more rigorous criteria for making the diagnosis of phobia, 18% were found to be severely phobic (Smail, Stockwell, Canter & Hodgson, 1984). Alcohol had also been used deliberately by the phobic and alcohol-dependent subjects to cope with fears. In a comparison group whose primary diagnosis was phobia, one-third, mainly men, had used alcohol in a similar manner.

Epidemiological surveys have also demonstrated a statistical association between anxiety neurosis and alcoholism. In a thorough study of a random sample of all Icelanders born between 1895 and 1897 and followed up 60 years later, Helgason (1964) recorded the lifetime risk of various categories of disorder. Neurosis was defined as a constant awareness of, and disturbance by, nervous symptoms for which a general practitioner or psychiatrist had been consulted. As has been found in most other surveys, females were more likely to have received a diagnosis of neurosis, males of alcoholism. When both sets of figures were added together, the prevalence of neurosis/alcoholism was virtually identical for each sex, at about 8%. Moreover, the most commonly observed combination of diagnoses (when these were broken down by types of neurosis, psychosis and psychopathic personality) was that of anxiety neurosis and alcoholism, but this was true of the males only. There were five times as many men as women with this combination.

Family Studies

Several investigators have interviewed the relatives of persons given an anxiety diagnosis in an attempt to study the heritability of the so-called anxiety disorders. Freud (1894) noted that anxiety neurosis seemed to affect members of the same family. This observation has been confirmed in later studies, which, incidentally, have also shown an association with dependence on alcohol. An early small-scale survey of the general population assessed the prevalence of anxiety neurosis to be 4.7% (Cohen, Balal, Kilpatrick, Reed & White, 1951). Among first-degree relatives of *patients* given this diagnosis, the prevalence figure was many times higher, with women outnumbering men by two to one. When the number of males in a family who were diagnosed alcoholic was added to the number diagnosed with anxiety alone, an equality between the sexes was obtained. In other words, it could be argued that a common factor was responsible for the expression of these two problems.

Crowe et al. (1980) observed a higher prevalence of panic in the sibs of subjects complaining of anxiety than was found in relatives of control subjects. There was no increased risk of other anxiety disorders in the relatives, but there was a greater than expected number who were dependent on alcohol, particularly in the males. In a family study by Cloninger et al. (1981), it was again found that there was a familial pattern of anxiety diagnoses, and dependence on alcohol appeared to be more prevalent in male relatives only. Amongst the first-degree relatives of patients given diagnoses other than anxiety, there were significantly fewer cases of anxiety neurosis.

In conclusion, it seems that there is a statistical association between various anxiety diagnoses and alcohol dependence. It appears to be the males who are given combined diagnoses or, if they are the first-degree relatives of a person who receives an anxiety diagnosis, to be regarded as dependent on alcohol rather than as complaining of anxiety.

POSSIBLE EXPLANATIONS FOR THE ASSOCIATION

I suggested in an earlier publication (Hallam, 1978) that staying at home and the use of alcohol were two alternative ways of coping with the distress associated with complaints of anxiety. Males were assumed to prefer the latter strategy, females the former.

Staying at home and the use of alcohol relieve distress in different ways. In the following discussion I assume that the probability of reporting anxiety is related to a balance of eliciting and inhibitory cues. The antecedents of reports of anxiety are probably wide-ranging (see Chapter 14) and are most likely to be present in novel, demanding, conflictual or threatening situations. Inhibitory cues (see Mandler, 1975, p. 195) are assumed to include human contact, familiar and predictable situations, pet animals, the availability of a telephone, and so forth. On balance, the home environment should contain more inhibitory cues than the public environment, and therefore the person who habitually reports anxiety should prefer to stay at home and avoid public places. However, in the presence of a trusted companion (a strong inhibitory cue), anxiety may not be reported at all in public places. In order to emphasise that complaints of anxiety in agoraphobics were not simply reported in response to features of the public environment, I renamed agoraphobia as staying-at-home behaviour (Hallam, 1978).

Staying at home is effective as a strategy because it acts on the environment to diminish the likelihood that antecedents for reports of anxiety will be encountered. Self-sedation, in contrast, acts on the individual, permitting freedom of movement and concealing any tendency to report anxiety in specific situations or to demonstrate behavioural avoidance.

I assume that the preference of females for staying at home as a coping strategy accounts for the very high ratio of females to males who are diagnosed as agoraphobic (Marks, 1970; Burns & Thorpe, 1977). This preference may derive from social incentives (Hallam, 1983) and also conformity with sex-role stereotypes (Fodor, 1974). The use of alcohol is more consistent with the fulfillment of male expectations, and therefore this strategy may be preferred by males. However, the issue is likely to be much more complex than appears at first sight. For example, sex biases in the perception of fearful behaviour need to be considered (Evans & White, 1981).

The hypothesis that staying at home and use of alcohol function to reduce complaints of anxiety must be modified to take into account short- and long-term effects of coping. As *maladaptive* coping strategies they are likely to exacerbate sources of distress in the long term. Staying at home leads to social isolation and failure to meet social obligations. Abrupt withdrawal from alcohol after a steady period of ingestion causes tremulousness, hyperexcitability and sleepdisturbance and thus increases the likelihood that anxiety will be reported. These negative effects are often overcome by further use of alcohol.

The presence of cycles of exacerbation when maladaptive coping strategies are employed raises a question about the direction of causality in the statistical association between anxiety diagnoses and alcohol dependence. Even if the presence of complaints of anxiety is a risk for alcohol dependence, over the long term, dependency may markedly increase the probability that anxiety will become a major complaint.

A retrospective study of the time course of phobic behaviour and alcohol use attempted to throw some light on this causal question (Stockwell, Smail, Hodgson & Canter, 1983). In subjects with both problems, it was found that for the majority, phobias developed before problem drinking. This was also found in the study by Mullaney and Trippett (1979) mentioned earlier. However, the phobias became most constricting some time after a dependence on alcohol had developed. In general, the amount of drinking and the intensity of the phobia covaried systematically, decreasing as fear lessened and vice versa.

Stockwell and his colleagues made an interesting observation about a phenomenon they called the dry shakes. This is an alcohol-withdrawal type state during an abstinent period. Approximately one-third of their sample recognised this phenomenon, and this subgroup was more severely dependent on alcohol and more phobic. They suggested that the terms *panic attack* and *dry shakes* do not really denote different underlying states but simply reflect different labelling habits.

If this is so, there is no reason to suppose that alcohol-dependent persons will *necessarily* complain of anxiety. However, alcohol will presumably be consumed to alleviate a distressing state which shares some common antecedents conditions with panic. These antecedents are assumed to interact with other factors related to gender, labelling habits and coping attitudes, and in doing so produce distinctive clinical phenomena. By adopting a multidimensional causal perspective on these so-called disorders, the overt behaviours which distinguish them might, on examination, be found to be related to common psychological processes.

7

Depersonalisation

INTRODUCTION

Depersonalisation, like a dependence on alcohol, has been put in the category of pathological disorders. It is examined here in the spirit of the last chapter, that is, as a phenomenon to illustrate the general point that a psychological perspective seeks common processes and mechanisms to explain clinically diverse problems. Depersonalisation has, of course, been mentioned in association with the putative anxiety disorders. It is an intriguing phenomenon deserving of renewed research interest.

DEFINITION

Depersonalisation refers to a certain strange, but commonplace, experience. It is described as a sense of detachment, as if the body and self are separate, and the self is observing the body. There may be a loss of the sense that actions are willed and an absence of reported emotion even though behaviours and physiological changes that are commonly associated with emotion are obviously present. The related experience of derealisation is described as a sense of estrangement from the world, which appears distant, remote, dreamlike or two-dimensional. The aforementioned experiences tend to be associated with each other, and this was confirmed by a statistical analysis of a questionnaire designed to cover a variety of unusual perceptual experiences (Dixon, 1963). Dixon referred to the cluster of items which included depersonalisation and derealisation as *self-alienation*. The other factors he obtained were *mystical experience* and *hallucinatory experience*.

Noyes, Hoenk, Kuperman and Slymen (1977) factor analysed a questionnaire of a similar nature with data obtained from two groups of subjects: accident victims and psychiatric patients. Accident victims described their experiences in the moments between the time they realised that the accident would occur and the moment of impact (a median time of 5 seconds). The psychiatric patients reported back on the previous 6 months. Despite the large difference in time span and situation to which the reports referred, a set of three similar factors was obtained from the analysis of the data from each group. The first was labelled detachment (from the world, body and emotions); the second indicated a clouding or hazing of consciousness including panoramic memory; and the third appeared to refer to a contrasting state of hyperalertness, sharpness of perception and reports of intensified emotional experience.

People who complain of anxiety and panic commonly report depersonalisation as well (Roth, 1959; Noyes et al., 1977). Depersonalisation has also been described as a psychiatric diagnosis. It appears that the diagnosis of depersonalisation can be made in the absence of any other pronounced psychiatric complaints (Davison, 1964). The age at which the complaint is registered and the sex ratio are very similar for the diagnoses of depersonalisation and anxiety (McClure, 1964). The events which precipitate complaint appear to be similar (see below), and like panic, an episode of depersonalisation is usually abrupt rather than gradual. It would appear that depersonalisation can become a source of complaint in the absence of reported anxiety (Davison, 1964).

The relationship between reports of depersonalisation and other mood states has been the object of considerable controversy. The association with reports of anxiety is particularly interesting because, in some cases, a report of depersonalisation can suddenly replace one of anxiety, leading some researchers to speculate that it is a mechanism to reduce sensory stimulation (Lader & Wing, 1966, p. 145). However, it is reported in the absence of complaints of anxiety, or sometimes appears to precede reports of anxiety.

Something like depersonalisation has been described by jet pilots and is called the 'break-off' phenomenon (Clark & Graybiel, 1957; Sours, 1965). It may occur when a pilot is flying solo at high altitudes with little to do. Up to 35% of pilots enter a detached, dreamy state with vivid fantasies which, for most of them, are exhilarating and pleasurable. The phenomenon was experienced as highly unpleasant by about 13% of the pilots in whom it occurred; they reported anxiety, loneliness and giddiness. An effort to become involved in flying manoeuvers often abolished the sensations. Individuals described as unstable were said to be more prone to experience break-off.

Depersonalisation is a common experience. McClure (1964) conducted a survey in the general population and found that 29% reported the experience in the previous 6 months. For 7% it was described as intense. Dixon (1963) observed that over half of his student subjects could recognise descriptions of depersonalisation as something they had experienced.

In the psychiatric context, where it is described as a symptom, depersonalisation is associated with many diagnoses. This is not surprising in view of its common occurrence in the general population. Davison (1964) described seven subjects who had few other complaints. Typically, each episode had an abrupt onset and offset, and lasted from a few minutes to several months. As one subject said 'Something goes click in my head'. The tendency to report depersonalisation often spanned several decades with episodes spaced years apart. Davison stated that his subjects were normal between episodes but that they were rather meticulous and conscientious.

DEPERSONALISATION AND PANIC-ANXIETY

An association between reports of depersonalisation and panic was noted by Roth et al. (1965). Depersonalisation was prominent as an initial feature of the phobic-anxiety-depersonalisation syndrome in 21% of the patients who fell into this category. In 60%, fears were the most prominent complaint when problems began, and in the remainder both features were equally represented when problems were first noted. The patients who complained of depersonalisation were younger, less often married, reported fewer panics and were less depressed.

Among students who had experienced depersonalisation, anxiety in public places was reported by one-third of the females but only 6% of the males (Meyers & Grant, 1972).

In Noyes' series of consecutive psychiatric admissions, depersonalisation was associated with the severity of reported anxiety and with panic (Noyes et al., 1977). There was a slight but nonsignificant association with depressed mood.

There seems to be some agreement that changes in normal sensory experience (e.g. due to fever, drugs, emotional shock, extreme fatigue and sensory isolation) can lead to a report of the experience. Saperstein (1949) believed that susceptible individuals are unable to bring into congruence their perception of the environment and the schema of the environment which they hold; for example, depersonalisation may be reported when a person is shown his or her own photograph, after a transitory deafness or any perceptual change, peripherally or centrally induced. Davison (1964) described one subject in whom depersonalisation was regularly reported after (the morning after!) taking alcohol. An impression that is gained from reading the studies cited above is that the events which elicit reports of depersonalisation and panic are very similar.

THEORETICAL INTERPRETATION

Sedman (1970) reviewed theories of the depersonalisation experience and concluded that it is a normal and innate functional response of the brain, which is not associated with the 'clouding' of consciousness observed in persons with organic brain syndromes. The assumption of innateness does not answer any theoretical questions. It may be more useful to study the circumstances in which reports of depersonalisation are made.

The verbal description of depersonalisation suggests that a sense of self-identity is retained but is assailed by information which cannot readily be accommodated. One might speculate that there are three ways in which the self-concept could be modified. (1) It could be modified by an alteration of sensory experience which, because it is initiated voluntarily (e.g. by taking a drug), cannot be attributed to public events and must instead be attributed to a change in the self. (2) Self-concept could change if information that is used in the construction of the familiar experience of self is missing an important component (e.g. feedback regarding peripheral physiological state). (3) Assuming that the self-concept requires continual confirmation from information supplied in personal interaction, sensory and social isolation might diminish the sense of self.

Given these possibilities, an asociation with reports of anxiety might be expected. Insofar as panic is reported as an intense and unusual experience, it might be viewed as novel information associated with the self. However, it is not clear why reports of panic (rather than other intense emotional experiences) should be specifically associated with depersonalisation.

Apart from the unfamiliarity of panic, certain behaviours associated with this cluster of complaints may induce a state of relative sensory isolation. For example, a preoccupation with future harmful events or repetitive behaviours might limit the range of cues to which a person attends. Thus, a lack of information which confirms the sense of self, rather than excess novelty, might be critical.

Further alternatives are that depersonalisation is an antecedent of reports of anxiety (because it is perceived as threatening) or that reports of both experiences are a function of a third, unidentified variable.

There is support for the view that interpretations of the experience of depersonalisation vary. Saperstein (1949) described a subject who developed a fear that 'there would be no thoughts in his head' (p. 71). Skoog (1965) described two main reactions to the experience of depersonalisation in persons who developed anankastic (phobic/obsessive) problems. A paralysing passivity was said to be characteristic of individuals who became phobic, whereas in persons with tendencies to act in an obsessive way, there was more likely to be an active, intellectual preoccupation with the experience (e.g. a desire 'to get to the bottom of it').

Cappon and Banks (1961) and Cappon (1969) offered the hypothesis that physical causes can give rise to disturbances in the perception of time and space, which are then elaborated into various types of psychological distress, including depersonalisation. Misinterpretations of the perceptions (e.g. 'I am going insane') are said to have emotional consequences which feed back and contribute to further orientation distortion. Certain laboratory stressors were found to increase disorientation and depersonalisation in both psychiatric and nonpsychiatric subjects. Sensory isolation produced significantly more reports of distress in the former group. The authors noted that only verbal data differentiated psychiatric subjects from controls; behavioural measures were identical. Verbal reports of disturbance correlated with the Cornell Medical Index and with a neuroticism questionnaire.

Self-report measures of depersonalisation have been found to correlate with a neuroticism questionnaire in other studies, but little, if at all, with extroversion (Dixon, 1963; McClure, 1964; Meyers & Grant, 1972).

Sours (1965) described three pilots in whom the complaint of anxiety and/or phobias for flying appeared to *follow* the break-off phenomenon. (see also Roth et al., 1965, above). It is possible that depersonalisation and panic are alternative ways of construing unfamiliar perceptual experiences. If the assigned meaning includes catastrophic interpretations, panic may be more likely to be reported.

Psychoanalytic writers have considered depersonalisation to be an ego defence against id drives whose associated affects are perceived as a threat to survival. This thread of ideas has been continued by others. Roth (1960) saw a similarity between the role of depersonalisation in his phobic-anxiety-depersonalisation syndrome and 'states of dissociation or clouding induced by the acute terror of battle where an adaptive mechanism is clearly at work' (p. 293). He also compared depersonalisation to patterns of defensive nonresponsiveness in animals, such as the death-mimic reflex.

Kelly and Walter (1968) did indeed find that, when subjected to a laboratory stressor, psychiatric subjects reporting depersonalisation had a lower forearm blood-flow than any other psychiatric group they studied. However, on self-report measures of anxiety they scored as high as subjects given a diagnosis of anxiety. Lader and Wing (1966, p. 90) had earlier made an interesting observation while measuring the heart-rate and skin resistance of psychiatric subjects who had been given an anxiety diagnosis. In one subject who reported an episode of depersonalisation while measures were being taken, there was an abrupt decline in heart-rate and skin conductance. It is clear from Kelly and Walters' results, however, that a general tendency to report depersonalisation is not associated with fewer complaints of anxiety, and so it is not a generally successful defensive strategy if that is supposed to be its function. It is worth noting that changes in autonomic responsiveness (including diminished arousal) are frequently associated with alterations in the meaning assigned to events (Grings, 1973). It is not parsimonious to infer, therefore, that depersonalisation is an innate defence mechanism against strong emotional experiences. However, experimental research into this topic has hardly begun.

PART II

Psychological Theory and Panic-Anxiety

8

Introduction to Part II

SURVEY OF THEORETICAL APPROACHES

The aim of the second half of this book is to place panic-anxiety in the context of psychological theory. This will be achieved in several ways. The first is a general survey of theoretical approaches to anxiety. I cannot hope to be exhaustive, and so particular attention will be given to theories and approaches which have attempted to explain panic-anxiety phenomena or can conceivably be applied in this attempt. Although the concept of anxiety has generated a large literature, relatively little research has been conducted on individuals whose complaints of anxiety appear to be unrelated to specific situations. However, in recent years there has been renewed interest in this area of study. Several models of agoraphobia have also been developed, and these will be examined in Chapter 12.

A further source of knowledge about panic-anxiety has come from therapeutic attempts to modify aspects of the phenomenon, in particular, avoidance of public situations. This literature will be reviewed with the limited objective of drawing out some theoretical implications of the results of therapeutic trials. Several evaluative reviews of the efficacy of anxiety-modification techniques have already appeared (e.g. Emmelkamp, 1981; Marks, 1978), but our concern here is with what can be inferred about causation from the benefits that the techniques confer.

Chapter 14 offers a conceptual orientation to the topic of anxiety. 'Anxiety' is regarded as a social construction that organises perceptual experience. This view may be contrasted with the idea that emotions are primary and universal perceptual experiences generated by 'affect' mechanisms in the brain. The constructivist viewpoint does not deny the importance of biological mechanisms but emphasises the multi-referential nature of emotional experience. The stimulus antecedents of emotional experience are thought to include a combination of internal and external events, in large degree resulting from sequences of diverse psychological processes. The latter can, of course, be approached at different levels of analysis and within different realms of discourse. Reference to the experience of anxiety is assumed to belong to a realm of discourse to which a scientific causal analysis does not apply. I will assume, then, that anxiety qua experience should not be viewed as *causing* behaviour, although the processes of recognising and reporting emotional experience can, of course, be studied objectively in an experimental and social context.

Emotions have also been regarded as hypothetical constructs in scientific (causal) theories. I will take the position that it is not very useful to conceive of anxiety in this way. I will assume that the perception of emotion as an entity derives from the way social perceptions are, in general, organised, for example, in the way that persons are perceived as unitary entities which cause things to happen.

Following a detailed discussion of these conceptual issues, a schematic model of panic-anxiety is presented in Chapter 15 in which I attempt to integrate the available evidence.

The task of surveying theories of anxiety represents a considerable challenge. Almost every school of thought in psychology has had something to say on this topic. Common themes continually emerge but often in parallel and in noncommunicating forms. Emotion is a subject in which everyday and scientific concepts are intertwined, and so it calls for careful analysis. Apart from confusion between lay and scientific discourse, models of emotion are often aimed at quite different levels of analysis. The problems that this presents for conceptualising the interaction between behavioural, physiological and verbal/cognitive processes is discussed in Chapter 14.

Rational Models

The survey will begin with Freud's thoughts on the irrational nature of some anxiety complaints and with the way he reconciled irrationality and psychological principles. The idea that certain human experiences are irrational must be seen against the background of the philosophy and psychology of the day. Given the concept of the mind as separate from the body and the locus of rational human action, it is not surprising that phenomena which did not fit the model were deemed irrational.

Panic-anxiety poses several problems for a rational view of man. First, the anxiety complaints may arise suddenly in the absence of a previous tendency to report anxiety with a greater than usual frequency. Second, the sufferer may be unable to point to any reasonable source of anxiety. Third, the problem is resistant to any rational attempt to alleviate it and usually becomes worse. Fourth, the cluster of panic-anxiety complaints includes diverse thoughts, behaviours, and somatic sensations which may appear incomprehensible and unrelated to each other.

Theories of anxiety can be divided into rational, mechanistic and holistic models. Rational theories build on a rational model of man and elaborate on cognitive evaluative processes which, though they differ from everyday understanding, do not usually depart too far from it. For example, anxiety has been defined as a response to an appraisal of harm. To appraise means literally to set a price, or generally, to assess the amount or quality of something. In the case of a harmful event, this might refer to an inventory of the intensity, probability, duration, quality or any other feature of the event. The appraisal concept has been elaborated to include a wide range of factors (e.g. coping resources) which influence the report of anxiety. However, these factors are appraised or evaluated rather than linked in a cause-and-effect manner, as in a mechanistic model.

Mechanistic Models

Mechanistic models depart to a greater extent from everyday understanding. Of course, many theorists, like Freud, have combined mechanistic and mentalistic metaphors. This tendency is an almost inevitable consequence of the assumption that there is an interaction between an individual's conceptualisation of his or her own behaviour and other behavioural and environmental processes. Models which attempt to encompass this interaction are likely to be of a 'mixed' type, for example, combining peripheral arousal with attribution processes. Several mixed models will be discussed following a critical examination of the appraisal notion.

The more purely mechanistic type of model is to be found within physiological and behavioural psychology. The physiological explanations of anxiety can be roughly divided into those that focus on central or peripheral mechanisms (the latter have been considered in Chapter

5). The principal learning models are derived from Pavlov's studies of conditioning.

Holistic Models

There are, in addition, a group of models that relate anxiety to a holistic view of the organisation of behaviour or cognition. The common thread in these models is that anxiety is related to a general psychological model of adaptive functioning. Usually, it is seen as an aspect of the *disorganisation* of cognition or behaviour, for example, as a consequence of stress, information overload, incongruity, interruption or inadequate problem-solving. However, some holistic models regard anxiety as adaptive (at least under most circumstances) or are silent on this point. It must be emphasised that no taxonomy of models is entirely satisfactory because they have developed from such a diverse set of philosophical and scientific traditions.

9

Rational Approaches: Appraisal, Verbal Mediation, Labelling and Attribution

FREUD ON IRRATIONAL ANXIETY

Freud constructed his theories when dualism was the most influential philosophy of mind. According to this philosophy, mind and body are divided as different substances or entities. The body is the sphere of action, and the mind informs the body what to do. The mind is said to have *intellect* for 'research and development', *reason* to assign priorities, *volition* as the centre of executive control and *affects* (feelings, motives, desires, passions, etc.) to provide a driving force and purposes. Anxiety that is reported without an object of harm is problematic in this scheme of things because it is considered irrational. Freud (1964) noted this problem, and he sought to develop a theory of unconscious causal determination. 'A psychical origin would be present, for example, if we found as the basis of anxiety neurosis a single or repeated shock, justified by the circumstances, which became the source of the readiness to anxiety' (Freud, 1894/1964, p. 107). In other words, if the report of anxiety could be related to a rational source of harm, it could be understood as a fear, and subsequent attempts by theorists to achieve this transformation betray the mentalism of their basic assumptions.

Freud's solution to the problem was first of all a neurophysiological one: Anxiety is the physical expression of dammed-up sexual energies. In a later revision of this theory, he replaced the idea of physiological

damming by one of psychological repression. This explanation is basi-
cally mentalistic except that cogitations and passions are transferred to
an unconscious realm; that is, to reasoning, desires and emotions of
which the person is unaware because they are repressed. Anxiety is a
conscious manifestation of the breakdown of the process of repression,
the breach in the psychological dam which produces the sensations that
form the basis of the experience of anxiety.

The phenomenon of unprovoked anxiety remained an enigma to
Freud, and he stressed that his ideas on the subject needed to be developed. The questions he posed himself were 'What are people afraid of in
neurotic anxiety?' and 'How are we to bring it into relation with realistic
anxiety felt in the face of external danger?' (Freud, 1932/1964, p. 82).

Having worked out his revised theory (Freud, 1964), he felt confident
that 'neurotic anxiety has changed in our hands into realistic anxiety,
into fear of particular external situations of danger' (Freud, 1964, p. 93).
Briefly, his new model stated that anxiety is brought about by a conflict
of impulses, a conflict which can be portrayed as a sequence of events as
follows: an anticipation of the unpleasant consequences of the conflict;
the production of anxiety, leading to the transformation of one of the
impulses; and resolution of the conflict. For example, a young boy loves
his mother, but his knowledge of this impulse leads to an awareness
that it can be punished by castration. That is, there is a realistic threat of
external danger. The unpleasurable feelings (anxiety), initiated by a perception of this danger, automatically cause a repression of the impulse
to love his mother (mother is renounced) or some other mechanism
leading to symptom formation is invoked.

Freud (1964, p. 90) recognised the metaphorical nature of his exposition, and wrote, 'I have tried to translate into the language of normal
thinking what must in fact be a process that is neither conscious nor
preconscious, taking place between quotas of energy in some unimagin-
able substratum'.

In order to account for reports of an anxiety which is consciously
perceived as irrational, Freud had to assume that rational processes take
place unconsciously; one of their products is a set of unpleasureable,
conscious sensations. At the same time the use of unconscious rationality is supplemented by various metaphors of depth, force and
energy, some of which have mechanistic functions that have nothing to
do with rational processes. Having adopted a mechanistic approach, it is
not clear why Freud insisted that neurotic anxiety be seen as the product
of a realistic anxiety about an external danger. Having drawn his metaphors from mentalism and mechanism, it is difficult to criticise his theory as a whole. It does not seem worthwhile to try to reconcile his ideas,

but simply to note that Freud had raised the difficult problem of how we should attempt to describe unconscious (or inferential) processes— whether new metaphors should be constructed, or whether unconscious processes should be modelled on conscious ones, or whether both approaches should be adopted. The way in which Freud posed the problem of irrational anxiety and his tentative solutions have had a continuing influence on subsequent theorising.

THREAT-APPRAISAL MODELS

Threat-appraisal models are founded upon cognitive evaluations that a state of affairs will lead to harm or danger. Concepts of threat are not, of course, as simple as this assertion suggests, and most models of threat take into consideration other cognitive evaluative processes as well. As noted in the introduction to Part II, some cognitive models are holistic; that is, they relate reports of anxiety to general aspects of central processes (e.g. to conflict, interruption or cognitive incongruity) rather than to specific threats (e.g. harm or threat). Construed as a process/ content distinction, holistic cognitive approaches can be compared to a process model and threat appraisal to a content model. However, the holistic perspective is compatible with various uses of the threat concept, and many models are of a mixed type. For example, when anxiety is defined as the *processing* of aversive and/or threatening information, the threat concept is utilised but is not central to the model. Similarly, when anxiety is related to the emotional processing of *information structures* (see Chapter 11), threat appraisal is considered to be merely one aspect of relevant information. The threat concept is not employed at all when the report of anxiety is viewed as a direct consequence of, say, conflict or information overload. However, it is natural to assume that any kind of cognitive/behavioural disorganisation (or inefficiency) which leads to a report of anxiety is also likely to have potentially harmful consequences. In some instances the harmful consequences of, say, physiological lability or speech dysfluencies can be seen as secondary to, and causally independent of, the prior process. Despite the difficulty of classifying models definitively as holistic or founded on threat appraisal, the distinction is a useful one for conceptual analysis.

Modern cognitive theory has come a long way from the view that anxiety is simply the conscious response to an appraisal of harm. Mandler (1982) stressed that the new cognitivism does not restrict its domain to the contents of consciousness or to those aspects that can be varbalised. He argued that common language terms were only borrowed in the early stages of cognitive theorising and that they are being replaced by new theoretical concepts.

The mental concepts of harm, danger and threat have been transformed into cognitive evaluative processes which take into account not only unpleasant outcomes, but also resources and coping skills. Lazarus (1982), one of the steadiest advocates of a threat-appraisal model, stated that cognition does not imply deliberate reflection, rationality or an awareness of the factors upon which it rests. He extended his model of emotion to animals, therefore going beyond what humans report as emotion. The concept of harm has also been extended to include symbolic 'abstract events' such as meaninglessness and loss of identity (Lazarus & Averill, 1972).

Despite attempts to radically redefine rational cognition, threat-appraisal models of anxiety often remain, at heart, mentalistic. When threat is inferred from verbal report alone, the concept adds little of theoretical value—one mental state (anxiety) is simply defined in terms of another(threat, harm, etc.). Kelly (1955) illustrated this tendency; for him, anxiety is 'the conscious awareness that the events with which a man is confronted lie mostly outside the range of convenience of his construct system' (p. 533). Definitions of this kind are not self-evident and depend too much on rational intellectual activity. Kelly assumed that an intellectual awareness of the limitations of one's constructs precedes the report of anxiety, but it is more likely that one cannot conceive of the limitations of one's constructs until they have already been invalidated, an event likely to have entailed emotional consequences.

Some of the difficulties with the threat-appraisal concept can be illustrated by examining the model of Lazarus and his colleagues (Lazarus, 1966; Lazarus & Averill, 1972; Coyne & Lazarus; 1980; Lazarus, 1982). Lazarus and Averill (1972) defined anxiety as an emotion which is based on several appraisal processes (in particular, an appraisal of 'symbolic threat') which mediate between two classes of antecedent (situational and dispositional variables) and several modes of expression, including emotion and coping responses.

It is apparent that the value of appraisal as an explanatory concept is weak because the terms it is supposed to mediate are confounded. For example, the primary appraisal of threat depends on dispositional variables (such as coping resources) and emotion is defined as a syndrome of responses which include cognitive appraisals. Development of the model has lead to even greater conceptual interpenetration of the explanatory terms. Coyne and Lazarus (1980) stated that cognitive appraisal is part of a continuum of psychological, social and physiological events. They describe their point of view as transactional and cognitive phenomenological. By transactional it is meant that there is feedback between components in the model, and firm notions of linear causality are rejected. If this is taken literally, we could not say whether the model was primarily cognitive, physiological or behavioural.

In fact, the primacy of *cognition* in threat-appraisal models seems to follow from an assumption that cognitive processes belong to a higher level of analysis than physiological or behavioural processes. The appraisal mechanism is usually presented as a kind of central processor which takes into account all the relevant information, rather like the pilot of an aircraft responding to the aircraft instruments. Behaviour is initiated to correct deviation from desired outcomes. If appraisal is *not* conceived as belonging to a higher level of analysis, it is difficult to see what is being suggested, that is, how cognitive processes are supposed to articulate with behavioural and physiological processes.

The phenomenological aspect of Lazarus' model presumably derives from the fact that appraisals are generally accessible to consciousness or that their effects are revealed in consciousness. However, the threat-appraisal concept fails us in our attempt to understand the phenomenology of panic or severe generalised anxiety. These experiences are usually reported as spontaneous, irrational or out of proportion to actual danger. In order to accommodate these potentially embarrassing features of reported anxiety, Lazarus and Averill (1972) resorted to two lines of argument. The first amounts to the transformation of a threat-appraisal model into a holistic model. They agreed with Cattell (1966) that anxiety is an experience *sui generis,* a consequence of motivational uncertainty and that it is not teleologically purposive. They stressed that they were more concerned with the structural and organisational properties of symbols than their content. Harm is conceived as falling along a dimension from the physical to the symbolic. Unfortunately, the nature of the link between the structural properties of symbols and reports of anxiety is not developed. In any case, the equation of holistic and threat-appraisal models must be rejected.

Their second argument to deal with the problem of anxiety that is reported in the absence of an awareness of threat resorts to the familiar Freudian theme of unconscious threat. They suggested, for example, that anxiety might be reported when a person unconsciously anticipates manifesting a latent disposition to hostility. However, the authors did not translate this assertion into the terms of their own model or show how it could be tested.

The views of Lazarus and his colleagues have, over the last two decades, successfully counterbalanced the influence of conditioning and biological models and have also generated their own theoretical offshoots. However, as the boundary definitions of appraisal have grown (Lazarus, 1982), the concept has become increasingly untestable.

It is perhaps not surprising that the new cognitive/behavioural therapies have been more concerned with the verbal reports that subjects *make* about their thinking processes than with inferred cognitive appraisals. This follows naturally from the emphasis given by Bandura (1969) to the *symbolic control* of behaviour. He drew attention to the fact that behaviour could be controlled by verbal instructions, awareness of reinforcement contingencies and the redirection of thought processes. This view is an extension of stimulus/response mediational theory rather than a new cognitive paradigm (Schwartz, 1982). The promise of a new cognitive paradigm has yet to materialise, at least from the appraisal tradition.

VERBAL MEDIATION

The mediational approach has been successfully applied in the analysis of severe irrational anxiety. Beck, Laude and Bohnert (1974) claimed to observe that subjects diagnosed as anxious were aware of danger just prior to or at the onset of reported anxiety. The most common danger themes were death and social rejection, and the content of the subjects' thoughts was meaningfully related to actual historical events. The danger was therefore usually assessed as plausible rather than irrational. In other words, Beck and his colleagues claimed that, by searching diligently, sources of threat could be found. Add to this the possibility that a person who complains of anxiety might also be mistaken about the probability of potentially harmful events, or even commit logical errors, then the seeming irrationality of severe generalised anxiety might turn out to be rationally related to verbal cognitive mediating processes.

This is a potentially rewarding avenue of investigation. A knowledge base, and habits of reasoning, can presumably generate information which corresponds sufficiently well with past circumstances in which 'anxiety' was actually related to harmful events. In other words, the problem lies with the individual as an information transducer. One suspects that, all too often, complaints of anxiety have been designated as 'free-floating' or generalised without proper investigation. If it can be shown that threats are perceived and that reports of anxiety are diminished by therapeutic exploration of, and exposure to, the relevant verbal cues, then the importance of covert verbal mediating processes will have been demonstrated.

Agoraphobics certainly hold irrational beliefs about the effects of being frightened (Chambless, 1982b), and it would be surprising if these beliefs were not relevant to an explanation of their fears, For example, agoraphobics may believe that they have a serious medical condition or that they will lose control of themselves or have a heart attack in a state of panic.

There is at least one possible objection to making an appraisal of potential harm a primary causal factor in panic-anxiety. It can be objected that perceiving threat is part of what it means to report anxiety. Having had a sudden and disturbing experience perceived as panic, a person might not entertain alternative interpretations of what has happened and simply describe the experience in terms of plausible dangers. Another person might simply report feeling strange, not describe their experience as panic and therefore not perceive their situation as threatening. It would be of interest to know whether individuals who develop the agoraphobic cluster of complaints have always had fears of the kind documented by Chambless (1982b). If so, then the fears and their associated beliefs are likely to be contributory causal factors. Of course, an explanation also needs to be found for the fact that individuals hold inappropriate beliefs or make verbal inferences which lead them to perceive their situation as threatening.

If appraisals of harm are a secondary consequence of panic (i.e. a way of comprehending a nameless fear or a reasonable interpretation of what fear might bring about), this does not detract from the potential importance of verbal mediating processes in maintaining or increasing the tendency to report anxiety. The distinction between processes responsible for the *origin* and *maintenance* of panic-anxiety is an important one, and this survey of theoretical models is more concerned with the former. In terms of explaining the persistence of panic-anxiety complaints, an understanding of maintenance processes are probably of greater importance. This will be considered later. At this point we need to consider the possibility that *coping appraisal* generates complaints of anxiety.

COPING APPRAISAL AND SELF-EFFICACY

Lazarus and his colleagues have distinguished between primary appraisal of harm/danger and secondary appraisal of coping resources and options. The two types of appraisal do not necessarily occur sequentially, and, in any case, degree of threat depends on joint appraisal. Thus, a potentially harmful situation, say, mountain climbing, can be approached without reported anxiety if mountaineering skills are adequate.

Lazarus and Launier (1978) divided coping skills into two types: coping with the source of harm/danger and coping with the disorganising effects of emotion (e.g. autonomic arousal and motor tremor). To continue with the mountaineering example, it follows from this that success in tackling a particular rock-face might depend not just on climbing skill but also on voluntary control of breathing, self-encouraging thoughts, and so on.

Different aspects of the threatening situation are said to have a bearing on which coping responses are selected. These are the extent to which important outcomes are perceived as uncertain or ambiguous, the severity of threat, conflict between alternative responses and the perception of potential control over harmful outcomes. In this multifactorial model, reported anxiety is just one outcome of the interaction of several appraisals.

As I have already remarked, no clear predictions about the kinds of coping appraisal which might lead to panic-anxiety can be made. On the face of it, anxiety is reported in situations which have not formerly represented a challenge or threat, or required the summoning up of coping resources, for example, situations such as walking down the street or taking a bus. Moreover, sufferers cannot usually point to any obvious change in their life circumstances which would account for their loss of confidence in these situations or lead them to perceive their situation as one of helplessness in the face of threat.

Even though we are dealing with coping appraisal, it is pertinent to ask whether individuals given anxiety diagnoses (including agoraphobia) are generally lacking in coping skills. This cannot be answered without begging other important questions. Persons who become psychiatric patients may have multiple problems or disadvantages and so may not be representative of the pool of people who demonstrate the phenomena of panic-anxiety. For example, members of the general population who differ in many ways from psychiatric patients may fall into the latter category (see e.g. Meyers & Grant, 1972; Torgerson, 1979). However, even amongst psychiatric patients given an anxiety diagnosis, Noyes et al. (1980) found that about half had no rated impairment of work, marital, sexual, social or family life. Compared to an age- and sex-matched control group, the average annual income of the anxiety group was about one-fifth greater than that of the control group. These are admittedly crude indicators, but taken together with the fact that anxiety complaints can disappear completely for long periods, it suggests that difficulties in coping with life in general are not specifically related to panic-anxiety. Some research has identified general behavioural problems such as lack of self-assertion (Chambless, 1982a), but assessments made after the onset of the anxiety complaint might confound cause and consequence of the problem (Hallam, 1983). Chambless noted that there might be several ways in which the features of agoraphobia arise, therefore leaving open the possibility that other behavioural problems are relevant in some cases but not in others.

Even if an inability to cope with day-to-day situations (or coping appraisals) are unlikely to account for the origins of the problem, the way in which distress is managed may determine maintenance. Of course, when the source of an anxiety complaint is unknown, the individual is left with little to do but manage discomfort as well as he or she can. Anxiety complaints can be modified by following certain general principles (see Chapter 13), and so to some extent the problem may be maintained through ignorance of successful coping techniques. However, other factors are likely to play an important part as well. For example, some people might hold attitudes that are incompatible with the adoption of successful coping strategies, or attempt to solve their problems in a way that actually undermines their positive coping efforts (see Chapter 11).

Bandura has proposed that the most important determinant of future coping efforts is the individual's appraisal of his or her ability to perform confidently in fear-provoking situations (Bandura, Adams & Beyer, 1977; Bandura, 1978). This 'self-efficacy' judgement is based on an assessment of many sources of information, including behavioural and physiological feedback obtained in previous fearful (or successful) encounters. Measures of self-efficacy were found to correlate better with subsequent approach than measures of previous behavioural performance (Bandura et al., 1977). It is perceived lack of efficacy in managing potentially aversive events which is crucial, according to Bandura, in determining whether anxiety is reported.

It is certainly true that panic episodes are likely to lead to a loss of self-confidence. Panic is often unpredictable and its effects may seem uncontrollable. The episode is usually suffered until discomfort declines of its own accord or until an escape can be made to a safer situation. If Bandura's assumption about the determinants of reports of anxiety are correct, an approach to therapy which develops the client's belief that panic can be managed and reduced should be successful. Given the multiple sources of information upon which such a belief might be based, several alternative methods are likely to be successful. In a study which measured the self-efficacy beliefs generated by two different methods of reducing a circumscribed phobia, Biran and Wilson (1981) concluded that self-efficacy beliefs are dependent on the nature of the information available. With a guided exposure method it was found that there was a high degree of agreement between self-efficacy judgements and subsequent approach in the feared situation. However, with a cognitive restructuring method in which subjects had no opportunity to monitor their own performance in the target situations, degree of congruence was much lower, and performance correlated better with previous estimates of fear and actual physiological reactivity. This suggests that even if anxiety reported in anticipation of a threatening encounter reflects perceived self-efficacy, subsequent performance is more powerfully governed by stimulus conditions which have controlled behavioural and physiological responses in previous encounters. Self-efficacy judgements presumably reflect the quality of information that is available about performance. When information is inadequate, self-efficacy judgements do not predict performance.

Self-efficacy theory combines concepts of verbal mediation with cognitive appraisal. As thoughts or judgements which regulate the behaviours that follow them, self-efficacy beliefs are assigned a causal role (Bandura, 1978). Self-efficacy has been measured by asking people to assess their ability to cope with a specified hierarchy of fear-provoking situations. Self-efficacy measures are considered as probes into mediating thoughts. However, Bandura also argued strongly for an a priori definition of an efficacy expectation (e.g. that it is an appraisal of an ability to perform confidently and *not* an expectation about the outcome of approaching feared situations). But, as he admitted that people confound the concepts of outcome and efficacy, his self-efficacy measure must be an innaccurate reflection of self-efficacy. This ambiguity illustrates the problem with appraisal concepts in general. As Biran and Wilson (1981) have shown, self-efficacy judgements can be manipulated by verbal therapies, but then they cease to predict subsequent performance very well.

Do we infer from this that self-efficacy measures are invalid indicators of self-efficacy appraisal? If so, self-efficacy shares with other appraisal concepts their intrinsic inaccessibility to measurement. If, however, it is argued that self-efficacy measures are valid indicators of self-efficacy appraisal and represent the subjects' best estimate given the information available, we must conclude that self-efficacy cannot claim any causal priority in the determination of reports of anxiety.

COGNITION AND AROUSAL

The theories discussed in the next two sections are included in this chapter because cognition is seen as operating *on* feedback from physiological and behavioural systems, that is, they are two-factor theories which assume independence between cognition and (usually) arousal. Mandler's interruption theory has developed out of two-factor theory, but it is included in Chapter 11 because it integrates the concept of anxiety within an holistic framework.

The concept of *physiological arousal* has played an important role in many theories of emotion. Broadly speaking, peripheral physiological arousal is taken to be the effect of autonomic nervous system activity; its nonspecific and diffuse nature has been inferred from the fact that stimulus material with different emotional effects tends to produce similar peripheral changes (see e.g. Levi, 1975). The concept of a diffuse arousal state continues to be useful despite definite constraints on its validity. These are, for example, the demonstration of individual differences in characteristic patterns of arousal (Lacey & Lacey, 1958) and stimulus/response specificity.

The attention given to arousal probably stems from the way that the James–Lange hypothesis, which concerns the source of emotional experience, has been understood. James (1884) and Lange (1885) reversed the traditional assumption that ideas cause feelings and suggested the opposite view that emotional feeling is the result of perceiving one's own bodily reactions. Although the subsequent debate focussed on visceral activity as the source of feeling, James also included motor behaviour in the gamut of responses which gave emotions their 'colour' and intensity. The self-perception of bodily activity has remained an important element in later developments of the James–Lange position, but the idea that reports of emotions are correlated with distinct patterns of physiological arousal has not been supported empirically.

In the theories of Schacter and Singer (1962) and Mandler (1975), physiological arousal is treated as a necessary but not sufficient condition for emotion to be reported. These theorists conceive of arousal as being a diffuse generalised state varying only in intensity.

The clue that factors in addition to arousal are necessary came from early investigations of the effects of injecting epinephrine (which has sympathetic-like effects) into human subjects (see e.g. Marañon, 1924). After receiving the injection, subjects variously reported palpitations, motor tremor and feeling hot, flushed and sweaty. The experience was not usually described as an emotional one, but some subjects said that they felt as if they were in a state of emotion. However, some subjects who were engaged in conversation about unresolved problems at the time of the injection, did report 'real' emotions. Also, psychiatric patients with anxiety diagnoses usually developed episodes of intense 'anxiety' (see Chapter 5).

In their classic experiment, Schacter and Singer (1962) set out to investigate the interaction between a subject's physiological state and his or her concurrent interpretation of the environment. They argued that subjects who knew what to expect from an injection of epinephrine, and who were given a correct explanation of their state of arousal, would not react emotionally. Some subjects were therefore informed about the effects they would experience, others were misinformed or not told anything at all. For the latter group there would be a need to evaluate their state of arousal; and in order to steer this process, different 'labels' were suggested by manipulations of the environmental situation. This was achieved by deceiving the subjects about the purpose of the experiment and by asking them to wait in a room with another subject (an accomplice of the experimenter) who acted either euphorically or angrily. Actual physiological arousal was manipulated by injecting epinephrine or a placebo saline solution.

The results were essentially in keeping with the experimenters' hypotheses that self-reported and behavioural indicators of emotion were related to an interaction between a need to evaluate a state of arousal (misinformation condition) and actually being in an aroused condition. The nature of the emotion was influenced by the situational cues provided. It was concluded that two independent and interacting factors—physiological arousal and cognitive evaluation—give rise to reports of emotion. Neither factor is sufficient in itself.

This complex and ambitious experiment has been criticised for methodological flaws and weak statistical effects (see e.g. Plutchik & Ax, 1967; Maslach, 1979). An attempted replication was not successful (Marshall & Zimbardo, 1979). The authors of this experiment and also Maslach (1979), who used an hypnotic method for producing unexplained arousal, found that arousal was perceived negatively whatever the environmental cues suggested.

Erdmann and Janke (1978) replicated the main features of the Schacter and Singer experiment and found only slight support for the potentiation of angry and happy moods by a concealed administration of ephedrine. Under threat of electric shock, subjects receiving either ephedrine or placebo reported anxiety; if anything, ephedrine diminished this effect. In a later study (Erdmann & van Lindern, 1980) utilising anger manipulation only, a beta-adrenergic stimulant increased *anxiety* ratings only, whereas with a placebo, 'anger' was produced. The pattern of physiological change differed in the two groups, and the authors suggested that subjects were responding to a pattern of physiological cues. Whether or not this is a correct interpretation, the results of the two experiments indicate that the interaction of arousal and cognition is far more complex than the two-factor theory suggests. The finding that anxiety is reported with a sympathetic stimulant, even when anger is suggested, is consistent with the results of Maslach (1979) and Marshall and Zimbardo (1979) mentioned above.

Why is it that subjects given anxiety diagnoses report anxiety when injected with epinephrine whereas 'nonanxious' subjects do not (see Chapter 5)? According to Schacter's theory, it might be supposed that (1) they are more frequently subjected to high levels of unexplained arousal and (2) they are more likely to label unexplained arousal as anxiety. Following this line of reasoning, it matters little how high arousal is actually caused, for example, whether due to pathology such as thyrotoxicosis, or to environmental stressors. If of pathological origin, arousal is likely to be unexplained (at least before medical diagnosis), and, if stress-related, it might also be unexplained if the individual is a poor interpreter of the social environment and cannot identify the sources of stress. The importance of arousal from whatever source is supported by clinical observations that individuals who are predisposed to report anxiety may do so when excited for any reason (e.g. watching an enjoyable football match) or when exerting themselves physically.

The complaint of anxiety is, of course, associated with organic pathologies that produce marked sympathetic arousal. It has also been established that subjects given an anxiety diagnosis are more physiologically responsive to stimulation and return more slowly to resting levels (see Chapter 10). If this is a biological characteristic, then it would be consistent with a two-factor hypothesis of the generation of 'anxiety' in these individuals.

It would also have to be assumed that subjects whose main complaint is anxiety label their unexplained arousal *as* anxiety and that these cognitive-perceptual biases are not sufficient to explain their complaints without the independent occurrence of high arousal. As Schacter himself assumed, in most instances, the *same* cues give rise to both cognitive evaluations and arousal.

Two-factor theory has stimulated a great deal of useful research, but it is not very compelling on logical grounds. Emotion is regarded as the product of the synthesis of the activities of two systems: arousal and cognition. First, this leaves the theoretical status of emotion as product in a rather ambiguous position. For example, what is the relationship of emotion to emotional *behaviours* or to the social practices of communicating emotion? Second, the assumption that arousal is independent of cognition may only be true in the rather trivial sense that arousal can be produced in a variety of ways. Thus, it is not as if a label is applied to arousal; arousal cues must surely partake in the acquisition of cognitive labels and supply meaning just as much as social/environmental cues. This can be deduced as follows: First, arousal is biologically necessary for the execution of behaviours described as emotional (e.g. anger or flight). Therefore, arousal cues are likely to be an intrinsic part of the meaning of emotion concepts. Second, arousal has publicly observable sensory consequences (change in respiration, skin colour changes, etc.) which are likely to be utilised in the social learning of emotion concepts. Therefore, there is no compelling reason to view arousal cues as more 'independent' than other cues. Recent research into two-factor theory (reviewed above) suggests that unexplained arousal is interpreted negatively regardless of the presence of additional labelling cues. This may be so because unexplained arousal is part of the *meaning* of negative mood states such as anxiety.

The necessity of arousal as a precondition of reports of anxiety also seems doubtful. The definition of an aroused state is somewhat arbitrary, and it could be argued that, if a subject required inferential support for the position that he or she was in a state of anxiety, attention to peripheral physiological cues could almost certainly provide it. Research has fairly consistently shown that the correlation between objective measures of arousal and the perception of internal states is rather low (Pennebaker, 1982).

ATTRIBUTION AND AROUSAL

As the autobiographical accounts in Chapter 4 illustrate, individuals attempt to understand the causes of their own behaviour. All three accounts mentioned unfamiliar sensations as precursors of their later problems. The sensations were usually identified as the effects of fear, but this realisation was not presented, in all cases, as a self-evident fact. The accounts contain evidence of further self-questioning which leads, in one way or another, to doubts about sanity, physical health and even the reality of ordinary experience.

Attribution theory is an attempt to understand how people arrive at causal explanations of behaviour. However, our main interest here is in the *effect* that attributions of causality may have on the development and maintenance of anxiety complaints. Some causal beliefs imply that acting in a certain way is likely to have aversive consequences. Other beliefs can produce a threatening interpretation of a bodily sensation. Causal beliefs are also associated with particular coping actions and therefore are related to the maintenance of a problem. The way that behaviour is interpreted might blind the individual to the means of changing it or lead the individual to believe that it cannot be changed at all.

Schacter's two-factor model of emotion prompted research into the attributions made by subjects in aroused states. In the Schacter and Singer (1962) study, arousal that could not be attributed to its true cause (because of deception) was *misattributed* to the plausible source of emotion provided by the experimenters. The process of misattribution seemed to permit, within limits, the arbitrary control of emotional states. That is, if subjects could be induced to believe that arousal associated with, say, the anticipation of an aversive event had a nonemotional cause (e.g. the ingestion of a pill), then the intensity of the reported emotion might be reduced (see Ross, Rodin & Zimbardo, 1969). Alternatively, if subjects could be led to believe, through false feedback, that they were more or less physiologically aroused than they really were in the presence of emotion-provoking cues, then emotional intensity might also be manipulated in this way (e.g. see Valins, 1970).

These ideas and the research they generated have demonstrated the great plasticity of emotional behaviour. They have not, however, convincingly shown that the ideas upon which the experiments were based are correct (see Zillman, 1978; and Brewin & Antaki, 1982, for reviews). In any case, the two-factor model of emotion has been shown to be in need of revision (see above).

Alternative explanations of their results were suggested by the attribution researchers themselves. Storms and Nisbett (1970) attempted to influence subjects who had difficulty falling asleep at night by persuading them to misattribute their assumed arousal state to another source. As the authors noted, their procedures might simply have modified the degree to which the subjects worried about the condition of insomnia. In other words, difficulty with getting to sleep, which may have a trivial and temporary cause, leads to concern about the *effects* of not getting to sleep, or worse, concern about the consequences of having developed the psychological disorder of insomnia. These beliefs then have physiologically arousing effects which produce an exacerbation of the problem.

Unlike earlier interpretations of the vicious-cycle effect in anxiety complaints, the attributional explanation stresses the individual's belief that unwanted behaviour is due to dispositional characteristics (e.g. 'basic' personality). It is assumed that an internal attribution to negative characteristics can lead to self-depreciation and in this way have a general effect on mood.

Storms and McCaul (1976) obtained experimental support for their view that dispositional attributions have maladaptive effects. Subjects who were told that their speech dysfluencies were due to their personal speech pattern and ability, rather than a situational stress, were more likely to stammer when the situation was actually made stressful. These authors suggested that exacerbation of dysfunction mediated by attribution to internal dispositions might be a common factor in many anxiety complaints. This suggestion cannot be accepted uncritically if it is meant that 'anxiety' is the cause of both the original problem and of the emotional effects of the dispositional attribution. This concept of anxiety reifies a description as a causal mechanism.

However, explanations of the vicious-cycle effect can be stated in more specific terms, and Storms and McCaul discuss several possibilities. For example, heightened awareness of the self in stressful situations might be associated with self-derogatory thoughts which distract attention from task-relevant cues and thought processes. This produces an impairment of performance which reinforces negative self-evaluation.

In some cases the effects of autonomic arousal *are* threatening. A client described in Chapter 4 was afraid of standing on a ladder because his legs 'turned to jelly' and could not support him. In practice, it is difficult to differentiate the specific effects of causal attributions on reports of anxiety from other verbal/cognitive mediators (e.g. see Beck, 1976).

Discussion of the effects of causal attributions often begins with some unwanted behaviour, sensation or 'symptom' which the subject needs to explain, for example, a pain, fatigue state, or arousal. Whether the dysfunctional element is psychologically mediated or has an independent physiological basis (e.g. tinnitus caused by auditory pathology; Hallam, Rachman & Hinchcliffe, 1984), the subject's *attention* to the element also needs to be accounted for. The causal beliefs which have an exacerbating effect might also produce attention to the dysfunctional element in the first place. Thus, linear cause-and-effect analyses of exacerbation phenomena are problematic. Peterson (1982) also pointed out that particular attributions cannot be viewed in isolation from a person's general framework of causal beliefs. However, these interpretive difficulties do not make the role of causal attributions any the less interesting or relevant to an explanation of exacerbation phenomena.

When considering these phenomena in general, it may be necessary to distinguish amongst (1) beliefs that determine which cues are attended to and considered to signify dysfunction, (2) beliefs which lead an individual to perceive a dysfunctional element as threatening or to perceive himself or herself negatively and (3) beliefs about the appropriate method of removing or dealing with the dysfunctional element.

Stricklund (1978) has reviewed research showing an association between reports of anxiety and the general attributional style described as a belief in an external locus of control. An external locus of control refers to the degree to which an individual perceives events happening as the result of luck/chance/fate, or powers beyond human control (in contrast to an internal locus in voluntary action). However, as Watts (1982) pointed out in his discussion of an attributional framework for medicine, either an external or an internal locus of control can be maladaptive in different circumstances. Also, a belief that a dysfunctional element has occurred as the result of fate does not necessarily imply that it is accepted fatalistically. Therefore, the idea that complaints of anxiety are related to a general attributional style is probably too simple.

A further point to consider is that the expression of beliefs about the origins of distress may have functional utility. For example, a woman described by Hallam (1976a) erroneously believed that she had body odour. It was concluded that her obvious discomfort in social situations was not directly related to this belief as an eliciting condition, but that the belief served to justify her avoidance of social interaction in general. As such, it was a reflection of her social timidity and not a reason for it. Her perception of the source of her problems was her way of dealing with them.

10

Learning Models and Central Mechanisms

INTRODUCTION

From its early beginnings in associationism and Russian neurophysiology, learning theory has drawn on many other traditions to the point where it is difficult to characterise it as a family of models. The influence of behaviourism remains as a strong belief in the importance of objective, replicable observation as the basis for an empirical science. Although the conceptual separation of environment and behaviour has come under strong attack, the basic terminology remains stimulus/response. Behaviour is analysed as a system of responses, habits or reflexes which are, in a sense, automatically controlled by stimuli in the environment. Complexity is built into behaviour by the development of new controlling relationships between stimuli and responses.

There are problems inherent in this framework which have been reflected in learning explanations of anxiety. As a lay construct, anxiety is a mental state, which, of course, behaviourally oriented theorists have shunned. Although in the early stages of associationism, the purpose was to analyse complex mental ideas by resolving them into learned compounds of a more basic nature, mentalism was later rejected, and sensation was replaced by the concept of stimulus. However, the mental or physical status of stimulus remained a problem. Strictly speaking, in order to confine ourselves to physical language, the stimulus should be described as a pattern of physical energy, and in some experiments this can be done. The perception of the stimulus is then taken to be one of the responses of the organism. In practice, though, in most experiments with human subjects, the stimulus is taken to be the *perceived* stimulus and not a pattern of physical energy.

The tendency to disregard perception of the stimulus as a response appears to have lead some behaviourally oriented theorists into regarding the verbal report of anxiety as simply the mental or epiphenomenal aspect of anxiety *behaviours*. The learning history of verbal statements such as 'I feel anxious' were hardly considered.

In spite of the objective emphasis on behaviour, a tendency has developed to infer the functional significance of stimuli from the *mental* qualities which are generally assigned to them, for example, that certain stimuli are painful or that response feedback from the behaviour from which anxiety is inferred is itself aversive. In this way it has been argued that this behaviour is self-reinforcing. Such arguments do not escape the charge that they are ultimately rooted in mentalistic concepts. Thus, it could be said that, by ignoring verbal reports of mental states (as behaviour), learning theory has reintroduced, through the back door, some mentalistic assumptions.

What then are the foundations of recent learning theory accounts of reports of anxiety? A learned association must begin somewhere, and so it is necessary to postulate an original or unlearned stimulus for fear/anxiety. This is plausible insofar as certain classes of environmental stimuli do elicit responses that incorporate signs that they are aversive and physiologically arousing, and/or there is evidence that the organism is attempting to defend itself. Some types of stimuli (e.g. heights, darkness) can be understood as having had significance for survival during the course of human evolution (Gray, 1971). In the literature to be reviewed, the unlearned component is usually described as a painful or an innately fear-producing situation.

The idea that the central feature of the agoraphobic cluster of complaints is a *phobia* of public places has strongly influenced learning models, and reports of anxiety which do not connect with specific eliciting stimuli have not received the same amount of attention. The psychiatric description of anxiety neurosis (Marks & Lader, 1973) as reports of anxiety that are independent of external stimuli and without a recognised source must have deterred attempts to formulate a stimulus/response account of the problem. The failure to discern elicitors during a psychiatric interview does not mean, of course, that they do not exist. The criteria specified by Marks and Lader (1973) are descriptive rather than aetiological. The idea of a rational source of anxiety should be distinguished from the concept of causal antecedents of reports of anxiety. For example, even when specific elicitors are reported by agoraphobics, it has been argued that they are mistaken about the actual events that elicit their distress (Goldstein & Chambless, 1978).

Learning theory accounts of panic and generalised anxiety, in which specific elicitors are difficult to detect, have not been very promising. Agoraphobia has received far more attention from authors who have drawn upon the research on phobias in general. The simplistic application of a conditioned fear model to agoraphobia is being abandoned and learning involving interoceptive stimuli is being emphasised; as this happens the two areas of agoraphobia and panic/generalised anxiety are coming together in a theoretical synthesis. The learning approach to phobias will now be reviewed.

THE PHOBIA MODEL AND CONDITIONING THEORY

Eysenck and Rachman (1965, p. 81) proposed a two-stage model of the acquisition of phobias; the first stage involved the classical conditioning of a fear response, and the second, the development of avoidance responses instrumentally reinforced by reduction of fear drive. The unconditioned stimulus (UCS) for the unlearned fear component was said to be a fear-producing state of affairs usually, but not necessarily, involving a painful stimulus. Subsequent reworking of the conditioning model of phobia acquisition has extended the range of conditions which can act as a UCS to include frustration and conflict, which Eysenck (1976) described as giving rise to 'mental pain'. The original two-factor theory has been considerably modified and partly abandoned (Eysenck, 1976; Rachman, 1977). Rejection of the model followed failure of attempts to condition fear in the laboratory, failure to observe the acquisition of fear in natural circumstances when it might have been expected and the frequent absence of identifiable frightening and/or painful events at the time of onset of clinical phobias (Rachman, 1978, p. 185). Furthermore, the persistence of phobias was inconsistent with conditioning phenomena observed in the laboratory such as the rapid extinction of the conditioned response (CR) with nonreinforced presentations of the conditioned stimulus (CS). As these inadequacies became apparent, the simple contiguity model of classical conditioning and the two-factor theory of avoidance learning, upon which early conditioning models were based, were shown to be deficient in the laboratory (e.g. see Thomas & O'Callaghan, 1981).

It must also be said that the behavioural indicators of fear in the animal learning experiments which formed the basis of this particular learning model provided a rather weak analogy with reports of anxiety in humans and with the general complexities of human avoidance associated with them. Given the rather low correlations between verbal reports and other behavioural measures in humans (Lang, 1971; Rachman & Hodgson, 1974), the animal analogy is doubly suspect.

It is unlikely that reports of fear/anxiety necessarily indicate the influence of an aversive stimulus. Within conditioning models themselves, the aversive element may include feedback from the CR and UCR, and so the simplest versions of a conditioning model are difficult to evaluate. In their theory, Eysenck and Rachman (1965) stressed the salience of the CS, repetition of acquisition trials, intensity of the UCS, CS generalisation, and confinement during acquisition. Although Rachman (1978, p. 192) concluded that a conditioning model is not a *comprehensive* account of the genesis and maintenance of fears, this is already implied by his earlier inclusion of several additionally important variables such as CS salience and confinement.

It would probably be agreed that certain patterns of stimulation which conform to the specification of a classical conditioning procedure do occasionally give rise to persisting reports of fear. The evidence tends to be anecdotal or dependent on subjects' recall, but traumatic experiences (e.g. dental trauma) can give rise to persisting emotional reactions (Lautch, 1971; Lindsay, 1984). The important issue is whether the various theoretical interpretations of conditioning phenomena assist in explaining these cases. The vast majority of human classical aversive conditioning studies have employed UCSs which were tolerable, familiar in their effects and under the subjects' control (Hallam & Rachman, 1972; 1976, p. 192). Under these conditions, the capacity of the CS to elicit an excitatory response usually peaks in a few trials and thereafter inhibitory processes diminish the size of the CR and UCR (Grings, 1969; Kimmel, 1965; Kimmel & Burns, 1975). Therefore, these experiments do not provide a good basis for a model of phobia acquisition if a phobia is regarded as a strong excitatory reaction. The model has been modified to allow for rapid acquisition and slow extinction with certain 'prepared' CSs (Ohman et al., 1978), but the response selected to index fear in these studies, has been criticised as inappropriate (Gray, 1982, p. 429).

A more promising conditioning model might incorporate the subject's perceived control (or tolerance) of the UCS. Although strictly speaking, subjects cannot prevent the occurrence of the UCS in a classical conditioning procedure, they might engage in preparatory activity which diminishes its impact. Moreover, in laboratory studies, subjects perceive they have control because they can request termination of the experiment.

One of the few experiments to demonstrate persisting conditioned autonomic responses lacked this feature (and for this reason may be regarded as unethical). Campbell, Sanderson and Laverty (1964) injected the drug scoline, once only, without their subjects' awareness of its precise timing or effects, and thereby produced a complete muscle paralysis. As the paralysis brought about a suspension of breathing, a loud-tone CS was sounded until respiration returned 90–130 seconds later. All subjects later reported that they felt they were dying. Conditioning was evaluated by comparing this procedure with two control procedures which consisted of tone alone or scoline alone. In spite of the small number of subjects in each group (three), the conditioned subjects produced significantly more autonomic responses which showed no sign of extinction over 30 trials delivered immediately afterward and 1 week later. The general sensitising effect of the UCS was not sufficient to produce conditioned-like responses, although variability of autonomic baseline measures increased following scoline injection alone.

Despite methodological weaknesses, this study has been detailed because it is unique and raises questions about the meaning of conditioning. There were strong indications that contextual and expectancy effects were operating. The subjects were inpatient alcoholics who volunteered for an experiment connected with a possible therapy for alcoholism. Some subjects requested clarification of the experimental instructions and reassurance that the UCS would not be repeated (the experimenter's response was not mentioned); some subjects later ran away from the hospital. The authors also noted that volunteer physicians who knew what to expect when they underwent paralysis did not report feelings that they were dying. The powerful effects of the procedure on alcoholic subjects given this form of aversion therapy (which did not in fact achieve therapeutic objectives) is documented in other studies (Sanderson, Campbell & Laverty, 1963; Laverty, 1966; Clancy, Vanderhoof & Campbell, 1967).

It would be tempting to conclude that the autonomic responses of the subjects were cognitively mediated (e.g. by an expectation that the trauma would be repeated) and therefore not examples of 'true' conditioning. This view is challenged by the argument that virtually all Pavlovian conditioning phenomena can be accounted for by cognitive processes reflected in reports of awareness of the conditioning contingency and instructional manipulations (Brewer, 1974). Theoretically, this leads to the proposal that a Pavlovian CR is just one indicator of a mediating expectancy (Reiss, 1980). This expectancy model would be severely stretched to account for *all* conditioning phenomena, for example, subtle changes in response topography over trials or interactions between instructional effects and other parameters of conditioning. Nevertheless a subject's interpretation of conditioning events *must* be relevant to an explanation of conditioning phenomena. The ability of humans to discriminate contingencies presumably gives a two-edged advantage; on the one hand, rapid detection of nonreinforcement may enhance the speed of extinction, but the capacity for symbolic representation makes a human subject vulnerable to potential, remote or fantasied dangers (Bandura, 1969, p. 38). The relevance of a conditioning model to reports of anxiety in humans therefore depends on the theorist's willingness to fashion the model with more or less emphasis on the complexity of human cognitive abilities. Eelen (1982), for example, has linked conditioning principles with predictions from attribution theory, and from such beginnings a model of greater relevance may develop. It is interesting to note that in one application of scoline aversion therapy (Farrar, Powell & Martin, 1968) all of the alcoholic subjects assumed a *causal* connection between the trauma and the ingestion of alcohol (the CS).

Conditioning Theory and Fears of Public Places

As an account of the origins of fear experienced in public places, classical aversive conditioning has been rejected in recent texts on agoraphobia (Mathews et al., 1981, p. 43; Thorpe & Burns, 1983, p. 167). It is argued that the hypothesis lacks credibility because anxiety is reported spontaneously in the absence of aversive events of sufficient intensity to engender severe, persisting fears. Thorpe and Burns (1983, p. 167) half-seriously suggested that an attack of influenza, general stress or fatigue might act as a UCS for fear, but they assumed that CRs acquired in this way would rapidly extinguish. However, in their survey of over 900 agoraphobics, 70% of the sample reported a precipitating event at the onset of their problem. The most frequently reported category was direct exposure to a traumatic event (32%), and the second most frequent was death of a relative or friend. Examples in the former category included near-accidents, mugging, and coming close to collapsing in a supermarket. The accuracy of these reports can be questioned, but it is difficult to dismiss them as irrelevant to a learning model of acquisition. But given that the events must occur fairly frequently without adverse long-term consequences, a classical conditioning explanation would have to be seriously modified and assume an interaction with other characteristics of the individual.

It might simply be the case that the precipitating event sensitises the person to pre-existing fears. If so, these fears are unlikely to be fears of public places but rather, as suggested by the nature of the precipitants, fears associated with tissue damage, death, illness, and so on. In any case, the hypothesis that the cues associated with public places are *conditioned aversive stimuli* must be rejected. Agoraphobics do not typically report a fear of supermarkets, buses, open spaces, and so on, but a fear of experiencing panic in these situations. The cues appear to function as conditioned discriminative stimuli which signal an increased probability of panic. In the presence of a trusted companion, or when travelling by car, the same cues do not usually elicit reports of anxiety.

Mineka (1983) overcame the difficulty that there is no obvious precipitating trauma in the development of agoraphobia by suggesting that unconditioned interoceptive stimuli can elicit 'anxiety responses'. It has been observed clinically that vertiginous episodes, depersonalisation and drug experiences can act as foci for complaints of anxiety and that the ensuing cluster of problems closely resembles panic-anxiety and agoraphobia (e.g. see Pratt & McKenzie, 1958). Mineka's suggestion is therefore plausible, although the interoceptive stimuli mentioned above are unlikely to be intrinsically aversive as they appear to be innocuous for some individuals at least. Interoceptive stimuli may be perceived as aversive if they signify other aversive consequences, for example, loss of control, potential embarrassment and death/illness. Even if interoceptive stimuli do not unconditionally elicit anxiety responses, this capacity may be acquired.

Having acquired aversive properties, interoceptive stimuli offer a convenient explanation for the generalised and 'irrational' nature of some anxiety complaints. That is, interoceptive stimuli occur regularly as part of everyday living, and the subject may be unaware of the cues to which he or she is responding. Further, interoceptive conditioning is known to be stable and resistant to extinction (Mineka, 1983).

Mathews and his colleagues, like Thorpe and Burns (1983), reject a classical conditioning account of the origins of panic but accept that panic is a traumatic experience leading to fearful expectations that the panic might recur, possibly in a worse form, and perhaps accompanied by some disastrous consequence (Mathews et al., 1981, p. 44). In the survey conducted by Thorpe and Burns (1983, p. 25), agoraphobics were asked about their worst fears of what could happen during an episode of panic. Fainting/collapsing was ranked first (28%), death second (13%) and personal illness third (10%). It need not be assumed that these fears would undergo extinction when the anticipated consequences failed to be confirmed in an actual panic attack. In fact, agoraphobics hardly ever faint (Connolly, Hallam & Marks, 1976), but they may feel close to doing so and continue to fear this as a possible outcome of remaining in the phobic situation.

A fear of experiencing panic can be logically distinguished from fears of disastrous consequences, but it is possible that panic would not develop at all unless some kind of future harm was anticipated. However, these fears may not be easy to elicit from clients. Nevertheless, it is reasonable to suggest that a variety of cues give rise to panic which in other circumstances or in other individuals might be interpreted as innocuous. For example, the experience of depersonalisation, which is quite common, might be interpreted as threatening (see the case of Miss C, Chapter 4). In some persons, sensations arising from a minor physiological irregularity could perhaps be interpreted as a threat (e.g. of illness) which is magnified by further evidence of autonomic disturbance mediated by threat.

This explanation of the origins of the first panic as a threatening interpretation of an interoceptive stimulus is not altogether convincing because it does not account for the timing of the panic, except perhaps by chance factors or the addition of stressor events. A different speculative hypothesis is put forward in the next section.

Summary

The simple notion that agoraphobia is a fear of public places is losing ground, and, hence, classical aversive conditioning seems less appropriate as a model for the development of this cluster of complaints. The application of classical conditioning theory to an understanding of phobias has, in any case, come into serious question. However, theories of conditioning are in continual revision; and as they begin to incorporate a cognitive component which does justice to human abilities, their relevance may, once more, become apparent.

It is not yet clear how a learning process might be involved in the first episode of panic, although subsequent maintenance and generalisation of avoidance of those situations in which panic is likely to occur is more amenable to a learning analysis. This is so because panic itself is an aversive event. It has been assumed by some that interoceptive stimuli associated with panic acquire aversive properties (see Chapter 12). The origins of the first panic remain a problem for learning theory.

DISINHIBITION, PANIC AND PHOBIA DEVELOPMENT

Conditioning models of phobia aquisition have generally sought support from studies of the conditioning of *excitatory* responses and have emphasised factors which influence the *growth* of the CR such as unconditioned stimulus (US) intensity and repetition of CS/US associations (Eysenck & Rachman, 1965). Eysenck's incubation theory, in similar fashion, implicates the paradoxical growth of an excitatory CR during nonreinforced CS presentation (Eysenck, 1976). Preparedness theory (Seligman, 1971; Ohman, Erixon & Lofberg, 1975) has appeal as a means of supporting an excitatory conditioning model and depends on assumptions that excitatory CRs develop more readily to certain prepared CSs and extinguish more slowly.

Gray's account of phobia acquisition, though differing in fundamental ways from the models mentioned above, relates clinical fear phenomena to the degree of activation (excitation) of the 'behavioural inhibition system' (Gray, 1982). Though the system is assumed to be innately elicited, one of the sufficient conditions for its initiation is a signal for a punishing event, a situation identical in other terminologies with a classic conditioning procedure. Inhibition in Gray's model refers to the inhibition of ongoing behaviour, and he was at pains to distinguish the concept from conditioned inhibition (Gray, 1975, 1978).

Pavlov himself theorised that the strong excitatory responses observed in psychiatric patients (neurasthenics) were due to inadequacies of *inhibitory* processes (Pavlov, 1961). In a development of Pavlov's ideas, Anokhin (1974) concentrated on mechanisms which give rise to conditioned inhibition, and he explored their implications for an understanding of neurosis. According to Anokhin's interpretation of his own and Russian research, conditioned inhibition arises as a result of the collision of two systems of excitation and is the means by which a stronger activity of the organism inhibits all the weaker activities present so that conflict is avoided. Neurosis is explained by conflict in which stable inhibition of a competing activity is not achieved. In this state, one activity may suddenly appear with increased intensity, especially the cardiac and respiratory components which are less easily inhibited.

Western research on conditioned inhibition has proceeded with few attempts to consider its possible relevance to clinical phenomena. Rescorla (1969) reviewed the concept and placed it in a general framework of the learning of CS/US relationships. In particular, discriminative stimuli, stimuli negatively correlated with the US and possibly long-delay CSs can aquire inhibitory properties. That is, in the context of a particular US and specific to that US, discriminative stimuli come to control a tendency opposite to that of a conditioned excitor. This tendency has not been viewed as a behavioural output which competes with excitatory CRs. Rather, it summates with excitation and diminishes responding; procedures have been specified by Rescorla for inferring conditioned inhibition from alterations in level of response.

Grings (1976) has reviewed concepts of inhibition in autonomic conditioning and has emphasised the complexity of studies with human subjects when symbolic representation of contingencies and other aspects of information processing are considered; for example, Grings pointed out that knowledge of negative contingencies is not readily acquired unless other events are positively correlated with the US in question. The message is, however, the same: The manifest behaviour of the moment is some net effect of excitatory and inhibitory tendencies. It should be noted that a designated CS+ can come to elicit an inhibitory tendency if it is presented in compound with a CS predicting absence of the US or there is a long delay between CS and US.

How might the concept of learned inhibition help to account for unpredictable episodes of panic which neither the sufferer nor an outside observer can reasonably link to any eliciting event which is sufficiently aversive to warrant the intensity of the response? One implication of the concept is that it cannot necessarily be inferred from absent or diminished responding that associative strength is zero. Therefore, even when there is little evidence of an excitatory CR, the unsignalled arrival of an event which is the same as or closely resembles the original aversive US might disinhibit the excitatory CR so that it occurs suddenly and possibly at a strength never previously made manifest in behaviour. Assuming that excitatory and inhibitory tendencies have been acquired gradually, the disinhibited response might be perceived as 'spontaneous' and even as unrelated to the disinhibiting stimulus.

Clearly, if such responses are included amongst the antecedents of panic, or become the focus of threat, then the process of disinhibition might partially explain one type of panic episode.

There are a few studies which at least suggest mechanisms for rapid fluctuation of excitatory response strength. Assuming that extinction involves learned inhibition, then fluctuations of response magnitude during nonreinforced trials might reflect disinhibition *or* differential forgetting of learned inhibition and excitation. With regard to the first possibility, Rescorla and Cunningham (1977) found that an extinguished excitatory CR (fear) could be reinstated to the CS by unsignalled presentation of the original shock reinforcer. (The subjects were rats.) This reinforcer did not reinstate fear to neutral stimuli. The nonreinforced presentation of a different fear elicitor prior to unsignalled shock attenuated the reinstatement effect, suggesting that reinstatement is a non-associative process. These authors inferred that reinstatement is related to a changed central representation of the US.

With regard to differential decay of excitation and inhibition, Henderson (1978) noted that if a single stimulus is used to measure spontaneous recovery of an extinguished fear CR, fluctuation in response magnitude might reflect either inhibitory or excitatory processes. By using different stimuli and a response suppression technique of measurement, Henderson was able to conclude that there was an assymetric forgetting of conditioned fear and of its inhibition, with inhibition being lost more rapidly. Henderson (1978) made the interesting comment that 'depending upon the conditioning history of the subject, this process could produce a variety of effects ranging from regression to the pattern of behavior which predominated prior to the development of conditioned inhibition, to the appearance of new excitatory processes that developed after and were masked by, inhibitory ones' (p. 30).

It might prove extremely difficult to predict the learned excitatory and inhibitory consequences of exposure to signalled aversive events under natural circumstances. The aversive event might occur extremely infrequently (e.g. a bad fall when parachuting) or not at all but remain a possibility (e.g. failure of parachute to open). Thus, in the context of predicted aversive events, individuals might be exposed to repeated nonreinforcement and therefore acquire strong inhibitory tendencies to warning signals. However, it is not clear from current research how the balance of excitatory and inhibitory associative strength might develop under these conditions especially if individuals differ in the kind of event sequences they cognitively rehearse. Even so, it might be preferable to conceptualise the process of adaptation/tolerance to signalled aversive events as one of conditioned inhibition rather than habituation, as is so frequently done.

The value of conceptualising adaptation/tolerance of signalled aversive events as learned inhibition rather than habituation depends on what differential predictions can be generated and tested empirically. Habituation may be defined as a decremental process which occurs with repeated, nonreinforced elicitation of unlearned responses (e.g. the orienting reflex [OR] or an innate fear response). Learned inhibition, by contrast, can be defined as a decremental process resulting from signals of nonreinforcement. Stated slightly differently, in habituation a stimulus which is not being used to establish a learned association with another stimulus is followed by nothing. In the case of learned inhibition, the stimulus is followed by nothing, but that nothing signifies the absence of a reinforcing event expected in that context.

Adopting Rescorla's theoretical position, changes in excitatory response strength that depend on inhibitory processes would be expected after (1) a change in learning contingencies (e.g. the degree to which a CS predicted the absence of US), (2) a change in the number or strength of conditioned inhibitors co-occurring with CS+ and (3) the occurrence of a disinhibiting stimulus, such as the unsignalled presentation of the original US. Turning now to habituation, the main factor affecting the decremental process is likely to be a mismatch between actual and expected stimuli, for example, if an unsignalled shock to which a subject was habituating suddenly changed in quality or intensity.

Nonassociative processes such as tonic arousal level, or motivational influences, might be expected to modify decrements in responding due to habituation *or* learned inhibition. However, the kinds of stimuli producing dishabituation or disinhibition should differ in their effects according to their similarity to the US. That is, if *any* novel change produces an increment in response strength, then the underlying process is more likely to be habituation. However, if novel events which relate only to the presumed US lead to a response increment, the underlying process is more likely to be disinhibition of learned inhibition. In the special case of the learned inhibition of the OR, any novel stimulus might reestablish the OR but not necessarily other anticipatory CRs subject to learned inhibition.

In Lader and Mathews' (1968) physiological model of phobic anxiety, they proposed that certain individuals are in a vulnerable state of high tonic arousal in which habituation to innately arousing stimuli is minimal or nonexistent. It was argued that, in such individuals, arousal may be pushed beyond a critical level above which a positive feedback process occurs. That is, the phasic arousal associated with novel stimuli adds to tonic arousal with the consequence that habituation fails to occur and physiological responses increment to the point that a panic attack is precipitated. The authors gave examples from Glaser (1966, p. 43) of cases in which a sudden recovery of physiological responses to an habituated painful stimulus occurred under stressful circumstances. The stressor was in both cases unrelated to the habituated painful stimulus (e.g. a social stressor and painful thermal stimuli). Furer and Hardy (1950), in a similar pain habituation experiment, noted that there was no relationship between resting levels of skin conductance and reports of emotional state but that, in one subject, dishabituation seemed to occur during nonspecific stressful events. These observations of Glaser and Furer and of Hardy are consistent with a nonspecific effect of novel events on an habituated response, but it should be noted that during the habituation experiments the aversive (painful) events were presented in such a way as to be predictable. It is therefore possible that disinhibition of conditioned inhibition might account for these observations.

Lader and Mathews (1968) also suggested that stimuli with a special (covert/symbolic) significance might trigger the chain of events leading to panic. Thus, although the situations which are typically avoided by, say, an agoraphobic are intrinsically arousing (noise, crowds, unfamiliar places, etc.), the particular meaning of the situation to the individual might also contribute to arousal. Of course, this is readily understood as fear of fear once a panic has been experienced, but for the first panic a different explanation is required. As I suggested earlier, one possibility is that events with a special significance for the subject might act as *disinhibitors* of learned inhibition.

Anecdotal examples of disinhibiting events in natural circumstances have been provided by Epstein and Fenz (1962, 1965) in accounts of their work on the stress and mastery of parachute jumping. Anticipatory excitatory responses were subject to a decrement with experience, especially in the period before the jump. This resulted in an inverted V-shaped curve of self-reported and physiological arousal. Epstein (1967) argued that repeated successful execution of parachute jumps leads to an expansion of a gradient of anxiety and the development of an inhibitory gradient with a steeper slope. An interaction between the two results in a forward displacement of the peak of arousal along *cue* and *time* dimensions, so that, for example, reported anxiety peaks a few hours before the jump itself. Fenz and Epstein (1968) obtained evidence that the inhibitory reaction is specific to parachute-relevant cues and occurs only on jump days. This suggests that the researchers were studying a learned inhibition controlled by warning stimuli rather than the habituation of responses to unconditioned stimuli or the extinction of CRs which subjects brought to the stressful task. Fenz (1975) noted anecdotally that mishaps, a change of normal procedure or a prolonged absence from jumping eliminated the learned inhibitory tendency, that is, there was a loss of control of excitatory autonomic activity. We may tentatively conclude that any US-relevant event (in this case the US is performance failure, mishap or death) occurring during the anticipatory period would act as a disinhibitor. Nonexposure to safety experiences following the CS would also appear to lead to forgetting of the inhibitory tendency (e.g. if a mishap occurs or there is a long absence from jumping).

The hypothesis I am putting forward is that the sudden occurrence of excess physiological arousal and/or 'fear responses' may be attributed to a disinhibition of a learned inhibition of excitatory reactions. Thus, in an individual who suddenly experiences panic, it is assumed that prior to the onset of panic he or she has been repeatedly subject to signalled aversive stimuli which have been successfully avoided and/or tolerated. If the successful management of aversive stimuli has been aquired gradually, the individual may not recall the process as especially noteworthy or memorable. However, it must be assumed that the excitatory powers of the US (if it occurs) are maintained and that the US still has at least a remote possibility of occurring.

The most likely precipitant of panic is an unsignalled presentation of a US-relevant event or an event which changes the central representation of the US (e.g. increases its excitatory potential). It is conceivable that the sudden emergence of excitatory responses would not be meaningfully linked to the precipitating event if the individual has underestimated the arousal potential of the US (because it has been successfully avoided and/or anticipatory excitatory responses have been inhibited). We need not, in any case, assume that individuals are always aware of the learning contingencies which influence their behaviour.

The disinhibition hypothesis is speculative, but the kinds of events which have been noted to occur at the onset of panic (see Chapter 3) would satisfy the condition that they are relevant to commonly expressed fears, for example, death of a relative is related to concerns about illness/death in oneself.

Another context in which anxiety is often reported is that of flying, which is presumably a stressful occupation for a proportion of pilots and navigators. Goorney and O'Connor (1971) studied a group of military aircrew who had started to report anxiety. The precipitants often included accidents (to self or comrades), but because a large proportion of active fliers are involved in accidents, an additional vulnerability factor must be inferred. It is tempting to speculate that this is a prior (mastered) anxiety about flying competence or death/injury. The authors noted that reports of anxiety precipitated by fatigue were associated with a return to full flying duty, whereas the fliers whose reports of anxiety were precipitated by accidents were more likely to be permanently grounded. In other words, it is possible that these pilots did not return to flying because their original fears were rearoused in an acute form. As experienced fliers, they could not overcome their fears by graduated re-exposure.

In a more recent study of military aircrew (Aitken, Lister & Main, 1981), 20 pilots or navigators who reported complaints attributed to anxiety while flying were compared with a control group of 20 aircrew without similar problems. The control group had had more flying accidents. The aircrew with complaints came from families in which more relatives had been injured or killed in flying accidents or air raids. Further, there were many more subjects in this group who reported childhood phobias, or adult phobias such as a fear of fainting, which pre-dated their anxiety while flying. It may be inferred from these results that flying had always represented greater danger (even if unacknow-ledged) and that learning to fly had, perhaps, involved a mastery of fears of various kinds. Accidents, then, may only be critical in pilots with a previous history of concern about death/injury. However, this study has also pointed to the potential importance of stressors of a nonspecific kind; the pilots who reported anxiety were experiencing more problems of a marital and sexual nature.

In summary, it has been argued that fearless performance in the con-text of signalled aversive stimuli is compatible with (1) the US maintain-ing its excitatory potential and (2) fearfulness returning as if spon-taneously if a learned inhibitory process is disinhibited. A study of disinhibitory phenomena may have more to offer as a way of under-standing panic than learning models based on the growth of excitatory responses.

CENTRAL MECHANISMS AND ANXIETY

Biological and ethological research into emotion has not, in general, concerned itself with phenomena such as panic-anxiety, and so discus-sion in this section is limited to the work of authors who have explicitly applied themselves to this problem. A large literature exists relating psychophysiological measures to specific reports of anxiety (sometimes called *state* anxiety) and to a general tendency to report anxiety in many situations (trait anxiety). Trait anxiety has sometimes been considered as a normally distributed behavioural disposition related to biological char-acteristics. This proposition will not be examined here.

Much of present-day research had its origins in an era when virtually all forms of distress were treated as illnesses which reflected biological dysfunction. Pavlov proposed that a clash of neural excitation and inhi-bition in the cerebral cortex could produce a functional disease of the central nervous system (this is similar to Freud's warring instincts). The illness view has recently received apparent support from family and twin studies of the inheritance of anxiety disorders. Carey (1982) tenta-tively concluded that the prevalence of anxiety neurosis and agorapho-bia is higher among the first-degree relatives of patients diagnosed as having these disorders than it is among the general population. Evi-dence for inheritance is also adduced from twin studies. However, the studies illustrate the problem of defining a disorder from a cluster of complaints, as shown by separate entries for questionable cases. Variations in the initial sampling of the probands was also shown to influence rates of prevalence in the relatives. The positive evidence included studies of diverse phobic features in the relatives of agoraphobic-like normals.

In a second review by Reveley and Murray (1982), the authors began by defining anxiety as a trait concept and end up by drawing conclusions about disorders. The influence of genetic factors in the expression of emotional behaviour has received considerable support but the strong genetic loading of a trait (e.g. intelligence) does not imply disorder. In any case, the *general* rather than the specific nature of the genetic influence, if substantiated, is indicated by the increased prevalence of alcohol abuse and specific fears and phobias amongst the relatives of persons who satisfy psychiatric criteria for anxiety disorders.

Anxiety as a Physiological State

The concept of state anxiety gives the impression that a report of anxiety is a report on a mental state corresponding to a discrete set of physiological and psychological indicators. This static concept will be rejected in favour of a processual view. An individual reporting on his or her mental experiences is assumed to be actively trying to comprehend them as well as responding to the total social and psychological context. The act of communicating a mental experience (i.e. the lay view of what is going on) is also likely to have functional consequences. As I will elaborate later, the situations in which such reports are made are assumed to involve complex interacting processes which cannot be frozen in time to constitute the psycho-physiological correlates of 'anxiety'. Furthermore, it is unreasonable to expect a lay construct to have discrete biological referents.

The assumption of psychophysiological parallelism still guides some biological research. For example, the physiological correlates of psychiatric diagnosis have been extensively investigated. Early in this century it had been established that neurasthenics (whose diagnosis resembles anxiety neurosis) could be distinguished from normals by their responses to physiological tests (Altschule, 1953). For example, neurasthenics' pulse rates rose markedly during stressful interviews, physical exercise, or voluntary overbreathing (hyperventilation). During strenuous exercise, systolic blood pressure was observed to rise to higher levels, and concentrations of sodium lactate in the blood were elevated. *Resting levels* of physiological activity were not on the whole found to differ. These observations are valuable only if they point to possible causal mechanisms rather than document a putative emotional or pathological state.

Malmo (1957, 1966) conducted further studies of patients given a psychiatric diagnosis of anxiety neurosis and showed that they were more reactive to a variety of laboratory stressors, motor tasks and other psychological tests. Again, differences in activation were not noticeable under resting conditions, but following stimulation, sustained afterreactions were observed in muscle tension, blood pressure and heart-rate. It became apparent that the stimulus conditions to which his subjects responded differently were not confined to those having a personal significance. Malmo explained his results by postulating that his subjects had a defective inhibitory system, probably inherited, although he thought that the inhibitory mechanism could be weakened by 'overuse' (Malmo, 1957). The physiological correlates of psychiatric diagnosis are still being vigorously investigated (see below).

Arousal, Orienting and Behavioural Inhibition

The finding that patients given a diagnosis of anxiety are more highly aroused in certain experimental situations has been interpreted as reflecting a *primary* abnormality in response to stimulation (e.g. Bridges, 1974). The psychological characteristics of the patients, that is, their tendency to report anxiety, then becomes secondary. This theoretical approach to anxiety disorders has been backed up by research which has replicated and extended the studies mentioned above (see reviews by Lader, 1975; Kelly, 1980). In general, a constitutional explanation for the abnormality is preferred.

The hypothesis that clients who complain of anxiety are constitutionally predisposed to develop their problems needs to be supported by longitudinal studies which show that problems can be predicted from prior psychophysiological characteristics. There is little evidence of this kind available. Causal inferences cannot safely be made from contemporaneous physiological measurements. For example, subjects who tend to report anxiety are likely to perceive laboratories as threatening places, and so response to stimulation under these conditions might not be representative. Lader (1975) noted that high resting pulse-rate in patients diagnosed as anxious may fall to normal levels during sleep.

Of course, a constitutional abnormality might only become manifest under stressful conditions, but this hypothesis is not convincing unless *some* discernible differences between predisposed and nondisposed subjects could be demonstrated prior to the development of psychological problems. Most studies do not report higher levels of *tonic* arousal in anxious subjects, but slower habituation of *phasic* responses (see e.g. Lader & Wing, 1966) or a slower return to baseline levels after stimulation. These features of responding could as easily be related to the perceived meaning of stimulation as to general biological characteristics.

Even if individuals complaining of anxiety were shown to have arousal characteristics which were predisposing, the question remains as to why *anxiety* is the reported emotion (Lader, 1982). Lader concluded that this is poorly understood but implicates cognitive processes. He speculated that anxiety is reported when 'emotional parts of the brain are active but disorganised' (p. 20). This phraseology is one of biological dysfunction, but the implication is that the problem is psychological, that is, disorganisation and emotion are properties of behaviour, not of the brain.

Psychophysiological studies of patients complaining of anxiety have suggested causal mechanisms which, even if they do not explain how the problem of anxiety begins, may account for its continued maintenance. Lader and Mathews (1968) based their physiological model of phobic-anxiety on studies which compared the physiological characteristics of subjects given different anxiety diagnoses. Compared with specific phobics or normal subjects, patients given the diagnoses of anxiety state or agoraphobia showed (1) more spontaneous fluctuations in skin conductance and (2) a lower rate of habituation of the orienting response to tones, the rate being inversely related to the level of spontaneous fluctuation. These authors therefore proposed that certain individuals are in a vulnerable state of high tonic arousal in which habituation to innately arousing stimuli is minimal or nonexistent. In fact, such individuals may be pushed beyond a critical level of arousal, above which a positive feedback process occurs. That is, the phasic arousal associated with novel stimuli adds to tonic arousal with the consequence that habituation fails to occur and arousal increases in increments to the point that a panic attack is precipitated.

This model has been influential in stimulating research, especially in the area of therapeutic process, but it has been difficult to prove or disprove. Although physiological measures usually show greater variability when anxiety is reported (e.g. during panic itself; Lader & Mathews, 1970), a consensus on the meaning of an arousal system (or systems) has not yet been achieved. Given also the problem of classifying events or situations as novel/stressful, it is difficult to demonstrate that variations in the levels of reporting anxiety are correlated with a central state produced by novel stimulation.

A related model has been presented by Costello (1971) who speculated that the experience of anxiety results from the continuing novelty of stimulus input to the nervous system. Persons who chronically report anxiety are said to have an overreactive autonomic nervous system, and so they continually receive stimulus information about the activity of body organs. The inputs of the autonomic nervous system are not readily matched with stored memories (e.g. because they are not associated with any particular external stimulus), and so the inputs remain novel. The explanation is therefore pinned on a constitutionally overreactive autonomic nervous system combined with a failure to habituate to internal (somatic) input. In order to account for the absence of reported anxiety in childhood or adolescence in some cases, Costello assumed that additional factors such as hormonal levels or conflict may be needed to overactivate the autonomic nervous system. The failure of habituation is not assumed to be constitutional but to result from an inability to form a model of stimulus input.

Gray's views on anxiety are more deeply rooted in laboratory experimentation (Gray, 1975, 1982), but they belong in our present discussion because they treat anxiety as an experience which corresponds to the activity of a structure of the central nervous system. This structure, the behavioural inhibition system (BIS), is initiated by several classes of stimuli, and Gray allowed for variation in the precise naming of the subjective experience according to the source to which the state is attributed (Gray, 1976). The different classes of initiating stimulus comprise signals of punishment, signals of nonreward, novel stimuli and innate fear stimuli. The functions of the system have been inferred from extensive experimentation, mainly on animals, using brain lesion and pharmacological approaches (see Gray, 1982). Apart from innate elicitation of the system, what is threatening or frustrating must be learnt and therefore anxiety in humans may take an apparent variety of forms.

Briefly, the main functions of the BIS are the inhibition of all ongoing behaviour, increased attention to environmental stimuli and increased level of arousal (as shown by an increment in the intensity of whatever behaviour finally does occur). The purpose of these activities is placed in the context of a general monitoring of the adaptive nature of expectations and learned behaviours. In its monitoring capacity, the BIS is sensitive to novelty and to stimuli which warn of aversive events. In its behavioural inhibition mode, initiated by mismatch between actual and expected stimuli, interruption of behaviour occurs, during which time alternatives are generated and checked and/or exploratory activity is initiated. The BIS may take direct control of behaviour which bypasses events disruptive to previously adaptive behaviour. If the disruption is relatively unimportant, the initial motor programme is resumed (habituation). Otherwise, an alternative successful response is found or the subject simply engages in other behaviour.

It must be noted that the BIS does not produce Pavlovian CRs (Gray, 1982, p. 437), although warnings of punishment are an adequate eliciting stimulus. In this sense, it is a state theory, but Gray's description of the functions of the state show it to be many-sided and of wide-ranging significance in the organism's psychological adaptation. Gray's direct equation of activity of the BIS with reports of anxiety therefore comes as a rather surprising application of psychophysiological parallelism. Gray (1976) asked what the BIS 'feels like' and replied 'anxiety'. Although individual variation in labelling is allowed for, his description of the functions of the BIS show that he was rather loosely characterising several interacting processes as a state. The lay construction of anxiety is certainly as a state, but the psychological substrate (if correct) belies this simple attribution. What appears to be required is an elaboration of the model to encompass the subject's construction of sensory feedback of his or her psychological functioning as an emotional state.

However, granted that Gray was sketching the broad outline of the functions of a brain structure, is the concept of the BIS useful in understanding panic-anxiety? He argued that all complaints of anxiety presented in a clinical situation are the manifestation of a personality disposition—reports of anxiety reflect degree of activation of the BIS which is more or less prone to activation according to personality type. If this is so, it is difficult to explain the *sudden* onset of panic episodes in individuals who maintain that they were previously of a stable disposition (e.g. see Chapter 4). The panic-anxiety cluster of problems is not usually brought to the attention of a clinician until the third or fourth decade of life, and so a lifelong disposition to report anxiety is an unlikely explanation. Alternatively, it could be argued that there is an interaction between disposition and environmental stressors, that is, that the onset of problems is associated with novel, threatening or disruptive life situations. However, there is only limited evidence for this view.

Moreover, measures of general emotionality (neuroticism or anxiety-proneness) do not load on the panic-anxiety dimension in factor analyses of data from subjects given diagnoses of phobia or anxiety. (Roth et al., 1965; Arrindell, 1980). Therefore, panic-anxiety appears to be unrelated to the general disposition Gray referred to. Also neuroticism and extroversion have not, in general, been found to predict therapeutic response to behaviour modification procedures for phobic problems which might have been expected if dispositional vulnerability is important. There is occasional evidence that introverts respond more poorly or more slowly to therapy (Gelder, Marks & Wolff, 1967; Mathews, Johnston, Shaw & Gelder, 1974; Hallam, 1976b), but greatest support can be found for the hypothesis that neuroticism and extroversion scores increase or decrease with change in affective disturbance but do not predict it (Kelvin, Lucas & Ojha, 1965; Ingham, 1966; Hallam, 1976b). It is therefore debatable that self-report measures of anxiety, upon which so much rests when theories on the grand scale are proposed, actually reflect enduring personality characteristics.

SUMMARY: CENTRAL MECHANISMS

It would be foolish to assert that there is no association between the behaviour of reporting anxiety and the activity of relatively specific central processes. What I have argued is that these processes cannot be conceptualised as a neurophysiological *state* which corresponds to a mental state of anxiety. This position is untenable on philosophical grounds, and the effort to produce evidence documenting a pathological state of anxiety is misguided.

First, the results of psycho-physiological tests performed in laboratories are unconvincing because they are obtained from individuals who are already complaining of anxiety and may well feel threatened by the testing situation. Second, the idea that panic-anxiety is the expression of a biologically constituted trait (or specific genes) is inconsistent with the fact that this form of distress often develops in individuals who were not previously noted for having an unstable or nervous disposition. A continuum notion only seems to apply to some of the individuals who complain of anxiety.

The neurophysiological mechanisms that have been put forward are inevitably fairly complex and assume an interaction between innate and acquired factors. In the last analysis, there is no resolution to the question of the relative importance of biological constitution and environmental factors in anxiety. It would be a mistake to view biological and social/cultural perspectives on anxiety as incompatible. What I have rejected is the idea that a psychological state is mirrored by, and can be reduced to, a physiological state.

11

Holistic Approaches

INTRODUCTION

Theoretical approaches to anxiety can be placed along an atomistic/holistic dimension. At the atomistic extreme, anxiety is explained by relatively discrete subsystems, mechanisms or conditionable responses, whose properties may be considered in isolation from an overall (holistic) view of the activities of the organism. At the holistic extreme, anxiety is placed within a general model of the organisation of behaviour. Holism in psychology takes a variety of forms, and this chapter deals with only three main approaches: Mandler's interruption theory, stress theory and information-processing models. These approaches have been selected because they have been applied, mostly speculatively, to an understanding of panic-anxiety. Apart from their holistic stance, they have little else in common, and I will not attempt to integrate the concepts they employ.

INTERRUPTION THEORY

Mandler (1975, 1979, 1982) developed the two-factor (arousal/cognition) theory of emotion (Schacter & Singer, 1962) and placed it within a much broader cognitive/behavioural theory. Moreover, he postulated a mechanism to account for the state of diffuse arousal, which is one of the two essential elements of two-factor theory. Like Schacter, he believed that arousal is necessary, though not sufficient, for emotion to be reported. In his view, arousal is automatically elicited whenever an organised action or thought sequence is interrupted. Any event, external or internal to the organism, that prevents completion of some well-established action, plan or thought sequence is considered to be interrupting. The reader is referred to original sources for a full explanation of these concepts, and only a brief exposition follows.

Interruption occurs when an action is inhibited or temporally delayed for whatever reason. Unexpected events, including whatever is novel or unusual, are interrupting by definition. Aversive events may interrupt as well as threaten. However, it is assumed that despite interruption, there is a tendency to complete the action, which remains as long as the situation is unchanged. The action may be repeated with increased force; or a similar action, or one achieving the same end-state, is substituted. For example, if in attempting to open the front door of one's home the key fails to turn the lock, the turning action may be repeated with increased vigour until, possibly, alternative response sequences are substituted. These may entail a violent forced entry or actions based on a sober appraisal of the problem such as entry by some alternative means. In some cases, even a minimally relevant organised sequence is repeated (e.g. turning the door handle).

Mandler's theory has the merit of doing justice to the diversity of emotional phenomena, suggesting that there is a loose clustering of a variety of effects. For example, in states reported as anxiety, one might expect to find cognitive difficulties, somatic discomfort and repetitive actions, as well as adaptive coping efforts. It should be evident that, as a general theory of psychological adaptation, Mandler's ideas have much in common with the views of Lazarus (1966) and Gray (1982).

For purpose of analysis, Mandler broke down behaviour into unitary sequences of responses (actions) with a natural end point. These actions are the final product of learning and eventually run off automatically without conscious monitoring. Even components of emotion can acquire this habitual property and when interrupted give rise to arousal. In this sense, some emotional responses do not differ in their development and maintenance from other human behaviours.

Interruption and arousal are not *sufficient* to produce emotional behaviour. Thus, performance in a stressful situation might be associated with arousal but no emotion. One example might be first attempts at riding a bicycle. The skills are partially present but not smoothly integrated and are subject to interruption by unforeseen circumstances. The subject is physiologically aroused but not emotional. Mandler assigns a crucial role to 'meaning analyses' carried out in the aroused state. As in Schacter's theory, the two factors, meaning and arousal, may have different causal antecedents or may be triggered by the same events. In the example of riding a bicycle, the arousal elicited by a sudden loss of support would be unambiguously attributed to the event bringing about a loss of balance. The arousal of physiological systems brought about in this way might be perceived as pleasureable or aversive depending on a full meaning analysis of the context. The emotional consequences for our unskilled cyclist of falling off accidentally or being distracted by another person might be very different. It is assumed that individuals are not always able to identify correctly the events producing arousal, and so arousal from one source may be misattributed to another or potentiate other emotional responses occurring at the time.

Mandler assumed that the arousal system evolved out of the more fixed and evolutionary adaptive patterns of the lower mammals. Physiological arousal associated with these fixed patterns became detached as a state of general readiness. Feedback from efferent autonomic discharge thus became, in Mandler's view, a signal system in its own right, alerting the organism that something needs to be done. In the short term and at a low level, arousal is assumed to facilitate scanning of the environment and effective coping. At higher levels of arousal, signals from body receptors can flood the limited-capacity attentional system and lead to a decrease in the organism's effective utilisation of information. When excess arousal results from interruption, cognitive efficiency returns to normal only when a means of dealing with the interruption is found.

Mandler was not especially concerned with clinical *complaints* such as panic, but he equated the state reported as anxiety with a stage of helplessness following interruption, that is, a stage in which no actions are available for substitution. He also speculated that signals of interruption to well-established future plans might provoke a similar state. It must be emphasised that emotional acts can on occasion deal effectively with interruption—emotion is not necessarily disorganising. Vigorous repetition of a response is also sometimes effective. It is only when *no* action is effective and alternatives are not available that interruption becomes problematic in its own right. *Panic* is said to be an extreme form of helplessness in which incremental arousal decreases cognitive efficiency, attention is narrowed, and the original ineffective action is likely to remain the dominant response, thus continuing a vicious cycle.

Can these ideas provide insight into the origins of panic episodes reported in a clinical context? Given the rather broad definition of interruption and the paucity of information we have about the circumstances in which panic first occurs, the answer must be speculative. A superficial examination of life events occurring at the time might miss the main point of Mandler's thesis. Immediate interruptions might not be the only cause of emotional distress. We may speculate that meaning analyses of the future significance of present events might lead the individual to perceive them as interrupting, or potentially so. The assigned meaning may not be one of threat or loss, but the disruption of planned activity, like that which might result from the incompatibility of organised plans. It is possible that even seemingly innocuous events can change the feasibility and outcome of established plans. Thus, marriage, or the departure of teenage children from the home, might have consequences not previously foreseen, or bring conflict between alternative actions into relief. For example, Goldstein and Chambless (1978) implicated conflict over dependency as one of the contributary causes of agoraphobia. These authors do not frame their model in terms of concepts of interruption, but their analysis is consistent with this approach. Conflict is assumed to give rise to arousal which is not attributed to its true source. In combination with other factors, arousal is eventually expressed as panic in public places (see Chapter 12).

Interruption is a *structural* concept in the sense that the emotional consequences of meaning analyses do not arise from meaning per se but from the relationship between organised response sequences (e.g. their spatiotemporal relations in particular environmental contexts). An event which in itself does not signify threat or loss may nevertheless demand an action at a time that it inevitably interrupts other organised actions. If the subject is verbally unable to articulate the various organised actions or plans in this scenario, or perceive their relations, the arousing consequences of interruption may be perceived as if spontaneous or incomprehensible. However, this is a speculative extension of Mandler's ideas. Stated less contentiously, if arousal is related to antecedent conditions which entail complex relations between environmental events, the individual might simply resort to simple explanations such as 'I am physically ill' or 'I am going crazy'.

The interruption concept can be used in a rather different way to help explain the spiralling distress of panic. Given that the person is in an aversive situation and that the dominant response is *escape*, arousal will be increased by physical and psychological barriers to escape (i.e. interruption).

The element of entrapment is certainly foremost in descriptions of conditions which increase fear. In a survey of agoraphobics, Thorpe and Burns (1983, p. 26) found that the situations which were said to increase fear were 'being trapped' and 'having to queue' (first and second most frequent reasons) and 'having a definite appointment' (fourth reason). These situations have in common an element of constraint or commitment which limits the opportunity for escape. The entrapment may be physical if it involves actual barriers such as being in a lift, in a crowded place or in a bus with automatic doors. Interruption of escape may therefore be conceived as giving rise to further physiological arousal which potentiates the ongoing emotional response.

An explanation of escalating panic in terms of the interruption of the dominant response (escape) does not depend on the presence of irrational cognitions or on the assumption that being trapped increases exposure to fear-provoking cues. However, it does depend on the reasonable assumption that the threshold for escape responses is lowered in aversive and/or fear-provoking circumstances. Many persons who report anxiety in specific situations do not, in fact, avoid them, but it is very common for them to describe strong urges to escape which they resist.

In summary, interruption theory has the merit of accounting for the broad clustering of diverse cognitive, somatic and behavioural responses in states described as anxiety. It may be applied in a speculative way to the phenomenon of panic. However, it shares the criticisms which can be made against two-factor theory in general (see Chapter 9). Furthermore, it is difficult, though not impossible, to operationalise the concept of interruption.

STRESS AND ANXIETY

Stress and anxiety are commonly linked, but this is an area of disagreement and incomplete conceptualisation. Stressors have been implicated as causal factors in agoraphobia (see e.g. Goldstein & Chambless, 1978; Mathews, et al., 1981, p. 40), and it has also been reported that threatening life events antedate the occurrence of a cluster of anxiety complaints which resemble panic-anxiety (Finlay-Jones & Brown, 1981). Before considering the role of stress in clinical and other real-life expressions of anxiety, I will attempt to clarify what might be meant by a causal connection between anxiety and stress. The large stress literature will not be reviewed, but some stressor explanations of the causes of anxiety will be critically examined.

At the outset, the meaning of the terms *stressor, stress response* and *anxiety* must be clarified. I will follow the practice of regarding the term *stressor* as interactional, that is, as indicating a theoretically conceived relationship between environmental and organismic processes. The term *anxiety* is commonly defined as a cluster of responses in several systems (self-report, behavioural and physiological). However, this conceptual approach presents a number of problems (see Chapter 14). It may be preferable to conceptualise the physiological and behavioural 'anxiety' responses within the terms of an adequate, interactional stress theory. The self-report of anxiety can then be regarded as a stress response but one which is dependent on, as yet, ill-defined parameters of stressors. A stress response may be defined as any measurable response which indicates or reflects that a stressor (or state of stress) is operating. A variety of stress theories have, of course, been proposed, and the causal relation between a stressor and the report of anxiety might be understood differently by each one. Broadly speaking, however, the domain of stress responses can be regarded as broader than the domain of subjective evaluations of situations as stressful, anxiety-provoking, aversive, and so forth. In other words, it is possible to develop models of (mal)adaptation to the environment without regard to the individual's self-report. For example, adaptation may be defined by criteria of efficiency or biological survival, but responses which might be regarded as signs of biological stress need not be viewed as stress responses when considered from the point of view of social or psychological criteria. Subjects may tolerate aversive experiences or stretch their biological capacities for the sake of ulterior objectives. For example, it has been found that the more stressful of two experiences involving electric shock administration (as shown by self-report and physiological measures) was also rated as more interesting and worthwhile (Houston, Bloom, Burish & Cummings, 1978).

It follows from the variety of motivations which subjects bring to stressful tasks that there is unlikely to be a consistent relationship between self-report measures and other stress responses. For example, subjects low on a questionnaire measure of trait anxiety were found to give greater heart-rate acceleration to warnings of a predictable electric shock than did high trait-anxious individuals (Lykken, Macindoe & Tellegen, 1972). However, in a study also involving warnings of electric shock, the most competent and experienced subjects (decorated bomb-disposal operators) produced the lowest heart-rate levels in the most stressful anticipatory period (Cox, Hallam, O'Connor & Rachman, 1983). Although there were important procedural differences between the two studies (e.g. the availability of an avoidance response in the latter), the results illustrate the variety of effects that can be produced under stressful conditions. (The authors of both papers could account for the adaptive nature of the physiological response).

Apart from a discordance between stress responses which may arise from varying task requirements and motivations, the subject's self-reports may not appear to be consistent with accompanying physiological or behavioural responses if (1) the subject cannot discriminate them or

(2) does not attend to stress responses and/or perceive the situation as stressful.

The relationship between stressors and reports of anxiety can be illustrated by taking the example of the effects of paced and unpaced industrial work. Paced work is associated with more frequent reporting of anxiety (Broadbent, 1982). In relation to this finding, we need not assume that pacing has effects *only* on reports of anxiety or that anxiety is actually attributed to pacing. For example, pacing might produce stress responses which some individuals perceive as aversive and others do not. Even if the effects of pacing are perceived, they might be attributed to other environmental sources.

Moreover, the effects of pacing might be mediated by cognitive evaluative processes. So, even if the increased information-processing requirements of paced work are not directly associated with stress responses, the perception of the work as paced and its implications in the work context might be sufficient to do so. (e.g. perceptions of employers' intentions).

As I noted elsewhere, some stress responses are likely to be perpetuated by feedback effects. This might come about in several ways. First, a stress response might interfere with the required response (i.e. the one that is judged to be adaptive) leading to interruption, conflict, and the like. For example, if paced work raises levels of central and peripheral arousal beyond an optimum point, stress responses may be elicited which interrupt work output itself, or, in common parlance, 'more haste, less speed'. Second, a stress response might be perceived as signifying an aversive consequence, for example, a deterioration of performance might produce embarrassment, or feedback from peripheral arousal might be thought to signify serious illness. Third, the method of coping with a stressor (or a stress response) might be inappropriate and only intensify certain parameters of the stressor, for example, attempts to solve a problem might make it more difficult to solve or create new problems.

The potential causal links between a stressor and reports of anxiety are therefore complex, and it is difficult to draw firm conclusions about causal connections in any particular case. This must be especially true of observations made in the natural environment.

Individual-difference factors are likely to be more determining when the response to a similar external situation is particular to a subject rather than common across subjects. However, common responses might be culturally specific. Individual differences have been played down as causal factors where an external stressor would appear to have arisen independently of subjects' choices (e.g. redundancy or death of relatives). However, the effects of events regarded as stressors have been found to interact with organismic variables (Brown & Harris, 1978; Henderson, Byrne & Duncan-Jones, 1982), and so independent stressor events, even if necessary to elicit a particular stress response, cannot be considered as sufficient causal factors.

Attempts have been made to account for anxiety in terms of just a few stressor parameters such as the uncontrollability and uncertainty of harmful outcomes. Garber, Miller and Abramson (1980) drew up a table relating the psychiatric syndromes of anxiety and depression to these event dimensions. Controllability and uncertainty are defined in terms of perceived probabilities rather than actual probabilities. These authors followed Seligman (1975) in their definition of uncontrollability, that is, an outcome is uncontrollable when the probability of its occurrence is the same regardless of what response the person makes. An outcome is controllable if the subject can produce it, remove it or prevent it if it is likely to occur. However, control may only be partial and the outcome occur anyway with a certain probability if the subject does or does not respond. Therefore, when making judgements about control, an individual is said to consider two independent probability estimates with respect to an outcome, that is, the probability of it occurring if no response is made and the probability of the outcome occurring if the response *is* made. Certainty is defined as the perceived net probability. Garber and her colleagues concluded that most theories of anxiety assert that a harmful outcome must be at least probable for anxiety to be reported. When the outcome is uncertain this may be due to the outcome being uncontrollable, in which case, some theories emphasise this factor rather than the uncertain probability of the outcome.

Uncertainty can be generated by different response/event conditions. Some types of uncertainty, such as those produced by a response which leads uncertainly to a good or harmful outcome, are said to give rise to normal anxiety. Abnormal anxiety is said to derive from uncertainty associated with a belief in uncontrollability. By its very nature, this belief is assumed to account for certain features of anxiety such as ruminations and lowered self-confidence.

Seligman's (1975) framework for the analysis of psychological events has provided an extremely useful foundation for research into depressed mood. Similar benefits may accrue in the field of anxiety. However, several cautions need to be stated. First, the coherence of the cluster of anxiety complaints as a statistical entity need not imply a corresponding unitary or coherent form to the underlying causal processes. Panic-anxiety (or the anxiety syndrome referred to by Garber et al., 1980) seems to consist of a diverse set of phenomena. Second, if the formulation refers to *perceptions* of event probabilities, then the question of why certain individuals have aberrant perceptions of, say, harmful outcomes, is not addressed. Third, if the assumption is correct that a set of beliefs produces a broad set of self-report, somatic and behavioural responses, then the theoretical account needs to be expanded to link the two in a plausible manner. It does not seem sufficient to assume that a belief in uncontrollability automatically produces behavioural disruption, or that, say, physiological arousal is proportional to perceived danger (Miller, 1979). Additional causal principles are required to explain how the beliefs acquired their causal efficacy. Physiological arousal in fear states can take quite different forms, for example, bradycardia with blood/injury stimuli (Connolly et al., 1976) and tachycardia with most other fear stimuli. This is only one example where a belief concerning the outcome might be insufficient to explain the nature of the stress response.

Stress and Anxiety in the Natural Environment

Studies of naturally occurring stressors have the advantage over laboratory studies that more severe testing conditions can be investigated over a longer time period. Rachman (1978, p. 67) came to the conclusion that individuals are, in general. remarkably resilient in the face of extreme stressors such as are found in wartime. When anxiety is reported by combatants or by the victims of bombing raids, a relationship with some parameter of the stressor can usually be observed, for example, the occurrence of near-misses during bombing raids and the number of dangerous missions for bomber crew. Rachman also noted the importance of a perception of control and a sense of personal competence, and the calming effects of social approval.

Combat fliers did not usually report the experience of anxiety when it was least adaptive, during a mission, but anxiety was often reported more intensely before setting out or some time after returning home (Hastings, Wright & Glueck, 1944). It was also commonly observed that crews became more fearful as they approached the concluding missions of their operational tour (Rachman, 1978, p. 52).

In their study of combat fliers in World War Two, Grinker and Spiegel (1945) reported that 90% of the men who were admitted to psychiatric hospitals were not overseas casualties but were recognised as needing hospital care after returning home from their tour of duty. In many cases, this group was more severely impaired and had a lower rate of recovery than the overseas casualties who prematurely terminated their tours. The psychological complaints were usually of the following kind: being restless, irritable, and lethargic; having insomnia: being easily fatigued and startled; feeling tense, depressed and anxious. The cluster of complaints obviously bears comparison with psychiatric descriptions of some anxiety diagnoses. Grinker and Spiegel explained the dysphoric condition as a combined consequence of a slow decrement of the physiological arousal brought about by military action and the effects of unresolved conflicts and fears.

One implication of the wartime studies seems to be that some emotional distress is due to immediate situational factors and some to longer-term temporal factors of adaptation. A more recent Norwegian study of trainee parachutists investigated the short- and long-term physiological effects of 11 days of training jumps from a mock tower. There was an expected decline in reports of anxiety, but only the tonic prejump levels of arousal, which included measures of cortisol and testosterone, declined as training progressed. Phasic levels of epinephrine and certain cardiac measures taken at the time of the jump remained elevated throughout training (Baade, Ellertsen, Johnsen & Ursin, 1978). These observations suggest that variations in phasic psychological arousal related to the performance of coping tasks can be differentiated from longer-term fluctuations of tonic arousal which may be associated with different emotional effects.

The presence of the end-phenomenon of training, consisting of a marked rise in physiological parameters and psychological test-errors, was noted by Basowitz, Persky, Korchin and Grinker (1955) in their study of trainee parachutists. An end-phenomenon was also observed in bomb-disposal operators who had carried out 4 months of duty in the demanding conditions of Northern Ireland (Hallam, 1983; Cox & Rachman, 1983). During the tour, some differences were observed between experienced and relatively less experienced operators on a mood checklist, but little anxiety was reported by either group. However, following the tour, a sizeable minority of operators felt restless or agitated and had unpleasant dreams for at least several weeks. A posttour questionnaire survey of over 200 operators, carried out to study the effects of the tour on the operators' feelings, attitudes and personality, revealed two main patterns of change. Operators who observed changes in their personality and behaviour after the tour (including positive as well as dysphoric effects) recalled more stress symptoms, unrelated to bomb disposal, during the tour itself. These soldiers were more likely to describe themselves as having become more mature and self-confident, and having achieved greater self-respect. The second pattern of attitudes consisted of an inverse relation between the operators' assessment of their bomb-disposal skills and the amount of 'anxiety' experienced while working on an explosive device; that is, operators who felt stressed or anxious while working on a device admitted to having weaknesses in their technical skills and to have made more procedural errors. Thus, we have one pattern of dysphoria which may be related to perceived competence and another which seems to be temporally related to a long period of demanding and hazardous work. It is interesting to note that one operator who had completed two successful tours, remarked that for a short period after his return he thought that he was becoming agoraphobic, having experienced anxiety unexpectedly in a supermarket.

In conclusion, it seems necessary to consider demand-type stressors as well as threat-type stressors as possible contributary causes of panic-anxiety. However, there can be no resolution to the problem of the relationship between stress and anxiety until these terms are themselves fitted into a common conceptual framework. As suggested above, it may be preferable to dispense with anxiety as a theoretical concept and regard the report of anxiety as just one of many possible stress responses. The definition of a stress response depends, of course, upon an adequate, and independent, conceptualisation of the interaction between organismic and environmental processes as constituting a stressor.

Stress and Panic-Anxiety

Although the evidence is rather limited. there is some indication that stressful events are commonly observed at the time of onset of panic-anxiety (Mathews et al., 1981, p. 40). Mathews et al. (p. 47) assumed that stress interacts with the subject's level of trait anxiety, and if this is high, an overaroused state is produced.

Research into the effects of stressful life events on affective state has tended to follow a medical epidemiological approach in which the psychological effects are conceived as disorders and the life events as pathogenic (or protective) factors, that is, a linear stress-strain model of adaptation is implicitly adopted. Affective disturbance is conceived as a syndrome of effects (of a disorder) rather than being seen as functionally related to other events according to the principles assumed to govern behaviour in general. The combined effect of these practices is to obscure the subtle interaction between organismic and environmental events. Unfortunately, a functional analysis of these interactions is time-consuming and hardly feasible on a very large scale.

Brown and his colleagues essentially followed a careful clinical-intuitive method in measuring this interaction (e.g. Brown & Harris, 1978). This approach has the merit of avoiding a spurious objectivity. In one study, complaints of depressed mood and anxious affect (including panic) were related to unpleasant life events in the 12 months preceding onset of complaint (Finlay-Jones & Brown, 1981). Raters were trained to scale life events according to 'how unpleasant the event would be for most people in the particular set of circumstances surrounding the event' (p. 805). Respondents' judgement of the event was ignored although biographical and background data were taken into account. Severely unpleasant events were classified as losses or dangers. Danger referred to specific future crises that might occur as a result of the event. The subjects, who were women of mostly middle-class origin seeing a general practitioner, were classified into those who had developed an anxiety or depressive disorder in the previous 12 months and those who had not. The former (i.e. the 'psychiatric' cases) reported severe life events at a rate four times that of the remaining subjects. Cases of anxiety did not have elevated levels of loss events (unlike the 'depressed cases') but experienced more events signifying danger.

The authors concluded that there is a causal link between a specific type of event and a specific disorder; they further concluded that this causal relation could not be accounted for by other nonmeasured variables such as personality characteristics.

The specificity of the link has, of course, only been demonstrated with regard to two effects. For example, events signifying danger might also be associated with alcohol use. The conclusion that other variables (e.g. personality) cannot be invoked to explain the relationship seems to be contradicted by their method of assessing unpleasant events, which took into account contextual and biographical details. A person's life circumstances cannot be considered as unrelated to individual difference variables. At the very least, the method depends on the subject's ability to describe the life situation and its stressing features.

It is claimed that the causal relation holds up even when only truly independent events are considered (e.g. being notified that one's house was to be demolished). However, life events of this kind were not *invariably* followed by anxiety complaints, and so some kind of interactive model of causality is required.

A further point concerns the definition of *caseness* in Brown's studies (Tennant, Bebbington & Hurry, 1981). It is interesting to find that events which portend danger are associated with anxiety complaints, but what determines caseness in a psychiatric context may be related to other factors. It is the persistence of complaints beyond a reasonable time which seems to characterise the psychiatric patient (e.g. complaints after the danger has been resolved). By and large, with panic-anxiety, we are dealing with complaints that are not perceived to be rationally related to life circumstances. This need not imply that threatening, unpleasant events are unlikely causal factors. However, additional explanatory principles are required, for example, that the person is unable to recognise or articulate that he or she is being threatened.

Some alternative hypotheses to account for persistence of anxiety complaints are (1) the development of unrealistic expectations of danger or (2) the exacerbation of stressor effects through an inability to cope effectively with actual or expected unpleasant events. These alternative explanations of persistence emphasise organismic variables rather than antecedent environmental events.

Problem-Solving and Anxiety

Enduring personality characteristics are unlikely to be the main explanation for the sudden development of panic episodes, but they may be important in interaction with other factors, for example, in the long-term maintenance of anxiety complaints as noted above. There are two aspects of problem-solving which might contribute to chronicity: cognitive premises and cognitive style. The relevant cognitive premises have been assumed to be absolutist beliefs about oneself and the world, which are maintained even in the face of contradictory evidence (Ellis, 1962). Examples are 'Things should be different from the way they are' and 'If others dislike me, that's their problem not mine'. Styles of thought which have been assumed to be maladaptive are selective attention to the evidence, dichotomous reasoning, errors in the process of drawing logical inferences, and the like (Beck, 1976).

Absolutist beliefs are likely to lead to the perception of threat. For example, believing that one must always be loved by significant others is likely to sensitise a person to possible cues of social rejection. Some evidence for this was obtained by Goldfried and Sobocinski (1975) who found a correlation between a measure of irrational thinking and self-reports of anxiety in social situations.

Stylistic features of thought might also impede an individual's attempts to deal with the source of problems or threats. In this way, conflict may increase or threat intensify. If the individual becomes markedly physiologically aroused, the general efficiency of information processing may be lowered, further reducing problem-solving capacity (see Janis, 1982).

A question which has yet to be investigated is whether complaints of anxiety are related to general characteristics of thought processes or to specific cognitive premises. At present, there is scanty evidence to decide this matter, but some preliminary findings indicate that social anxieties and situational phobias are differentially related to cognitive characteristics (Sutton-Simon & Goldfried, 1979).

INFORMATION-PROCESSING MODELS

I earlier drew the distinction between cognitive appraisal and cognitive holistic models of anxiety. In the former, specific appraisals (meaning information) is crucial, whether appraisal is carried out with or without awareness. A cognitive holistic model, on the other hand, may be defined as a formulation which relates the report of anxiety to a general view of the operation of cognitive processes.

In contrast to the idea that emotion is the product of a specific set of cognitive appraisals, information theorists have defined emotion *as* the processing of information, that is, it is not product but process. The idea that the categories of cognition and emotion represent fundamentally different psychological processes may, in this sense, be incorrect and may be derived from an outmoded rational conception of human beings.

Emotion has traditionally been conceived as disrupting cognition. In a review of the literature concerning cognitive performance and arousal, Easterbrook (1959) concluded that the number of cues utilized in any situation tends to become smaller with increases in emotion with the effect that performance is disrupted. Mandler (1975, 1979), drawing upon the work of Baddeley (1972), provided an explanation of this finding in terms of the effects of autonomic arousal on the limited capacity system of conscious attention. With increasing autonomic arousal, attention is given to peripheral sensory feedback, thus occupying some of the limited attentional capacity. The remaining capacity is devoted to those cues that have originally been perceived as most salient (i.e. this is the narrowing effect).

Note that autonomic arousal need not be understood as caused by emotion, although the perception of salient stimuli (e.g. danger signals) might contribute to it. Emotion may in fact be reported because high autonomic arousal has lead to narrowed attention and decreased task performance, that is, it is a consequence of features of information processing.

A model of neurotic anxiety which combines appraisal and information-processing concepts has been described by Hamilton (1979). He gave prominence to the processing of 'aversive and/or threatening information' and to 'aversive schemata' which provide a 'consistent predisposition to apply threat-oriented inference and search processes in the analysis of the environment' (p. 394). Aversive information is simply defined as the stimulus and response characteristics usually associated with reports of anxiety. Hamilton was mainly concerned with the effects on performance of an interaction between task-relevant information and aversive information and how this interaction can, itself, constitute a stressor. The parts of the model concerned with neurotic anxiety do not attempt to show how information becomes aversive, and so I will not consider it further.

McReynolds (1976) took the position that anxiety is the consequence of a stage of information processing. In his account, anxiety is defined as an unpleasant feeling state which is ascribed to a 'backlog of unassimilated material'. Unassimilated material of whatever kind contributes to this backlog. In brief, the theory states that each perceptual experience is pigeon-holed in memory as a category with various attributes. Some perceptions are incongruent when a person is aware of having simultaneously pigeon-holed a perception as belonging to two or more categories which have discrepant attributes. Incongruities can be assimilated into the mental system, and a certain degree of incongruity is said to be novel and exciting. Incompatible percepts must be utilised simultaneously in awareness in order to add to the backlog of unassimilated material; the existence of incongruous categories, as such, is not assumed to have any emotional effect. Anxiety is said to be reported when the backlog builds up to a critical level.

This model is speculative and requires measures of incongruity in order to be tested. In particular, it does not seem reasonable to reduce all kinds of disconfirmation of an expectation to conceptual incongruity; for example, uncertainty, conflict, and interruption are not so much the effects of incongruity as aspects of the spatial and temporal organisation of behaviour.

The most promising information-processing model of emotion to date is that of Lang (1977, 1979, 1983). The model is an account of the way multiple sources of information about an emotion-provoking situation are stored in an integrated form in long-term memory. The structure performing this function is an 'emotional image' which has response-evocation properties when it is called up and processed in short-term memory. One result of processing is a restructuring of the image, so that, for example, autonomic arousal is no longer evoked.

The image represents the stimulus properties of an emotion-provoking situation as well as the behavioural and physiological responses with which they are associated. In fact, emotion is regarded as an action program for efferent expression. Information is held in the image in the form of an associative network of 'propositions' which are broadly identified with the brain's 'software'. The image includes information which defines the meaning of stimulus and response data. During active imagery the pattern of effector activity is determined by the response propositions, which are held in the image structure.

The emotional image is accessed when a subject attends to environmental information which matches propositions that make up the image. Conceptual networks are triggered as a unit when enough propositions are accessed. If, say, some visceral propositions are already 'active', less stimulus information may be required to trigger the emotion program. Emotion can therefore be defined as an 'action set' controlled by an image made up by varying propositions.

Lang (1979) proposed only to deal with 'focussed mental imagery of specific objects and situations' (p. 499), although more recently (Lang, 1983) he has proposed the outline of a taxonomy of anxiety complaints based on the nature of memory structures. In his research on specific fears, he has shown that by varying the verbal instructions which are assumed to access the image and by training subjects in certain types of imagery, specific patterns of behavioural and physiological responding can be produced. The effect of a response emphasis in imagery training is to encourage response processing, resulting in a psycho-physiological pattern of efferent activity which duplicates, at a lower amplitude, the pattern of responses observed with actual stimulus confrontation (Lang et al., 1980). Subjects who describe themselves as good imagers are more likely to develop affective responses. Progress in the elimination of specific fears during therapy is associated with heart-rate accelerative responses during active imagery (Lang, Melamed & Hart, 1970). This has been taken to indicate that autonomic response propositions must be processed for change to occur. Lang did not imply that each emotion corresponds to a specific pattern of responses. He made clear (Lang, 1983) that there is no state of attention nor any unique behavioural act which covaries consistently with reports of anxiety or diagnoses of anxiety. Instead, it is assumed that there is an 'affective response organisation' in which the different aspects of anxiety responding are linked. The information which must be accessed for anxiety to be reported is heterogeneous in terms of our contemporary response classifications. What links emotional states together (according to Lang's view of the pragmatic layman and scientist) is the presence of shared response dimensions. The most important dimensions underlying judgments about emotion are assumed to be arousal, valence and control. An action is judged to be emotional when it approaches the extreme ends of these affective dimensions.

Affective response organisation is seen as hierarchical, moving from context-bound acts to relatively stereotyped emotion programs, through to dimensional dispositions. The conclusions Lang (1983) reached from his research findings (which generally focus on the emotion program level) is that the information networks of phobias, social anxieties, agoraphobia, and so forth, are different, though they have overlapping features, for example, the networks of specific phobics are 'coherent' with high associative links, whereas agoraphobics have a more diffuse and less coherent affective memory structure. In the specific phobias, fear is elicited under minimal but discrete external instigating conditions; but in agoraphobics, the relationship with external cues is less consistent.

In some respects then, Lang proposed a correspondence between anxiety diagnoses and qualitative characteristics of separate memory structures. Given that the information content of emotion programs can be accessed by activating different propositions (which then spreads to the whole network) it need not be assumed that a particular set of propositions (e.g. relating to conscious appraisal of harm) is a necessary antecedent of reports of anxiety. A wide variety of antecedent conditions may be sufficient to access the network as a whole. Thus, the meaning assigned to situation cues can prime expressive/motor responses, and physiological arousal (produced by whatever means) may prime associated thoughts about the current situation. As noted above, conscious evaluation is not assumed to be necessary for emotional processing to occur. Presumably, some propositions of an associative network can be activated without awareness and excite others, which leads to an experience of anxiety which lacks some of its usual accompanying intellectual activity, for example, it may lack an identified source, as in panic-anxiety. In the most generalised anxiety complaints, Lang suggested that 'affective response propositions float in memory' (p. 52) being prompted by many stimuli and exciting a variety of memory structures with which they are associated.

This general approach to emotion is supported by research showing that an anxious mood can act as a cue for the recall of other thoughts and behaviours which were acquired in a different context but in a similar mood state (see review by Lang, 1983). In other words, an anxious mood, however instigated, facilitates the retrieval of worrying thoughts, images, negative self-evaluations, avoidance behaviours, and so forth, acquired in an earlier anxiety-evoking but otherwise unrelated context. Further support for the model comes from studies showing that arousal associated with one emotional state can transfer and modify another emotional state elicited in close sequence to it (Zillman, 1983). In Lang's terms, certain response propositions may be shared by different emotional states, and their activation in one state may facilitate another.

What Lang has essentially provided is a necessary integration of the separate systems of his three-systems conceptualisation of fear (Lang, 1971). He integrated the systems at the level of memory structures which are programs for behaviour. However, he did not attempt to show how the programs are formed or how they are changed, and so the objectives of his model are strictly limited. The difficulties associated with the earlier 'lump' theory of fear (Lang, 1969) have been bypassed through dropping the assumption that verbal reports of anxiety reflect an underlying 'state of feeling'. The verbal report is simply a response which is moderately associated with the other components of a response cluster referred to, on the grounds of empirical observation, as anxiety.

At the level of memory representation, no distinction is drawn between verbal stimulus/semantic propositions and other states of affairs which are not ordinarily formulated as logical propositions, for example, postural adjustments, facial expressions, and pilo-erection. Lang assumed that all the components of emotion are ultimately encoded in the same deep structural code. This is clearly a conceptual advance on the mentalistic position that it replaces.

Because Lang dealt only with memory representations, the theoretical problems associated with a functional or developmental *causal* account of the relationship between different types of anxiety response can be ignored. However, as a result, the image concept tends to be descriptive rather than explanatory. This is shown by the proposed taxonomy of anxiety complaints which seems to translate terms from one descriptive language into another without apparent theoretical advantage. The problem here is that inferences about the nature of the memory network may reflect present conceptual inadequacies; for example, with reference to agoraphobia, if it was known what to access and how to access it, inferences about memory structure might be very different. There is also the danger that emotional reactions which do not correspond to the 'normal' pattern are explained in terms of individual differences rather than antecedent historical conditions. For example, Lang (1979) assumed that an excessive ease or difficulty in evoking response propositions might account for different forms of pathology.

Lang's theoretical position therefore still leaves us with the problem of understanding the causal relation between the different components of the anxiety response cluster. Even if conscious appraisal is not a *neces-*

sary part of emotional processing, the powerful effects of verbal mediation and cognitive evaluation need to be explained in a way that is an advance on the assumption that verbal responses and meaning information are simply associated with other anxiety responses. These conceptual issues are explored further in Chapter 14.

12

Theories of Panic-Anxiety and Agoraphobia

INTRODUCTION

Panic-anxiety refers to a factorially derived cluster of complaints, whereas theories have been developed to account for the behaviour of persons falling into psychiatrically defined categories. The main implication of this is that theorists have tended to look for explanations for each psychiatric disorder, whereas I have argued that psychiatric categories may not fit the needs of psychological theorising at all (Hallam, 1983). Certain limitations of the panic-anxiety concept should also be noted when it becomes the object of theoretical analysis. First, we are dealing with a wide range of phenomena, some of which are shared with other clusters of psychological complaint. Second, without sequential observations of the complaints over time, it is difficult to detect interactions between them or to know whether there are any aspects that have temporal priority. Involved in the chain of causal interactions is the individual's attempts to understand the sources of his or her problems. These cognitive-interpretative processes may themselves be instrumental in maintaining the problem. For example, labelling oneself as having a 'disorder' may have these undesirable effects (Storms & Nisbett, 1970). Finally, the factorially derived clusters are based on self-reports and psychiatric observations with their attendant biases (Hallam, 1983).

It has to be admitted that there is no widely accepted framework for classifying psychological distress and problem behaviours which can encompass these complexities. What seem to be required are descriptive dimensions suited to a psychological explanation of the phenomena. An attempt of this kind has been made by Foa and Kozak (1983) in their classification of anxiety complaints based on the internal or external nature of the salient cues, the presence or absence of anticipated harm, and avoidance behaviour.

Psychological theories of agoraphobia (e.g. Mathews et al. 1981; Goldstein & Chambless, 1978) have generally adopted multicausal hypotheses and imply that a multidimensional descriptive framework for the complaints are required. Once such a framework is available, there would appear to be no reason to retain the categorical disorder-model which is at present in vogue. With these cautions in mind, theories of panic and agoraphobia will now be considered. As might be expected they focus on different sets of variables, which I have grouped as (1) acquired vulnerabilities, (2) interpersonal, (3) endogenous factors and (4) integrated models.

ACQUIRED VULNERABILITIES

Family Influences

It is not surprising that in a climate of psychoanalytic theorising, the dependency of agoraphobics (i.e. their desire to be accompanied and to stay at home) was viewed as a consequence of early parental handling (Andrews, 1966). With admittedly little evidence to go on, Bowlby (1973) suggested that fear of public situations is based on a displaced anxiety about an absence or loss of an attachment figure or some other secure base. He speculated that in the majority of an uncontrolled series of patients, agoraphobia could be understood as the product of a pathogenic pattern of family interactions. He explained the displacement of anxiety as a consequence of a Western cultural bias toward stressing external danger and an underemphasis on the significance of being alone. It is interesting to note that he found some subjects intractably resistant to the idea that there were difficulties at home.

Researchers have examined two separate factors of early experience. These are inadequate care and maternal overprotection. Solyom, Beck, Solyom & Hugel (1974) found that phobic subjects (nearly all agoraphobic) perceived their parents as having more psychological problems than did age- and sex-matched controls (hospital employees and volunteers). Perception of overprotection did not differ significantly, and separation experiences were equally represented in both groups. In a later study of the mothers of the same phobic subjects, the authors could not reach a conclusive opinion about their protective attitudes (Solyom, Silberfeld & Solyom, 1976). Snaith (1968) compared a group of agoraphobics with other types of phobic subjects and found a small tendency for greater instability in the home backgrounds of the former. They did not appear to have experienced rejection or overprotection as children.

In a better-controlled study, Buglass et al. (1977) could find little evidence of greater parental deprivation, separation or psychological problems in the families of the agoraphobic group. There were no differences in attitudes of affection or dislike for the mothers during early development, but later in adolescence and at the time of assessment, the agoraphobics showed greater ambivalence between positive and negative feelings about their mothers. There was an awareness of dependence and resentment about this. This result could, of course, be interpreted as a consequence rather than a cause of the need to be accompanied.

In a more recent controlled study, agoraphobics perceived their mothers as less caring but not more overprotective (Parker, 1979). The correlation between the subjects score on an agoraphobia scale and a parental care scale, was, however, extremely low ($r = 0.16$).

Unfortunately, there are no prospective studies to throw light on the question of predisposing parental or family characteristics.

Other Characteristics

The psychological characteristics of agoraphobics as a group have been reviewed by Chambless (1982a). Nearly all the subjects in the studies she reviewed were obtained through psychiatric referral, and so it is difficult to say how much their general characteristics reflect psychiatric status per se. We have also to consider the effect of agoraphobic behaviour itself, for example, the consequences of social isolation, and failure to fulfil social obligations. Presley (1976) found that, although agoraphobic wives perceived themselves unfavourably (as also did their husbands), there was no suggestion that *prior* to onset of their problems, perceptions of self or their spouse were unusual. They did not differ from the way a control group of women perceived themselves an equivalent number of years previously.

INTERPERSONAL FACTORS

After reviewing a number of clinical descriptions of the agoraphobic woman's personality and selection of mate, Hafner (1982, p. 82) summed up by saying that 'agoraphobic symptoms emerge or are exacerbated as part of the couple's attempts to adjust to one another and to the constraints, demands, and conflicts of marriage' (p. 82).

The suggestion here is that interpersonal factors are important in both the cause and maintenance of the agoraphobic cluster of complaints. Goldstein and Chambless (1978) were more specific and proposed a distinction between *simple* agoraphobics (mostly precipitated by drug experiences and physical factors) and *complex* agoraphobia (in which interpersonal factors are implicated in cause and maintenance). A difficulty with this distinction is that all agoraphobics in whom the interpersonal context is not considered relevant may be relegated to the 'simple' category.

Hafner (1982) argued that preagoraphobics choose partners who are likely to act assertively and independently, that is, tend to be the problem-solver in the partnership. This arrangement is said to be inherently unstable, and the unassertive partner may later reflect this instability by developing agoraphobia. However, in some cases, it is argued, agoraphobia stabilises the relationship, and the spouse may become distressed if the agoraphobic can function normally again (Hand & Lamontagne, 1976; Hafner, 1977).

In the light of lack of evidence concerning the personality characteristics of agoraphobics, the hypothesis that preagoraphobics are excessively dependent or unassertive must be viewed with caution. Also, the argument that agoraphobia is *necessarily* associated with an unstable interpersonal relationship is untenable because some married agoraphobics have no obvious difficulties in this respect (e.g. Milton & Hafner, 1979; Bland & Hallam, 1980). In these studies, agoraphobics judged to have a poor marriage did not maintain the gains they had made in an exposure-based behaviour therapy or did not improve at all on some measures. This indicates that interpersonal factors are sometimes related to maintenance or to the success of therapy but does not prove that they are of causal significance in producing the initial complaints. A more recent study confirmed that marital adjustment was related to the success of an exposure therapy (Monteiro, Marks & Ramm, 1984), but better social, sexual and work adjustment also predicted outcome at a 2-year follow-up assessment. These authors argued that poor marital adjustment is an aspect of problem-solving capacity in general and that therefore interpersonal factors have no specific significance beyond this.

These issues are unlikely to be resolved without more sophisticated assessment of interpersonal relationships and their interaction with psychological problems. At present, there seems no reason to doubt that in many instances, complaints of anxiety and a fear of venturing out are functionally related to the quality of interpersonal relationships. It would be surprising if this were not the case.

Do interpersonal factors have a contributary causal role in agoraphobia? This hypothesis has been argued by Goldstein (1973, 1982) and Goldstein and Chambless (1978). Preagoraphobics are assumed to be particularly sensitive to the experience of aloneness or separation and therefore are overdependent on others. They are said to be unassertive, lacking in social skills and feel helpless unless attached to a strong partner. In addition, their style of dealing with stressors is claimed to have the following characteristics: (1) a tendency to label all arousal states as 'anxiety/fear' (i.e. they cannot recognise subtle distinctions in feeling states) and (2) a low ability to connect feeling states with antecedent events, especially interpersonal events.

The tendency to misattribute distress (e.g. that caused by arguments) to external situations is assumed to be rooted in childhood experiences of stress with which the individual could not cope. A misattribution of this kind is thought to be consistent with (1) panic being experienced as spontaneous, (2) an avoidant style of coping with any form of interpersonal confrontation and (3) a strong denial of interpersonal conflict.

A final precondition for the development of agoraphobia is the occurrence of a panic episode which is conceptualised as an unconditioned emotional response to prolonged stress or conflict. The interoceptive cues which are contiguous with the panic become conditioned 'anxiety cues', and a second-order conditioning follows from an association between panic and the situation in which it occurs. Avoidance of the situation is strengthened by stimulus generalisation, the anticipation of unrealistic catastrophic consequences, and the perception of being trapped in the situation and being unable to return to a safe place.

This complex model, illustrated in Figure 12.1, is perhaps the most developed account of the causes of agoraphobia. There is a clear distinction between factors which lead to the onset of problems and those that maintain them (e.g. panic may occur without situational avoidance). Attention is focussed at this point on the role of interpersonal conflict and other parts of the model are considered later.

Goldstein and Chambless (1978) found evidence of conflict (not necessarily of an interpersonal kind) in 20 out of 24 'complex' agoraphobics but information was sometimes obtained retrospectively or by recollection. Subjects who had hypochondriacal phobias or panic without phobia were excluded from this series. The model is presumably only partially or not at all applicable to them. The manner of selecting subjects suggests observational bias, and this is indicated by their comment that the therapist was often alerted to the existence of conflict by the absence of clear-cut conditioning events in the development of symptoms.

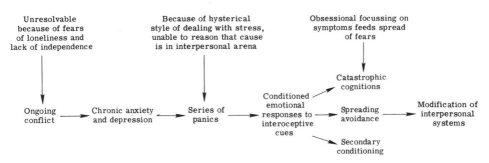

Figure 12.1. Goldstein's model of the development of agoraphobia. Reprinted from *Agoraphobia: Multiple perspectives on theory and treatment*, D. L. Chambless & A. J. Goldstein (Eds.), with permission of John Wiley & Sons, Inc. Copyright © 1982 by John Wiley & Sons, Inc.

The assumed importance of interpersonal conflict does not accord with what agoraphobics themselves say about the precipitants of their problems (see Thorpe & Burns, 1983, p. 24), but this is not damaging if agoraphobics do, in fact, deny their interpersonal problems. However, the hypothesis is difficult to test for this reason.

The hypothesis that interpersonal factors play a causal role can be questioned generally, on the basis that it is unlikely to apply to all agoraphobics (or even to all complex agoraphobics). A proportion of clients respond well to exposure-based therapies in which no attention is paid to interpersonal relationships. However, it was noted earlier that marital difficulties are associated with a poorer response to exposure-based therapy, and so interpersonal conflict may be relevant, in at least some clients, to the cause, precipitation or maintenance of fears of public places.

Sex-Role Conflict

With respect to the alleged personality characteristics of agoraphobics and the obvious sex-bias in the prevalence statistics, it could be argued that regardless of pre-existing personality characteristics, interpersonal (and sex-role) conflict is an endemic feature of late twentieth-century marriage. The constant mention of sex-role conflict by clinicians is reminiscent of the emphasis given to sexual conflicts at the beginning of the century. In other words, conflict may be an important factor regardless of its precise content. Because women are generally more dissatisfied with the current position of the sexes than are men (Steinman, 1974) and generally have fewer resources to deal with the conflict in more adaptive ways, it might be they who are more likely to report anxiety or panic.

This argument is different from that of Fodor (1974) and Al-Issa (1980) who have suggested that agoraphobia is an extreme expression of stereotypic feminine characteristics such as an avoidant response to stress. Instead of emphasising the personality characteristics of the pre-agoraphobic individual, we may instead point to general social conditions which perpetuate and enhance sex-role conflict and limit the range of options for coping with it. Staying at home may be regarded as consistent with sex-role expectations and pragmatic considerations (Hallam, 1983). Thus, in a survey of agoraphobia club members (Marks & Herst, 1970), it was observed that women with higher educational qualifications; or who were single; or, if married, had fewer younger children, were more likely to fight their fears and go out to work. The women who wanted to work but did not complained that they were unable to get the help that they needed because of their phobias. This suggests that pragmatic rather than personality factors influenced coping style.

As a general feature of present-day society, sex-role conflict must be commonly associated with problems of all kinds. Although no specific association with panic-anxiety can claim to have been established, it is worth noting the results of one detailed study of spouses' perceptions of each other in a marriage in which the female partner was agoraphobic (Buglass et al., 1977). The spouses were interviewed at home by a sociologist who questioned them about the allocation of household tasks, decision-making, and social activities. The interaction was tape-recorded and rated on scales of 'assertion–compliance' and 'affection–dislike'. It was found that, for phobic wives, joint decision-making was associated positively with the amount of affection shown toward husbands and negatively with assertion; that is, wives were more assertive when there was less joint consultation. These correlations between the variables were not significant for the husbands of the phobics or for the nonphobic control subjects (husbands or wives).

This finding might tentatively be taken as evidence of sex-role conflict in the marriages of the phobic group, although disagreements may have arisen as a consequence of the impact of agoraphobic behaviour on the marriage. For example, only about half of the husbands were perceived by their wives as sympathetic to their difficulties. Moreover, in a related study which utilised a semantic differential technique, there were no differences in the way that the phobic and control groups perceived their marriage partners *prior* to the development of the phobic problem (Presley, 1976).

The interaction between social conditions, sex-role conflict and other factors is probably too complex to permit any simple interpretation of the sex prevalence figures for agoraphobia. It is interesting to note that most cases of agoraphobia reported in the nineteenth-century literature were male (Mathews et al., 1981). A change in present ratios may be expected if women continue to move toward a less home-centered lifestyle.

ENDOGENOUS FACTORS

Although biological causal hypotheses have been reviewed elsewhere (Chapters 5 and 10), the theory of Klein (1964, 1981) deserves special consideration because his emphasis on *panic* in the causal development of fears of public places has had a significant academic and practical impact. Klein observed that anxiety was often initially reported as if it occurred spontaneously or 'out of the blue'. These episodes are commonly described as panic attacks. The stricken individual subsequently becomes fearful of having further similar episodes and avoids situations in which they might occur. In the development of a theoretical understanding of agoraphobia, Klein should therefore be credited with shifting the emphasis from a *phobia* of public places to an anticipatory fear of experiencing a panic attack in public places.

Klein (1981) postulated two types of anxiety: *anticipatory (conditioned) anxiety* and *panic.* His reason for doing so rested primarily on the differential effects of imipramine and other antidepressant medication on the two types of anxiety. This class of drugs was said to suppress panic but have little or no effect on anticipatory anxiety. Anticipatory anxiety is assumed to be reduced when the person learns (on medication) that panic does not occur.

Klein's double blind drug study (Klein, 1964, 1967) included a placebo and imipramine group but only two subjects in a third, chlorpromazine group. Imipramine significantly reduced reports of affective distress, panic and cardiorespiratory complaints, but there was no overall difference between the imipramine and placebo groups on measures of psychiatric syptomatology. Chlorpromazine led to increased distress according to psychiatric ratings. The claim that two drug-responsive syndromes had been delineated seems overstated as no reliable and independent measures of panic and anticipatory anxiety had been developed. Klein (1981) has suggested that in the psychiatrically defined disorders involving panic, there is a lowering of the threshold for an innate distress signal which is said to be part of a distress/despair mechanism. This mechanism would normally be called into play by maternal

separation. Other followers of Klein have argued for a genetically transmitted biochemical abnormality (Sheehan et al., 1980).

If anxiety, as a lay construct, is multireferential (see Chapter 14), it is
plausible to suggest that the episodes experienced as panic are invoked
by a set of antecedent conditions which differ in some respects from
those that elicit reports of anxiety in anticipation of an aversive experience. These antecedents may well include biological changes of an as-
yet-unidentified nature. The fact that certain physical abnormalities (e.g.
caused by phaeochromocytoma or thyrotoxicosis) are associated with
reports of anxiety is well established. However, this does not imply that
the reports of anxiety associated with these physical abnormalities are
different *types* of anxiety. It is sometimes stated that thyrotoxicosis
should not be mistaken for an anxiety neurosis, but these diagnoses
should not be regarded as alternatives. In other words, thyrotoxicosis
may have effects which produce the cluster of complaints I have termed
panic-anxiety. It has been found that thyrotoxic subjects who complain
of anxiety do not respond to antianxiety medication or an inactive
placebo in the same way as nonthyrotoxic subjects complaining of anxiety (Ramsay, Greer & Bagly, 1973). However, it should not be inferred
that this differential drug response establishes two types of anxiety:
thyrotoxic and nonthyrotoxic. It need only be inferred that some of the
referents of reports of anxiety are differentially affected by pharmacological and psychological influences. For example, thyrotoxic subjects did
not respond to placebo medication, which suggests that they were less
influenced by the social and psychological context of drug administration. This might be explained in terms of their understanding of the
causes of their complaints, that is, that they could be attributed to a
medical condition.

Although the apparently spontaneous and irrational nature of the
initial episodes of panic encourages the search for endogenous causes,
alternative psychological explanations can be put forward. In fact, physiological changes triggered by events defined at the psychological level
of analysis can also be described in terms of physiological mechanisms.
The two levels of explanation are not therefore necessarily incompatible.
It should also be added that the initial episodes of panic do not occur just
anywhere. As Klein (1981) observed, certain situations contribute to the
elicitation of panic, especially enclosure. Klein believed that enclosure
enhances the fear of having a panic while *helpless*, that is, it lowers the
threshold for a distress/despair mechanism. This hypothesis does not
account for the first episode before the fear of panic develops. It seems
more likely that enclosure contributes *directly* to the evocation of panic
because the first episodes are commonly reported as occurring in vari-

ous forms of public transportation, crowded shops, and so forth. In other words, the situational specificity of the initial episode cannot easily be explained in terms of a hypothesised *consequence* of panic.

Serious doubts can be raised about the pharmacological differentiation of anticipatory anxiety and panic and the definition of panic itself. The DSM III criteria (American Psychiatric Association, 1980) for determining the presence of panic are rather vague. During the episode itself, which must be discrete and occur at least some of the time in the absence of circumscribed phobic stimuli, the person need only demonstrate any 4 of 12 different 'symptoms'. These include feeling unreal and fear of the consequences of panic. Granted that there are some definitional problems, evidence that antidepressant drugs have an antipanic effect can be obtained by testing two hypotheses.

1. Imipramine should have a greater therapeutic effect on clients who report panic as one of their anxiety complaints versus those who do not.
2. Within individuals who complain of both anxiety and panic, imipramine should have a greater effect on panic than on other anxiety complaints.

In a test of the first hypothesis, Zitrin, Klein, Woerner and Ross (1983) compared imipramine and placebo in a double-blind trial with three groups of phobic client. These were simple phobics, agoraphobics, and a third group who reported panic attacks like the agoraphobics but showed much less situational avoidance. The subjects received either supportive therapy or supportive therapy combined with several behavioural techniques (imaginal systematic desensitisation and assertion training). There was a significant drug effect on many of the outcome measures. Panic was self-rated on 5–7 point scales. The main drug effect was significant on two out of four panic measures, but what the changes meant in practice is not clear. Significantly, the main drug effect was found only in the two groups of subjects who reported spontaneous panic attacks. It was concluded that the result was due to the behavioural characteristics of the clients. However, the simple phobics appeared to score almost as highly on the panic scales (and changed significantly in this respect), and so the scales do not appear to be measuring the phenomenon which allegedly differentiates the groups. If the scales are valid it must be concluded that panic can be modified in the absence of drug action, and it is more parsimonious to assume that imipramine facilitates a psychological process rather than assuming that it has a specific antipanic effect. Furthermore, the drug effect was observed on measures other than panic (e.g. the Taylor Manifest Anxiety Scale) therefore raising doubts about the specificity of the drug's action. Evidence that antidepressants have a generalised effect on psychological measures of distress can be found in the studies of Sheehan et al. (1980), McNair and Kahn (1981) and Mavissakalian and Michelson (1983).

Other groups of workers have found no superiority of antidepressant medication over placebo in producing change in agoraphobic clients (Solyom et al., 1981; Marks, Gray, Cohen, Hill, Mawson, Ramm & Stern, 1983). Almost all the subjects in the study by Marks and his colleagues reported unpredictable episodes of panic. Two forms of behaviour therapy were compared in this study, and it is interesting to note that one (involving therapist guided exposure to feared situations) produced greater change in frequency of panic than the other. It is clear from other studies, too, that panic frequency can be reduced by behavioural methods of therapy. Antidepressant medication is typically administered over several months, and so the extent to which the action of the drug is to suppress panic or to facilitate extinction mediated by psychological processes, cannot easily be determined. In a study by Mavissakalian and Michelson (1983), imipramine treatment was combined with a programme of exposure therapy and compared with exposure practice alone. The combined procedure was clearly superior. The research findings in this field are therefore full of inconsistencies, and the precise role of imipramine when added to other behavioural procedures is uncertain.

The antipanic effect of antidepressant drugs has been tested more directly by seeing whether they prevent the panics reported during infusion of sodium lactate (see Chapter 5). Eight subjects who were diagnosed as having a panic disorder or agoraphobia with panic-attacks and who had been prescribed antidepressant medication were infused with lactate or a (placebo) dextrose solution (Appleby, Klein, Sachar, Levitt & Halpern, 1981). Six of the eight had reported panic during an infusion before being placed on antidepressant medication, but none did so following successful drug treatment.

The interpretation of this finding depends partly on whether the panic-free state of their subjects prior to reinfusion can be attributed to their medication and not to other factors. However, a third reinfusion is planned after subjects have been withdrawn from medication (and remain panic-free) (Liebowitz & Klein, 1982). Results with two patients have been reported so far, both of whom were said to panic during infusion of lactate. This suggested to Leibowitz and Klein that vulnerability to lactate-induced panic is a trait rather than a state phenomenon. If that is so, then subjects who no longer report panic following behaviour therapy should continue to demonstrate the phenomenon.

No data of this kind is available. It remains to be shown that the pharmacological prevention of lactate-induced panic is specific to the antidepressant class of drugs or whether it could also be demonstrated with alcohol, barbiturate, benzodiazepines, and the like. As noted above, there are still problems in reliably measuring a state of panic.

INTEGRATED MODELS

Mathews and his colleagues speculated that the preagoraphobic individual is genetically predisposed to report anxiety in many situations, that is, has high trait anxiety (Mathews et al., 1981, p. 47). High trait anxiety, in combination with nonspecific background stress factors, is said to cause a generalised anxiety state. At this stage an acute episode of anxiety occurring away from the home is experienced as a panic attack. This acute episode is assumed to be the joint product of a state of generalised anxiety and exposure to arousing environmental cues; together these provoke an upward spiral of autonomic responses. Other causes of panic, including anxiety-provoking thoughts, are also suggested. The tendency to the agoraphobic pattern of behaviour is then reinforced by two other factors: (1) an avoidant/dependent style of coping with stressors which, being associated with sex-role learning, accounts for the predominance of women amongst agoraphobic clients and (2) an attribution of anxiety to external provoking stimuli (e.g. crowds, shops) rather than more internal causes such as worry and stress (Mathews et al., 1981).

Once the pattern of avoidance behaviour has been initiated, several factors are assumed to maintain it. One factor is a fear of provoking further panics, which arises because panic is inherently aversive and might possibly have other harmful consequences. In addition, a secondary conditioning process is assumed to occur by means of which incipient autonomic responses, elicited by situations in which panic occurs, come to signal the danger of an attack. Agoraphobic behaviour is also reinforced by such factors as attention provided by the 'sick role' or the willingness of family members to accommodate the phobic behaviour.

This integrated model represents a substantial departure from phobia conceptions of agoraphobia, and it emphasises the affinity between fears of public places and complaints of anxiety of a more general kind (Hallam, 1978). The model offers useful pointers to further research investigation, in particular, to clients causal attributions and coping style. Research into the features of the public environment which are physiologically arousing for both individuals who do or do not complain of anxiety is clearly indicated.

Evaluation of the model is hampered by lack of crucial information. For example, it is by no means certain that the majority of persons diagnosed as agoraphobic have had a pre-existing tendency to report anxiety with greater frequency than usual. Further, the differentiation of a predisposition to report anxiety (high trait anxiety) and a generalised anxiety state is not made clear. The latter would appear to entail complaints of anxiety in the absence of 'reasonable' sources of anxiety. It needs to be explained how nonspecific stress transforms trait anxiety into a problem having the features of panic-anxiety. Moreover, the mechanism proposed to account for the precipitation of panic is not entirely consistent with clients' reports that the first episode appears to come out of the blue with an unexpected intensity. If life stressors interacted with trait anxiety in the manner proposed, a more gradual development of problems would be predicted.

Goldstein's account of the development of agoraphobia (Goldstein, 1982) considered earlier (see Figure 12.1) is similar in many respects to the one provided by Mathews and his colleagues. Panic is explained as an unconditioned emotional response to stress and conflict, but no experimental models for this reaction are offered. Additionally, in Goldstein's model, panic is assumed to be a state that is discontinuous with anxiety reported as intense; the basis for this assertion—Klein's pharmacological differentiation of anxiety and panic—is questionable (see earlier).

Like some other authors, Goldstein stressed aversive conditioning to interoceptive cues that signal panic; irrational beliefs about the consequences of panic are assumed to reinforce this fear-of-fear component. As a result, the first signs of bodily arousal are said to bring into awareness thoughts related to these beliefs.

A striking implication of both models is the number of different causal processes (developmental, conditioning, cognitive, etc.) that need to be considered. For example, Mathews and his colleagues suggested that panic can be explained by several hypotheses which are not mutually exclusive. Therefore, even if agoraphobic clients have a similar cluster of complaints, it seems likely that a number of subgroups can be identified on the basis of psychological dimensions which are relevant to causation. Researchers would probably profit from giving up the 'uniformity myth' (Kiesler, 1971), which, in this instance, is based on the assumption that clients labelled as agoraphobics can be regarded as a homogeneous group.

13

Theoretical Implications of Exposure-Based Therapies

PROBLEMS OF INTERPRETATION

It is hazardous to use the outcome of therapy as a source of hypotheses about the cause and maintenance of psychological problems, although this is commonly done. The main purpose of therapy outcome studies is, of course, to demonstrate that clients can be helped to a meaningful degree. A secondary aim is to identify which components of a therapeutic procedure are essential and effective. Studies of therapy can also be informative about the process of change, and this may suggest how problems are maintained. Certain psychological variables have been shown to influence the amount of behavioural change (or to predict change), and these variables are clearly of theoretical interest.

For several reasons, the results of therapeutic trials are difficult to interpret in terms of underlying processes of change. Although most studies involve a comparison between different procedures, many variables typically either remain uncontrolled or cannot be controlled. Behavioural change can be produced in a variety of ways, and so it cannot be attributed with certainty to the processes assumed to underlie the procedures employed. Also, clients do not mention isolated and readily specifiable problems when they first begin therapy. Problem behaviours may be functionally related to other problems or to social/environmental factors which do not remain constant throughout the course of therapy. It is perhaps not surprising that response to therapy is highly variable and that success is difficult to predict.

As just one example of the interpretive problem, Mathews et al. (1981, p. 91) asked why graded retraining in the phobic situation was so ineffective with agoraphobic clients when first tried about 25 years ago. They suggested that location of therapy (hospital versus home), severity of problems (outpatient versus inpatient), and the assumption that it was countertherapeutic to distress the client, are all possible explanations. It might be added that behaviour therapy was in its infancy, that therapists were not confident of their techniques and that clients referred for therapy at that time tended to be difficult or unresponsive to other forms of therapy. It is noteworthy that success with a therapeutic procedure tends to be attributed to supposedly critical variables (e.g. exposure), whereas failure has a plethora of explanations.

The presence of problems in addition to the one being modified adds considerably to the burden of interpretation. Agoraphobic clients who are dissatisfied with their marriages appear to change less with exposure-based therapies (Milton & Hafner; 1979, Bland & Hallam, 1981). It has been argued that the presence of additional interpersonal problems is causally related to the genesis and/or maintenance of agoraphobia (e.g. Goldstein, 1982; Hafner, 1982). Other researchers have pointed out that the presence of additional problems must be expected by chance and that no causal relationship need be implied (Monteiro et al., 1984). However, if a multifactorial model of causation is adopted, no strict division can be made between those additional problems that are causally related to the main problem and those that are not. Taking agoraphobics as a group, a number of different variables may play a contributory causal role so that, for example, marital factors may be causally relevant in one subject but not in another. For a similar reason, a low association between a variable (e.g. organic dysfunction) and the agoraphobic cluster of complaints need not imply causal irrelevance if causation is multifactorial.

This chapter does not aim to compare the efficacy of different therapies or to review what is known about the processes of change during exposure-based therapies. This task has been performed by others (e.g. Marks, 1978; Marshall, Gauthier & Gordon, 1979; Mathews et al., 1981; Emmelkamp, 1982; Foa & Kozak, 1983). There is a consensus that behavioural methods which require the client to confront fear cues, imaginally or in real life, have transformed the outlook for agoraphobic clients (see Foa & Kozak, 1983).

There is also increasing optimism that clients who have complaints of anxiety of a generalised nature can also be significantly helped. The theoretical implications of therapeutic trials with this group of clients are, as yet, limited, and so they will not be discussed. The main aim of the present chapter is to comment on the methodology of the outcome research and to discuss some of its underlying assumptions in the light of my own perspective on anxiety.

Methodological Considerations

The evaluation of therapeutic efficacy has generally followed a medical conception of the task, that is, isolating specific techniques that are effective with specific disorders. Much of the significant work has been performed in England under the direction of psychiatric researchers (in particular, M. Gelder and I. Marks) whose principal aim has been the rapid and effective treatment of mental disorders. This service aim and medical orientation, understandable in a hospital context, has to some extent limited the theoretical implications of the research.

The disorder model has lead to a reliance on psychiatric diagnostic criteria for subject selection. Agoraphobics have been regarded as a homogeneous group even though psychiatric description of the agoraphobic syndrome has emphasised the multifaceted nature of the complaints. The principal target for therapeutic intervention has been phobic avoidance of public places. This is often the most disabling problem, but selection of this target was heavily influenced, at least initially, by the assumption that a phobia of public places was the *core* feature of the cluster. There have been attempts to measure panic, depersonalisation and other anxiety complaints; but assessments have been crude, and subjects have not been assigned to groups on the basis of these or other measures.

The concept of agoraphobia which underlies contemporary psychiatric definitions is that of a phobia of public places; for example, DSM III groups agoraphobia with the phobias. Therapeutic methods and assessment techniques have been devised around the phobia concept (Hallam, 1978; Gray & McPherson, 1982). In the early stages of behaviour therapy, agoraphobia was conceived theoretically as a conditioned emotional response elicited by stimuli associated with public places. Staying at home was equated with an avoidance response reinforced by anxiety reduction. For example, it was considered countertherapeutic for a client to withdraw (escape) from a phobic situation while feeling anxious. The imagery used in the method of systematic desensitisation (Wolpe, 1958) concerned leaving the home and entering public situations (see, e.g. Yorkston, Sergeant & Rachman, 1968), whereas it is now known that other cues (faintness, thoughts of death, etc.) are relevant. These types of cue were later incorporated into imaginal 'flooding' techniques (Boulougouris, Marks & Marset, 1971).

The view that agoraphobia is the manifestation of an emotional response which has been conditioned to cues found in public situations is still influential. In a review of therapy procedures, Jansson and Ost (1982) noted that real-life exposure is the most effective technique and that the process of modification most likely involves the extinction of a conditioned emotional response. They proposed that researchers adopt a uniform definition of agoraphobic problems. Their definition is entirely in line with a unitary disorder model of the underlying mechanism, namely, that 'agoraphobics should show marked phobic avoidance with relatively little anxiety when not in phobic situations' (p. 313).

It could be argued that, because of the way agoraphobics have been selected for outcome studies, they are a sufficiently homogeneous group for the purpose of showing that the available methods are effective for a substantial majority. However, the claim that currently used 'treatment packages' are *adequate* can be disputed on a number of grounds. Response to therapy is variable, and some of the established outcome measures are of doubtful validity (see later). The ability to predict who will respond to the most successful method to date (real-life exposure) has hardly improved in the last 10 years.

Outcome studies have characteristically employed a variety of measures and recorded improvement on some or most of them. However, there have been few attempts to predict the *pattern* of improvement, which has not been adequately explained. Furthermore, the methodological adequacy of the studies does not reach minimal standards according to Gray and McPherson (1982). These authors questioned any general conclusion about the value of behaviour therapy for the problem of agoraphobia.

Comments on the Efficacy of Exposure-Based Therapies

What then is the efficacy of behavioural methods? Jansson and Ost (1982) concluded that meaningful changes in the avoidance of public places take place in 67% of clients assessed at a follow-up duration of 6 months or more. This estimate is based on (1) a mean rating of 3 or less on the commonly used 0–8 scales of anxiety and avoidance in the main phobic situation (Watson & Marks, 1971) and (2) a reduction from the pretherapy mean of at least 50%. They note, incidentally, that a long-term follow-up study, in which assessments were made 5–9 years after therapy (Munby & Johnston, 1980), failed to achieve significance by these criteria. Emmelkamp and Kuipers (1979) used a 2-point change on the 0- to 8-point scales as their minimum criterion for improvement; 75% were found to be improved on this basis.

It should be noted that there have been differences in the precise form of the Watson and Marks scales over the years and that phobic targets vary between individuals. There is, therefore, no guarantee that studies are comparable on this basis. On the whole, standardised tests (e.g. of trait anxiety) have not been used for evaluation, or if they have, results have not been presented in such a way as to permit comparisons to be made between studies.

A rating of 3 on a combined anxiety/avoidance scale indicates a report of fear somewhat greater than unease together with a slight tendency to avoid. The rating refers to the main phobic target(s) on which greatest change would be expected. A mean score does not indicate the distribution from which it is calculated, and so some outcome data obtained during a therapist training programme (Marks, Hallam, Connolly & Philpott (1977) were reanalysed. Results for phobic subjects, in general, equalled or bettered results achieved in earlier trials, although the mean rating for 26 agoraphobics at 6-month follow-up was 3.3, slightly outside the Jansson and Ost criterion. Of this group, 50% had a rating of 2 or less, 27% showed essentially no improvement, and the remainder rated between 3 and 5. Significant reductions in questionnaire measures of other fears and of psychiatric symptoms were obtained, but the mean scores of the agoraphobic clients were still higher at 1-month follow-up than the scores recorded *before* therapy of clients with specific and social phobias.

The amount of change on scales or ratings of anxious mood is variable between studies. If a phobia of public places is the *core* feature of the agoraphobic cluster of complaints, then measures of trait anxiety or anxious mood should decline along with elimination of anxiety reported in public situations. Psychiatric description and psychophysiological measures (Lader & Wing, 1966) certainly suggest that generalised anxiety and high physiological arousal typify the agoraphobic client. These characteristics should, therefore, be incorporated in an overall assessment of improvement. Mathews et al. (1981) stated that scores on the depression and anxiety factors of the McNair and Lorr mood scale did show modest reductions during the therapy period. At long-term follow-up (Munby & Johnston, 1980), these changes were broadly maintained. An exception to this trend was the clinical assessment of anxious mood. The assessor judged that, in this respect, clients had returned to levels obtaining before therapy. Mavissakalian and his colleagues noted that of several outcome measures, generalised anxiety, as measured by the Zung anxiety scale (Zung, 1971), changed least (Mavissakalian,

Michelson, Greenwald, Kornblith & Greenwald, 1983). Some of the subjects in their trial had received a combined procedure of medication (imipramine) and a programme of exposure practice.

Changes on the 0- to 8-point phobia scales must be interpreted cautiously. In a study which used real-life exposure to modify a fear of driving alone (part of an agoraphobic cluster of fears), Williams and Rappoport (1983) found that subjects who showed little or no improvement in driving performance changed 3.8 points on the 0- to 8-point scales. Scores on the main phobic rating failed to correlate significantly with actual driving ability at any phase. Of course, the description of the main phobic item (driving alone) may have had different meanings for different clients according to their initial driving ability; indeed, the meaning may have changed over time. However, a low correlation between behavioural measures and the 0- to 8-point scales was also noted by Mathews et al. (1981, p. 22). These authors remarked that agoraphobic fears are complex and do not fall on a dimension which is common to all clients. They therefore constructed individualised hierarchies of phobic situations according to difficulty of approach, and the client was behaviourally tested on key items. This is not a purely behavioural measure because construction of the scale depends on the client's concept of a range of difficulty and the therapist's ability to elicit the appropriate information. The behavioural hierarchy measure correlated highly ($r = .74$) with psychiatric ratings of the phobia, but the latter were unrelated to a more purely behavioural measure derived from clients' diaries of time spent out of the house. Change in the diary measure over therapy was found to be independent of change in an assessor's rating of phobic disability (Mathews et al., 1981, p. 30).

These brief comments on assessment illustrate the problem of putting any percentage figure on therapeutic success with agoraphobic clients. Although advances in therapy have certainly been made, the outcome is variable, difficult to predict and not always of a generalised nature. The partial success of present techniques poses problems for the phobia concept of agoraphobia. Given that exposure-based therapies are highly effective in modifying phobic behaviour in many instances, how is it that some agoraphobic clients fail to respond at all, or if they do respond, still retain their tendency to complain of anxiety? An exponent of the phobia view might argue that there has been insufficient exposure, insufficient time for generalisation to occur or insufficient exposure of the right kind. Additional problems, or general deficits in problem-solving (Monteiro et al., 1984), have also been considered as factors which reduce the degree of success. A logical extension of this view would be that 'simple' agoraphobia is more easily modified than 'complex' agoraphobia. However, apart from marital dissatisfaction, there are few indications that any other measures of the severity and generality of problems predicts outcome. Furthermore, the idea that problems are additive in this manner is oversimplified.

The suggestion that some as-yet-unidentified parameters of exposure are critical for reduction of fear and avoidance will be taken up later.

EXPOSURE-BASED THERAPIES: IMPLICATIONS
OF RESULTS WITH AGORAPHOBIC CLIENTS

A consensus has emerged that the most effective way of modifying avoidance behaviour in agoraphobics is to confront the client with cues for fear. Clients can be confronted by imaginal or real-life stimuli, using mildly fear-arousing or strongly fear-arousing methods. The length of exposure varies between techniques; in general, longer durations are used with more intense evocations of fear. In systematic desensitisation (Wolpe, 1958), exposure is imaginal, brief and only mildly fear-arousing. Relaxation is employed to reduce arousal level and to reciprocally inhibit fear. In imaginal flooding (Boulougouris et al., 1971), clients' fears are evoked by a continuous narrative, lasting 45–90 minutes, describing the worst eventualities that might result from confrontation. The effects of fear on mental and bodily state are vividly described. Real-life exposure involves confrontation beginning with the least frightening situation but usually progressing rapidly to the most feared situations depending on the client's willingness to proceed and the extent to which reports of fear are reduced. Readers are referred to Marshall et al. (1979) for a detailed discussion of the exposure concept and its specification in practice. Chambless and Goldstein (1980) provided an extensive guide to the application of exposure methods with agoraphobic clients (see also Mathews et al., 1981, p. 76; Emmelkamp, 1979, 1982).

There is evidence that all methods of exposure modify reports of fear, physiological measures and behaviour, to some extent. Real-life methods are usually preferred because they produce greater change and minimise the problem of generalisation from the therapeutic situation to the real world. Reviewers are generally agreed that systematic imaginal desensitisation produces little if any change in agoraphobic clients, although this method can be effective with specific fears (e.g. Paul, 1966; Davison, 1968). As this is one of the few generalisations about exposure therapy that relates specifically to agoraphobia, it will be examined in more detail.

The Inefficacy of Systematic Desensitisation
with Agoraphobic Clients

Early studies of systematic desensitisation (SD) were conducted on mixed groups of phobics, and so it is difficult to draw any definite conclusions about agoraphobia from them. Mathews et al. (1981) concluded that, with nonhospitalised clients, SD carried out with instructions to confront actual phobic situations between sessions, is more effective than psychotherapeutic techniques. Instructions to practice can have powerful effects, and so the specific role of SD in this combined procedure is uncertain. In a study in which clients were told *not* to practice between sessions, SD had no discernible effect on behaviour or self-report (Yorkston et al., 1968).

Foa and Kozak (1983) interpreted the inefficacy of SD within their emotional processing model of therapeutic change. They argued that the therapeutic medium must access fear representations in memory, and fear responses must be elicited for therapeutic change to occur. The exposure medium must also present elements incompatible with fear responses. These authors do not conceive of agoraphobia as a fear of public places but as a fear of fear (Weekes, 1976). In other words, there is assumed to be a fear of self-produced stimulation such as cues derived from arousal. It follows that SD, which minimises arousal during exposure, is likely to be ineffective. In other procedures such as imaginal or real-life flooding, it is assumed that arousal cues are elicited and found to have no harmful consequences; for example, the client does not become insane, have a heart attack or lose control. The apparent effectiveness of exposure to intense fear imagery which is *unrelated* to agoraphobic fears (Watson & Marks, 1971) lends support to Foa and Kozak's argument.

If Foa and Kozak were correct, it is possible that SD to a hierarchy of interoceptive cues and their anticipated dire consequences would be an effective procedure with agoraphobic clients who demonstrate a fear of fear of this kind. As I have already noted, scene presentations in the early studies of SD were usually limited to public situations. These scenes might not, therefore, have been critical cues for effective exposure.

Drugs which suppress peripheral physiological arousal should, theoretically, minimise the therapeutic efficacy of real-life exposure or imaginal flooding with agoraphobic clients. Unfortunately, research on the effects of combined drug and exposure procedures have suffered from methodological weaknesses, and results have been contradictory (Mathews et al., 1981, p. 97; Sartory, 1983). Psychotropic drugs can produce unfamiliar sensory experiences which are threatening to some individuals. Sergeant and Yorkston (1968) observed that 4 out of 18 agoraphobic clients (who were not fearful of injections or of losing control) became 'uneasy, dizzy or even terrified' (p. 654) when injected with a fast-acting barbiturate (methohexitone). Some of their other subjects enjoyed the effects of the drug, but three more failed to relax before falling asleep. It has been discovered that, in a minority of clients, *relaxation* is a cue for reported anxiety (Heide & Borkovec, 1983). In any event, it is probably unsafe to assume that a tranquillising drug will necessarily have its anticipated psychological effect, and therefore studies predicated on these presumed effects may be unsound.

In conclusion, the apparent inefficacy of SD with agoraphobic subjects raises some interesting questions about the relationship between theory and experimentation. Systematic desensitisation has been regarded as a technique which does not work with agoraphobic clients rather in the manner that a drug might be evaluated as ineffective. This medical view of the matter follows from the assumption that all agoraphobics have the same disorder and therefore should either respond or not respond to a standardised technique.

Systematic desensitisation was introduced as a method for extinguishing responses to hierarchies of relevant fear cues. The assumption that agoraphobia is a unitary disorder based on a fear of public places seems to have inhibited attempts to identify the relevant cues in each client and structure therapy accordingly. There has, in reality, been a shift of emphasis over the years from situation to interoceptive cues and the consequences of panic. Because the nature of the relevant interoceptive cues and anticipated harms vary considerably from client to client, it might have been expected that subjects for research would have been selected on this basis. Clients who do not avoid public situations but who share the features mentioned above could be selected along with agoraphobic clients. However, these developments in mainstream research have not taken place. Agoraphobia has been taken as a real entity rather than an intervening variable which has grown out of earlier psychiatric conceptualisations.

WHEN DOES CONFRONTATION REDUCE FEAR AND AVOIDANCE?

Although there is good evidence that exposure to feared cues is an effective vehicle for the modification of avoidance behaviour, exposure is not a theoretical mechanism. On the original two-factor model of avoidance learning (see Chapter 10), it would be predicted that exposure to a fear CS allows extinction of a conditioned emotional response to occur. This implies that agoraphobic complaints persist because fear cues are avoided. Of course, since the two-factor model of agoraphobic avoidance was first suggested, assumptions about the nature of the CSs and UCSs in agoraphobia have changed; that is, there is now less emphasis on situational cues and more emphasis on interoceptive stimuli and feared consequences of panic. Mathews et al. (1981, p. 148) speculated that agoraphobic clients avoid situations in which they expect their emotional distress to rise to unacceptable levels. Therefore, it is predicted that, to be effective, exposure experiences should demonstrate that the distress is less aversive, occurs less frequently or is tolerated better than expected. Hence long-duration exposure is important so that the client can experience the decline in emotional distress that usually occurs. Mathews et al. (1981) interpreted the decline partly as an extinction process (i.e. nothing especially aversive or disastrous happens) and partly as habituation of autonomic responses to cues in the public environment (e.g. to its intense, complex and demanding stimulus features). These authors also speculated that confrontation is facilitated by social reinforcement, a feeling of mastery, and attainment of rewarding goals.

The importance of mastery over anxiety is emphasised by Williams, Dooseman and Kleifield (1984). It was found that during exposure therapy, the addition of 'mastery aids' led to greater change of a more generalised kind. The aids that were used included breaking down the task of confrontation into smaller steps, eliminating defensive manoeuvres and varying the manner of approach. In the comparison condition in this study, subjects were instructed to carry out a number of confrontation tasks as rapidly as possible despite distress; duration of exposure was equated in the two groups. The results suggested that the ways in which clients typically manage their emotional distress and, presumably, whether they believe themselves to have any control over it, are important determinants of the outcome of confrontation methods. By inference, they may be important as maintaining factors for the agoraphobic cluster of complaints.

In the new self-help, home-based exposure methods of Mathews et al. (1981, Chapter 8), the emphasis has shifted from exposure per se to helping clients find methods of managing distress when it occurs. In the manuals provided for the client, there are 10 rules of anxiety management, which include reminders that anxiety symptoms are not harmful, that they will dissipate in time, and so forth. The rules are aimed at undermining what the authors consider to be the major factor maintaining avoidance, namely, the fear of provoking an attack of panic.

The first trial of the new method (Mathews, Teasdale, Munby, Johnston & Shaw, 1977) indicated that, unlike hospital-based therapy in which change occurred mainly during therapy, home-based programmes lead to continuing change throughout the follow-up period. The instruction manual also appeared to help members of a society for agoraphobics who received it by post (Mathews et al., 1981). Given that a few agoraphobic individuals hardly avoid the situations which make them anxious (and may avoid only partially), the efficacy of self-exposure and instruction manuals needs to be explained.

The importance of what actually happens during exposure has been underscored by the results of some recent research on self-exposure (Mavissakalian & Michelson, 1983). In this study, all agoraphobic clients received self-exposure instructions and learning rationale. The importance of a graded approach and long-duration exposure was emphasised, but anxiety-management strategies were not mentioned. Clients kept detailed diaries of numbers of outings and the distress they experienced over a 3-month period of therapy. The clients were allocated to one of four experimental conditions: (1) real-life exposure in groups, (2) antidepressant medication (imipramine), (3) antidepressant plus real-life exposure and (4) discussion groups in which self-exposure homework was monitored and practical suggestions were made. The results showed that in the first three conditions, clients improved on nearly all outcome measures and to a significantly greater extent than in the fourth condition. The subjects in this group (self-exposure plus group monitoring) improved on some self-report measures of phobic severity but did not change in terms of their behaviour or distress during a standardised behavioural avoidance test or in their behaviour during an individualised avoidance test.

The unexpected and significant finding was that the four groups did not differ in the amount of self-directed exposure practised between sessions; nor was there a difference in this regard between subjects who improved most and least on other outcome measures. The clients who had improved most at the end of therapy had, however, showed cumulatively less distress during their self-exposure practice. One implication of the study is that self-directed exposure produces relatively little change unless some other factors (which are supplied by group exposure and antidepressant medication) are also included. The authors suggested that these are cognitive factors which facilitate habituation.

An earlier study of self-managed exposure (Jannoun, Munby, Catalan & Gelder, 1980) also raises doubts about the adequacy of an unmodified extinction/habituation model. Self-managed exposure was compared with a problem-solving approach also delivered on a self-help basis. One of the two therapists employed in the study achieved results with problem-solving which were comparable, at 6-month follow-up, with home-based exposure. This result was achieved despite the fact that the clients were not given direct suggestions to go out more frequently. It appeared, then, that clients changed in some general way which made it easier for them to go out. For example, there was a significant decline in a measure of trait anxiety in the successful problem-solving group. Unfortunately, distress experienced while out of the home was not recorded, and so the problem-solving and self-exposure groups may have differed in this respect.

An advocate of an extinction theory of the effects of exposure might argue that exposure in all its variations reduces reports of fear to the extent that there is *effective* exposure to relevant CSs. Anxiety management techniques, mastery aids, and so forth, are simply seen as providing optimal conditions of exposure. This view, in an extreme form, would relegate clients' perceptions and coping techniques to the role of facilitating or obstructing extinction/habituation. Reduction of complaints of anxiety would presumably follow automatically from the change in physiological and behavioural responses. While this position may have some validity, it cannot be sustained as a general account of the relation between cognitive and behavioural processes. Self-reports are related in a complex way to changes in behaviour and arousal, and there is a lack of synchronicity between measures of change in the three systems (see e.g. Barlow, Mavissakalian & Schofield, 1980). Rate of change in the three systems during exposure therapy was investigated by Mavissakalian and Michelson (1982) in groups of agoraphobic clients. Over a long time span, the majority of subjects demonstrated synchronicity with rate of change occurring in the order behaviour, self-report and physiology (heart-rate). In a few subjects, however, heart-rate increased while self-reports of anxiety declined. Desynchrony was greatest early in therapy, in line with hypotheses put forward by Hodgson and Rachman (1974).

The relation between physiological activity, cognitive variables and therapeutic change has been investigated systematically in a series of experimental studies by Borkovec and his colleagues (see Borkovec & Grayson, 1980; Borkovec, 1982). Using imaginal presentations, Borkovec and Grayson (1980) found that changes in heart-rate and self-report measures were influenced by expectations of therapeutic benefit which had been generated in the subjects by instructional set. Compared to a neutral expectation, positive expectancy lead to higher initial fear and heart-rate but greater subsequent decline in these responses. Lang, Melamed and Hart (1970) had previously shown that a similar pattern of responding was associated with greater improvement with imaginal desensitisation. In another study, Borkovec found that a SD procedure, compared to control procedures, produced greater initial responsivity regardless of therapeutic expectancy. Expectancy effects were only observed with the less effective comparison procedures. Borkovec concluded that positive expectancy, and elements of the SD technique (e.g. progressive muscular relaxation), promote 'functional exposure', that is, exposure which facilitated extinction. Individual differences in awareness of physiological sensations and direction of attention to these cues have also been shown to influence the course of fear reduction (Borkovec, 1982).

The importance of instructional set and attentional processes suggests that an extinction/habituation model of change should take account of the client's interpretation of what it is that the therapist is trying to do and whether it is plausible and/or likely to be helpful. Before being asked to confront their fears, clients are typically given an explanation of fear and its bodily effects and are provided with a therapeutic rationale. The therapist may request withdrawal of psychotropic medication, which itself is a powerful message of the therapist's expectations. If the client complies, this may be interpreted as a major change of attitude towards the anxiety complaint.

The information provided during diagnostic assessments has proved influential in some cases. Hand, Lamontagne and Marks (1974) reported that two subjects, on discovering the principles of exposure, confronted their feared situations and found that they could tolerate them. Can the role of instructional set, a therapeutic rationale, and information about the responses that are associated with reports of anxiety be regarded as factors which simply facilitate or impede extinction/habituation?

Bandura has persuasively argued that certain beliefs held by the client have a primary and independent causal status (Bandura, 1977). For Bandura, self-efficacy beliefs (i.e. a subject's belief that he or she can execute a given response to produce a desired outcome) are grounded in the feedback information provided by extinction/habituation (and other) processes but do not *directly* reflect this information. For example, it is assumed that self-efficacy beliefs partly determine choice of activities and how much effort will be expended in overcoming obstacles. Elaborating on Bandura's ideas, Goldfried and Robins (1982) stated that learning experiences are 'cognitively processed'. In their opinion, the ultimate aim of therapy is a lasting change in self-schemata.

Bandura (1977) and Goldfried and Robins (1982) have drawn attention to some general cognitive factors which are likely to be influential in the therapeutic process. These include individuals' generalised perceptions of themselves, attributional styles, and biases in the evaluation of potentially corrective information. To accept the importance of these factors does not necessarily involve adopting the extreme cognitivist position that anxiety is primarily a response to perceived inefficacy (Bandura, 1978). However, it does underscore the limitation of current descriptions of clients in therapeutic trials. If the cognitive attributes of subjects are as important as it is supposed, then new taxonomies which incorporate them need to be developed.

MORE RECENT THEORETICAL DEVELOPMENTS

In more recent theoretical developments, learning theory accounts of the mechanisms of exposure have been modified to incorporate an information-processing dimension. This tendency has partly arisen in order to supplement a rather bald stimulus/response account of human behaviour. Attention to factors which make information processing more efficient is likely to enhance therapeutic effectiveness. Other developments in behavioural theory have been stimulated by research on affective memory processing (e.g. see Lang, 1977) and affective recall. These developments may be interpreted as providing a more complete account of the processes underlying behavioural change rather than a change to a cognitive paradigm.

A rather different cognitivist position is that certain general assumptions about the world, self-referential beliefs and other beliefs of a more specific nature might be of paramount importance in mediating or moderating the effects of exposure; this view has not received much empirical investigation apart from the work of Bandura discussed earlier. It has, of course, received considerable, and deserved, discussion (e.g. see Ellis, 1979).

Rachman (1980) argued that failure to respond to fear-reducing procedures might be related to a family of phenomena (e.g. obsessions, unresolved grief, nightmares) which can all be regarded as indices of incomplete 'emotional processing'. Rachman listed a number of factors which are likely to impede emotional processing, which are also the factor assumed to give rise to maladaptive emotional reactions. The conditions which are said to promote processing are repeated presentations, long duration exposures, graded stimulus presentations of low intensity/complexity, minimal distraction, low level of arousal, breaking down information into manageable proportions and absorption over an optimal period.

Foa and Kozak (1983) have developed the theme of emotional processing, basing their model on Lang's theoretical views of fear change (Lang, 1977, 1983). It is proposed that emotional processing involves the structural modification of a fear (memory) prototype. For this to occur, the exposure medium must contain elements that evoke reports of fear, the individual must attend to the elements, and the process of exposure must introduce elements that are incompatible with the existing fear representation in memory. The findings from a large number of clinical and experimental studies of fear reduction are consistent with this general view; for example, that the activation of physiological arousal and reports of fear and their reduction during, and between, exposure sessions appear to be positively related to outcome of therapy.

Foa and Kozak suggested that exposure might be ineffective if there is a mis-match between the information contained in the exposure medium and in the memory structure such that responses associated with fear are not evoked. However, if the medium is too effective, clients might be prompted to escape or defend themselves in other ways, for example, become detached and deny the reality of their experience. Factors which promote attention (e.g. relaxation) or impede information processing (e.g. distraction or high arousal) are expected to influence the amount of emotional processing, and this expectation is indeed supported by various studies (see Foa & Kozak, 1983).

The information that the client receives during exposure sessions, which is assumed to be incompatible with the pre-existing memory of fear, comes from evidence of diminished physiological responding and disconfirmation of expected harmful consequences. Repeated exposures may be necessary to disconfirm beliefs about the long-term consequences of confronting the feared situation.

With regard to failures of emotional processing, a number of relevant factors have already been mentioned. In addition, Foa and Kozak pointed to features of the higher-order integration of new information that might impede processing. These might parallel, though not duplicate, the kinds of perceptual and recall biases observed in depressed individuals (Abramson, Garber & Seligman, 1980). Foa and Kozak noted that clients with obsessive-compulsive problems who believe that their fears are *realistic* fail to show habituation in exposure therapy between sessions.

Foa and Kozak's model suggests a number of client characteristics and process variables that may help to account for the variability of outcome with exposure therapies. Indeed, they proposed their own classification scheme for anxiety problems. The axes include the presence or absence of avoidance behaviour, of external fear cues, and of anticipatory harm. Nonexternal fear cues are assumed to occur in every anxiety problem, so the taxonomy yields eight categories. Although some of the DSM III categories map onto this scheme, many others do not. As Foa and Kozak pointed out, the DSM III criteria are not founded on theoretical criteria, and so it is not surprising that their review of the implications of the outcome studies on exposure techniques can conclude only that a given technique is more or less successful with a given disorder.

SUMMARY

The practical demands of therapy place severe constraints on the amount of control that can be exerted over critical variables in outcome studies. However, the design of outcome studies also demonstrates underlying conceptual weaknesses that limit their theoretical implications. Behavioural therapies have not been administered in a manner that is consistent with their theoretical foundations, and so it is often difficult to draw theoretical conclusions from their overall efficacy. A cornerstone of behaviour therapy is the assumption that an individual's problems are produced by individual learning experiences. Given the great variety of circumstances which shape and control behaviour, therapeutic techniques should proceed from a detailed behavioural description and from a functional analysis of learning contingencies. The favoured strategy, however, has been to group subjects for evaluation on the basis of the diagnostic label that attaches to them. Diagnostic labels are not, it is generally admitted, assigned on the basis of a consideration of learning history and processes of maintenance.

The current approach to evaluation has demonstrated that behavioural techniques, administered in a standardised manner, are reasonably effective for certain diagnostic groups. It has been important to demonstrate this, but the disorder model on which the selection of subjects was based need not be retained.

Only modest success has been achieved with the diagnostic groups agoraphobia, panic disorder and generalised anxiety disorder. A brief review of recent outcome studies and new theoretical conceptions of the process of change suggests that the existing diagnostic categories are of little value in selecting subjects for research. Earlier psychological concepts of agoraphobia (e.g. the conditioned emotional response model) are also being replaced by more complex models emphasising interoceptive conditioning, information processing and general attitudinal factors. From these new conceptualisations, a classification of greater heuristic value may develop.

14

Anxiety: Theoretical or Lay Construct?

INTRODUCTION

The sheer amount of thought and research that has gone into the analysis of anxiety is testimony to the theoretical puzzles posed by this elusive concept. The reviews of Chapters 10–12 have covered only a fraction of the existing literature. This degree of interest may be due to the fact that a number of contentious issues coincide in the topic of anxiety. First, there is the question of the status of self-reports as psychological data; self-reports refer to 'private events', but these events do not appear to be the proper objects of scientific study. Second, an issue related to the first, is the concern with the analysis of psychological events at a *causal* level, that is, the problem of human agency versus environmental control. The debate about reciprocal determinism has, for example, centered on differing accounts of anxiety (see Bandura, 1978, and accompanying articles). Third, a problem which permeates all attempts to relate the findings of the biological and social sciences is that of interpreting the covariation between changes in biological systems and changes in behaviour and self-report. This problem is acute in the area of emotion and will be discussed in this context in relation to the three-systems conceptualisation of fear and anxiety. The three systems refer to physiological, behavioural and verbal/cognitive processes.

My conceptual approach to anxiety (and indirectly to the three issues noted above) will follow the line of Sarbin (1964) and Averill (1980a) that anxiety is best regarded as a *social construction*. By anxiety, I refer to the meaning given to this, and similar terms, in everyday discourse. It follows that, as a social construction, anxiety is an *acquired* meaning which, I will assume, allows the individual to organise, label and therefore talk about certain kinds of perceptual experience. The social constructivist approach does not leave anxiety in the position of being an unanalysable private experience but, instead, encourages attempts to study the social practices which surround the development and use of emotion terms. According to Averill (1980a), the most relevant discipline to an analysis of emotion is the sociology of knowledge. Contributions can, of course, be made at several levels of analysis. However, one danger of relying too heavily on analysis at the biological level is that a social construction (viz., anxiety) may be reified as an objective entity which is viewed as independent of its social origins. The physiology of individual organisms cannot reveal social, cultural and historical influences which have gone into the making of a construct of emotion (unless, of course, they are studied philogenetically with that intention).

I assume that an important feature of the construct of anxiety is that it is *multireferential*. The perception of a limited number of states as emotions presumably stems from the need to communicate simply about events that are determined in a complex manner. In other words, the anxiety construct fits a variety of circumstances and serves sufficiently well to convey important meanings, albeit of a stereotyped kind. I assume, then, that the appropriate use of the construct of anxiety does not entail the presence of a fixed and invariant set of referents. Whether there is a *necessary* set must be determined empirically, although it seems likely that there is a *modal* set, of which some are evaluated as aversive. In its everyday use, *anxiety* may therefore be regarded as a construct that has both public and private referents. Furthermore, it is a construct which can be linked semantically to a broader set of beliefs about the nature of mental life and to other interpretive schemata. An analysis of anxiety as a multireferential lay construct has implications for the general conceptual problems mentioned earlier, in which anxiety has figured so prominently.

THE SCIENTIFIC STATUS OF VERBAL REPORTS OF ANXIETY

In the debate about the scientific status of self-reports, the objectivity of public events has often been contrasted with the subjective and unreliable nature of observations of private events. Thus, objective public events have been regarded by some as the proper subject matter of a *science* of psychology. I will argue that both public and private events have the same status vis à vis scientific theory. There are two reasons for asserting this. First, the public/private distinction is not a *given* property of events and must be learned, that is, we are not dealing with fundamentally different kinds of events. Second, the suspicion that self-reports are unreliable or do not constitute a valid source of data stems from a mistaken assumption that the events to which self-reports refer are substantive (rather than figurative) entities. Consequently, I suggest that a *causal* model of the interaction between organism and environment needs to be formulated in terms of *internal* and *external* events that are defined within the framework of a causal scientific theory. In other words, the public/private distinction is part of the lay construction of reality and therefore not a suitable starting point for a causal analysis. It may, of course, have value in other kinds of psychological analysis. I suggest that the internal or external nature of an event is defined in relation to its spatial and temporal disposition with respect to a suitable (but arbitrary) physical boundary such as the skin or central nervous system. Anxiety is usually defined in lay terms as a private event. I will assume that the referents of reports of anxiety are, in fact, public and private and that a causal analysis of reports of anxiety must deal with both internal and external antecedent (and consequent) events.

In his early writings, Skinner (1953, p. 257) implied that a private event can be treated in the same way as any other event apart from its limited accessibility, for example, *your* sore tooth does not give *me* a toothache. He claimed that the distinction between public and private events is not a question of the physical location of stimulation (i.e. my body and your body) but of public accessibility. That is, even sensations which arise from stimulation beneath the skin are interpreted as public events (roughness, stickiness, etc.) if their source is publicly accessible (p. 262). Skinner concentrated his causal analysis on relations between public events, stating that 'a private event, at best, is no more than a link in a causal chain' (p. 279).

It is clear from Skinner's writings that private events are not given the same scientific status as public events. He supposes a private realm of experience which is more or less poorly described by self-reports. 'The verbal report is a response to the private event and may be used as a source of information about it' (p. 282). However, for Skinner, the difference in scientific status of public and private events should not have been fundamental. Skinner claimed that we do not have infallible access to private events, but it could also be asserted that we do not have infallible access to public events. Just as a *purely* private event is not a discriminable event, so a public event is equally inaccessible (given Skinner's analysis of learning) if we are not trained to discriminate it. There should be no difference in scientific status between the two kinds of events but merely a difference in the ease with which the conditions of observation can be replicated and reinforcement consistently applied.

Public events are, of course, often equated with external events and private events with internal events. This tendency may stem from the readiness to identify the entities postulated by scientific theory with the entities described in everyday language. However, whether we are dealing with public events (e.g. sounds) or private events (e.g. emotions) it can be argued that the relationship between scientific hypothesis and the human observation of an event is in each case the same. That is, the explanation of the world which derives from the physical sciences is as much a *hypothesis* about public events as, say, biological or cognitive processes are an hypothesis about private events.

How the common designation of an event as public or private is related to scientific hypotheses about internal or external events or their interaction is an empirical question. Any suggested solution will need to take into account the 'private' aspects of our perception of public events and the fact that the public or private nature of some events may be debated. Skinner wrote as if private events would ultimately yield their secrets to advanced techniques of physiological analysis. However, this is to confuse a metaphor of privacy with an internal location in the body.

A simple example illustrates the point that private events do not stand in a substantially different relationship to scientific theory than do public events. Individuals who hear noises in their head which others do not hear learn rapidly that the noises (tinnitus) do not have a public source and are private events. Their privacy does not automatically reveal itself. In fact, some individuals develop a set of delusional ideas to support their belief in a public source while otherwise appearing quite rational (Walford, 1979). The group of people who fall into this category almost always report noises which are assumed to be low-frequency sounds. Low frequencies are difficult to locate spatially and are therefore more resistant to disproof as public events.

It is true that a science of *purely* private sounds (i.e. whose presence could not be discriminated in any way by another person) would be an impossibility. However, a private sound can be matched to a public sound (or simply compared to a public sound) so that scientist and subject can jointly identify it and correlate reports of its presence with other variables. The question to consider is whether the experience of a real public sound stands in any different relationship to scientific theory (e.g. the nature of sound waves and the structure of the ear) than does a private sound. In the case of tinnitus, as with public sounds, a report of the experience of sound is correlated with operations which satisfy certain methodological conventions and are linked to a scientific theory. The self-report confirms or disconfirms predictions from an hypothesis, but the event to which the self-report refers does not become *part* of the explanation, that is, it is not incorporated into the hypothesised chain of causal events. Similarly, the experience of sound is not incorporated into the physical account of sound waves and sound perception.

If public sounds were not reliably correlated with certain antecedent conditions, it would hardly be claimed that our ability to *describe* them in a reliable way would exceed our ability to describe, say, emotional states. Our superior understanding of sound perception probably stems from the relative ease with which specifiable antecedent conditions can be varied over a wide range and correlated with verbal reports, crude as they are (present/absent, higher/lower pitch, louder/softer, etc.).

The antecedents of emotional reports are presumably more complex and less easy to manipulate, but, in principle, the scientific investigation of reports of emotion should follow the same general strategy. However, certain differences of approach are evident in some contemporary research, and this seems to derive from an assumption that emotion is a private experience of which we have direct and immediate knowledge. Thus, laboratory experiments tend to remove reports of emotion from their social context and rely on the subject's introspective access to a private event. Subjects are requested to consult their 'mental measuring grids' for specific emotional states rather than respond freely to the situation by reporting their varied thoughts and feelings. For example, in snake avoidance tests, the subject is constrained to stop at predefined points and consult their fear 'thermometers'; measures of overt behaviour or physiology are not constrained in this way.

In general, theories of emotion have tended to reify emotions as unanalysable but measurable mental states. In this way, a more rigorous and scientific treatment of verbal reports of emotion has been avoided. This state of affairs is probably the result of a residual influence of mentalism on psychology, which clings to feeling as an irreducible datum of psychology. Consider, for example, writings on the assessment of private events. Hollon and Bemis (1982) compared the methodological problems associated with the assessment of self-reported events as analogous to the problem of assessing public events. They conceptualised three distinct events: the stimulus event, the covert observing event and the overt report of the observation. It is certainly true that the value of self-reports as data from which inferences can be made varies according to the instructions given to the subject and, of course, the design of the experiment. However, I suggest that a self-report of anxiety involves reporting as if anxiety was a substantive entity. It there-fore makes little sense to speak of improving observation of that 'event' in the sense that, say, observation of a public object might be improved by different lighting conditions, a different vantage point, and so forth. The assertion 'I feel like a mouse' conveys a meaning in a wider context than the reporting of something purely private. Pushed to greater preci-sion, our hypothetical subject would not go on to describe the mouse but come up with new metaphors involving different entities. Hollon and Bemis (1982, p. 153) argued that the limitations on directly observ-ing cognitions are of a technical nature though it is difficult to see what might be meant by direct observation in this instance. For these authors, the event to which a report of anxiety refers is not a cognition but an affective/autonomic event. It is not clear whether the terms affective and autonomic are intended as synonyms or whether Aff/auto represents a disjunctive proposition. With the social constructivist approach there would be no grounds for either assertion.

The idea that emotions are private events with the same spatial and temporal properties as behavioural and physiological events is encour-aged by the manner in which emotions are constructed in everyday language. Emotions are said to be states which we 'have' and words and symbols are said to refer 'to' emotions and represent them. But this manner of speaking is based on metaphor, and the states to which allusion is made are only devices or tools of communication (Sarbin, 1964; Jaynes, 1976, chap. 1). If we treat emotions as substantive entities, then we confuse figurative for literal language and may be led into applying an inappropriate causal framework.

FEAR AND ANXIETY AS THEORETICAL AND OPERATIONAL CONCEPTS

Fear and anxiety have long been regarded as useful psychological concepts in work on animal behaviour. In this work there is no question of the meaning of self-reports, and 'anxiety' is simply used to describe a cluster of responses or a hypothetical central state inferred from be-haviour. In work with humans (and also to some extent with animals), it became apparent that a central unifying construct of anxiety had certain limitations. Physiological changes and behavioural responses which were assumed to index this state did not always co-vary systematically. The variable or nonexistent correlations between self-reports of anxiety and other measures taken in situations in which anxiety was reported also raised doubts about the meaningfulness of anxiety as an integrating concept (Lang, 1969; Rachman & Hodgson, 1974; Rachman, 1978, p. 3ff.).

There followed a sensible retreat into an empirical approach towards the investigation of anxiety. Lang (1971) proposed that emotions such as anxiety be conceptualised as a system of multiple responses (verbal/cognitive, overt motor, and physiological) which are partially independent yet highly interactive. Components of emotion were said to enter into augmenting, sustaining or attenuating feedback loops (Lang, 1971). Methodologically, this new three-systems conceptualisation implied that response systems should be measured independently; theoretically it implied that the components might be controlled by different higher neural centres; and in practice, *desynchrony* (an absence of positive linear correlations between intensity characteristics of the components) could be expected under certain circumstances. For example, a person might avoid or respond autonomically in a situation which typically engenders anxiety, but not report fearful feelings.

The problem of interpreting the covariation between the three systems has not disappeared and recent models of anxiety (e.g. Bandura et al., 1977; Lang, 1979) may be seen as attempts to put the components back together again in a new way. Rachman (1978, p. 24) defined fear as a 'complex of imperfectly coupled response systems' and he viewed self-report, overt behavioural, and physiological measures as imperfect indices of what is, presumably, an operational concept of fear. Rachman and Hodgson (1974) predicted that concordance between measures (synchrony) or the absence of concordance (desynchrony) would be related to the intensity of emotional arousal and to the level of demand (e.g. demand for courageous approach).

The concept of synchrony implies that under indubitable conditions of fear there is concordance between the behavioural, physiological and self-report measures which are unambiguous indices of fear. These would be absent in states of calmness in which a different kind of synchrony would hold sway. At intermediate levels of fear arousal, the demand to act courageously, or other factors, would create desynchrony between the components.

It is doubtful, however, that there *is* a unitary, synchronous state of fear composed of unambiguous fear components in the three systems. There are, for example, different fear behaviours with different physiological accompaniments. 'Running to escape', 'being paralysed with fear', 'fainting with fear', 'anxious anticipation', 'panic', and 'ruminating about possible dangers', are all examples of what the layman might describe as fear or anxiety. However, it is hardly possible to order these states on a dimension of emotional arousal, and the pattern of activity in the three systems is likely to vary considerably between them. A dimension of fear/anxiety arousal might be defined by arbitrarily assigning weights to the different components, but this raises additional problems. For example, the direction of heart-rate change seems to be diametrically opposed in different situations where fear is reported (Connolly et al., 1976).

Lang (1971) referred to a *system* of interacting components, which might imply that there is a higher-order principle of emotional organisation. Other writers (e.g. Mandler, 1975, p. 86) have suggested that emotion does not constitute a unique class of behaviours. This means that great care must be taken in postulating the hypothetical construct of anxiety.

There has inevitably been a tendency to interpret the correlations between verbal and overt behavioural or physiological measures in a causal manner. However, the various levels at which, say, verbal self-reports can be analysed makes any causal interpretation problematic. A verbal report can be regarded as an event with time and space coordinates and as having a causal history. In an experimental context, verbal reports may be viewed as social communications which are subtly controlled by the demand features of the experiment. Verbal reports have also been interpreted by various authors as pointing to a subject's private feeling state which the subject might assume to be causing his or her behaviour. Given these various ways of interpreting self-reports, it is not surprising that scientific and lay constructs have been confused.

THE RELATIONSHIP BETWEEN SCIENTIFIC
AND LAY DISCOURSE

In effect, I have argued that it is necessary to distinguish two types of discourse about anxiety: scientific discourse and lay discourse (everyday understanding). By lay discourse is meant the set of hypothetical entities and ideas about causality and motive which lie behind talk about emotion. A causal scientific explanation will be taken to refer to concepts and their relationships which are explicitly defined for the purpose of developing a causal explanation of events. Unlike lay explanations (which are taken for granted), scientific hypotheses are formulated in such a way as to allow their validity to be tested by other scientists.

Lay explanation is related to scientific explanation in several ways. One possible implication of the assumption that the two types of explanation are associated with different hypothetical entities and rules of operation may be that the contradictions that do arise between them are linguistic confusions rather than fundamental philosophical problems. For example, confusion may arise when the ground rules for one discourse are applied to the entities postulated by the other. It is not denied that people make statements about the operation of their minds which are perfectly intelligible within the assumptions of lay discourse. From a scientific standpoint it is simply argued that research on anxiety should not begin with the assumption that it is an entity that can be regarded as having an existence independent of its social origins. The influence of lay discourse can be seen in theories of emotion which take mental contents as their basic constructs. For example, 'primary' emotions have been thought capable of mixing, rather like paints, to produce secondary emotions of a different hue.

What then is the relation between scientific and lay discourse? Although they may be regarded as independent, the two types of discourse have mutual connections through their shared use of a common figurative language. Metaphors for mind are taken from the public world, and the perception of the public world is strongly influenced by physical theories about the nature of that world. At the same time, scientific discourse could not be conducted without mutually understood and given meanings (e.g. convenient analogies) nor could scientific observations be made at all. As noted above, confusion may arise when metaphorical devices are taken to indicate substantive realities.

Some confusion may be generated by the power of verbal stimuli to control human behaviour. Rather than treating the causal efficacy of verbal stimuli as deriving from a learning history, the mental entity to which the verbal symbol refers are invested with these causal powers. For example, it may be assumed that the verbal transmission of threat is effective because the stimuli employed have had significant consequences in the past (for self or others). Thus, the concepts of threat and danger are not explanatory per se, except in the sense that they are commonly understood.

ANXIETY AS A MULTIREFERENTIAL LAY CONSTRUCT

As our emphasis shifts from taking the self-report of anxiety as an indication of an underlying emotional state, we are lead into the implications of studying the social practices which surround the development and use of emotional terms. I suggest that anxiety is a multireferential lay construct and that the process of construing anxiety entails the interpretation of information from a wide range of sources. These include

1. specific and contextual environmental events;
2. sensory feedback from autonomic and other somatic processes;
3. overt and covert behaviour such as escape, postural adjustments, and facial expressions;
4. combinations of these classes of referent, for example, the disruption of cognitive and motor skills under certain conditions;
5. conceptual schemata representing beliefs, attributions of causality, and the like.

Accepting that the referents of anxiety are of this diverse nature, a single psychological *causal* model of the behaviour of reporting anxiety may be an impossibility. We do not possess at present a general theory of human behaviour which encompasses the biological, psychological and social levels of analysis, and so our understanding of reports and complaints of anxiety is bound to be fragmentary. At best, separate causal models may be developed for explaining the different sources of meaning information mentioned above, for example, escape behaviour and peripheral physiological arousal.

In general, the process of construing anxiety is assumed to entail meaning analyses of an essentially self-referential nature, for example, schemata relating to personal resources and presentation of self in public. However, it need not be assumed that self-referential meaning analyses are a *necessary* element of construing anxiety. For example, there may be an awareness of an aversive state of affairs in the absence of an identified source of threat to the self.

The question of what referents are required for anxiety to be reported is an empirical one. It seems safe to assume that there is a modal (common) set of referents for meaningful communication to occur at all. However, one might expect to find considerable cross-cultural and individual variation in the conditions necessary for reports of anxiety and similar socially constructed states to be made. With regard to cross-cultural and historical variations, I assume that some potential referents receive heightened attention while others may become functionally irrelevant. For example, Leff (1981) has noted the difficulty of translating the term *anxiety* into non–Indo-European languages. Similar concepts in other languages appear to consist of expressions referring to states of the body. Leff speculated that there has been a progressive historical change in the referents for words denoting distress in the Indo-European languages. At first, the earliest words are thought to have referred to the perception of actual bodily events; later these words were used to refer metaphorically to bodily events; and most recently the referents are assumed to be psychological experiences. Whether these speculations are correct or not, it is clear that the referents of emotion words appear to differ historically and cross-culturally.

If anxiety is a multireferential construct, it is plausible to argue that several classes of referents may individually be sufficient in themselves to give rise to the report of anxiety. In the case of panic we appear to have an example of a complaint of anxiety that is unrelated to a rational source of danger or to a lack of coping skills. A report of anxiety in the absence of the modal referents may be explained in several ways. One reason so far provided is that the central representation of the referents of anxiety, once established, may be accessed by minimal sensory input. This view has been put foward by Mandler (1975) in terms of an 'autonomic image' and by Lang (1977) as an 'emotional image'. In behavioural terminology, evocation of reports of anxiety by cues which only remotely resemble the modal (consistently reinforced) cues has been explained by individual learning experiences and by stimulus and semantic generalisation. It should also be noted that the use of the term *anxiety* may be extended by figurative language to nonaversive contexts (e.g. as in 'anxious to please'). However, the use of figurative language is likely to be less important than the influence of individual differences in selective attention to the referents of anxiety, or to the employment of meaning analyses which evoke the referents. The source of these individual differences is still largely speculative.

THE MULTIREFERENTIAL MODEL AND MEANING ANALYSIS

Meaning will be considered here at two levels. At one level meaning is unquestioned and part of what is a taken-for-granted reality. No conscious intellectual work is required. However, a second level of meaning analysis takes over if a meaning is not readily available (e.g. see the response to the first episodes of panic, Chapter 4). A search may be initiated for a reasonable interpretation of an unfamiliar experience. For example, subjects may question whether their experience is of the type called emotional and perhaps choose the label of anxiety or panic. According to a social constructivist perspective, the category of anxiety is the product of social practices and historical conditions and therefore a product of the creation of meaning. Meanings such as anxiety may be seen as immediately and intuitively appropriate in a given circumstance because this meaning is already embodied in social practices and social products, and is internalised during the socialisation of the individual (see Averill, 1980a, for a discussion of the construction of emotion as a dialectical process).

At the second level of meaning, an individual attempts, sometimes quite deliberately, to interpret experience and respond in an innovative way to problematic situations. In some of the earlier models of emotion, the creation of meaning did not enter as a factor at all. In James' model, emotion was said to be the conscious perception of peripheral somatic and visceral activity. According to Schacter, the cognitive evaluative element was more active but essentially provided labels for a peripheral state. These models can be criticised on two grounds: (1) for assigning to conscious processes too *pivotal* a position in the generation of emotional experience and (2) for ascribing to conscious processes, when invoked, too *passive* a role.

As Lang (1983) pointed out, conscious evaluation is simply not a necessary part of the processing of emotional information. Lang suggested that 'meaning information' is part of an associative network in memory (see Chapter 11). Activation in one part of a network can spread to other parts with the consequence that expressive-motor responses might evoke conscious evaluation or vice versa. Lang's model is concerned with emotional memory, and so the question how meaning is generated and interacts with overt behaviour (i.e. how memories are formed) is not specifically addressed.

It cannot be accepted that the social construction of emotion is merely a process of *associating* meaning with stimulus and response information. If memory is regarded as the product of the internalisation of real-world events, then memories should also encapsulate the transformative relation between meaning and overt behaviour. That is, subjects are not mere passive recipients of external and internal influences, even when they accept the meaning of events without question. Furthermore, as products of social practices, emotions can be regarded as functionally related to aspects of social organisation (Averill, 1980b). At an individual level, assigning emotional meanings can have a controlling and transformative relationship to overt behaviour. Through attempts to understand their own experience, subjects restructure their perceptions and initiate responses to change their environment.

While meaning information may constitute an essential element of the central representation of an emotion, memories are not accessed in isolation from other cognitive interpretive processes. The danger of representing emotion as a cognitive structure (or any other kind of entity) is to remove from view the active contribution of the individual and the social matrix (Sampson, 1981).

Furthermore, the antecedents of labelling and interpretive processes must be differentiable in part from the antecedents of overt behaviour and physiological responses which constitute the source of potential referents for reports of anxiety. One implication is that there is no one-to-one relationship between a set of potential anxiety referents and the self-report of emotion. This fact has been observed as desynchrony between measures of emotion in the cognitive/verbal, overt behavioural and physiological systems. If, as I suggest, the potential referents of anxiety are wide-ranging and often related in complex ways to antecedent conditions, the subject's report of anxiety might depend on subtle attentional factors, competing activities, and so forth. It would not be expected that the report of anxiety relates in a one-to-one fashion with other measures. The two most interesting examples of desynchrony are, first, the case in which potential anxiety referents are present but the subject does not report anxiety, and second, where anxiety is reported in the apparent absence of potential anxiety referents.

The failure to report anxiety when it might be expected in the light of normal responding can be explained in several ways. If threat is a salient feature of the situation, the subject might possess special skills for dealing with it (e.g. as in mountaineers or bomb-disposal personnel) or, through repeated exposure, have become thoroughly familiar with the situation. Alternatively, the subject might be engaging in a competing response or have his or her attention diverted from potential anxiety referents for other reasons. Some authors have, of course, suggested active, but internal, defensive processes.

In the second type of desynchrony, anxiety is reported in the apparent absence of its referents. This general case draws attention to possible instrumental aspects of the verbal report. Anxiety has traditionally been regarded as the outcome of a state of helplessness or as causing helplessness. Inverting these assumptions, there may be a sense in which anxiety is a *claim* to helplessness, that is, anxiety is a socially institutionalised means of escaping social obligations or demanding challenges. I have argued all along that anxiety is not inflicted by a deranged biology, but an assumption of this kind might help to sustain an 'ideology' of helplessness.

The individual who complains of anxiety but who perceives this state as irrational might simply be unaware of events that are threatening or creating a conflict between alternative actions. These may be obvious to an observer. Further, although threats may be acknowledged, there may be no comprehension of their relationship to complaints of anxiety. For example, a person might acknowledge a fear of illness but not recognise that this fear is relevant to the elicitation of panic.

The chaining of responses might also obscure the perception of a connection between a verbal report and its antecedent conditions. Fear of fear probably involves response chaining, as discussed in Chapter 5.

A person may lack control over the links in a chain of responses if they include reflexive or habitual (automatic) responses. It is evident that physiological and behavioural responses can be controlled in an automatic way by essentially symbolic stimuli such as films and imagery. Chained responses involving positive feedback processes might lead to anxiety being reported without any accompanying comprehension of the processes that are occurring, that is, anxiety is reported as irrational.

Evidently, the human response to meaning information is not always based on rational appraisal. Some forms of culturally transmitted information (e.g. snakes are dangerous, incest is wrong) may be internalised without conscious evaluation. In other cases of irrational fear, learning of a traumatic kind appears to override subsequent rational considerations, and anxiety may be reported to events which merely resemble, physically or symbolically, the events surrounding the original learning experience.

In conclusion, lack of concordance between verbal reports of anxiety and potential anxiety referents is not surprising. The links between reports of anxiety and its potential referents may be sufficiently complex to tax the constructive powers of the subject as well as the investigative abilities of the experimenter or therapist.

15

A Schematic Model of Panic-Anxiety

INTRODUCTION

As I have discussed elsewhere, the idea that each cluster of complaints requires a discrete explanation is based on a disorder model of psychological problems. I assume that the panic-anxiety cluster of complaints shares common underlying determinants with other problems such as dependence on alcohol (see Chapter 6). Furthermore, if the antecedents of reports of anxiety are exceedingly diverse, a model of panic-anxiety would need to account for many different psychological processes such as the effects of the anticipation of aversive events, response conflict, uncertainty, novelty, the psychological mediation of autonomic activity, and so on. A complete explanation would also have to consider the processes underlying familiarity and safety, that is, processes which inhibit or otherwise modify the antecedents of complaints of anxiety. Although it is beyond the scope of this book to produce an integrated account of this nature, it will suffice for my outline of a schematic model to assume that there are two classes of eliciting conditions (excitatory and inhibitory) and that, broadly speaking, the probability of reporting anxiety depends on a balance between them. Some authors have used the concepts of trait anxiety or generalised anxiety as a simple starting point, but these concepts have the disadvantage that they are represented as attributes of the subject with all the conceptual problems attendant on reifications of this kind.

The concept of inhibitory and excitatory cues can be illustrated by considering fears of public places. The presence of a *normative* element in designating fears of public places as abnormal or irrational is not always recognised. It seems likely that, by gradually extending the concept of a public place, a point would be reached at which any person would baulk if asked to encounter the situation alone. For example, foreign travel can be conceptualised as falling along a dimension with local travel from a home base. Foreign travel represents unfamiliarity, challenge and possible dangers. Many people fear travelling alone, even within their own country. However, balanced against the sources of fear (the excitatory conditions) are a number of compensating factors (the inhibitory cues) such as the presence of a trusted companion, local contacts, an ability to speak the local language, and so forth. I suggest that the concept of a balance of factors can be applied equally well to the individual labelled as agoraphobic who is venturing out into the local high street.

Fears of public places cannot simply be explained away as an altered threshold of response to excitatory and inhibitory cues, but this concept does emphasise the continuity between what is considered to be normal and abnormal behaviour. Many persons given the diagnosis of agoraphobia appear to be exquisitely sensitive to cues that affect the average person to only a slight degree, for example, the ambient noise level, the need to choose between similar brands of goods in a supermarket, the state of the weather, the distance in inches from the edge of a railway platform, and so on.

A continuity between normal and abnormal responses to architectural spaces has been demonstrated with respect to perceived enclosure and its hedonic attributes (MacNab, Nieuwenhuijse, Jansweyer & Kuiper, 1978). Perspective drawings in which parameters of the architectural space were varied were presented to normal subjects and a group of subjects described as agoraphobic. Perceived enclosure was found to be related to the ratio of the height of the boundary wall to wall distance; degree of perceived enclosure was in turn significantly correlated with ratings of the drawings on scales of displeasure, insecurity and suffocation. This was true of each group, suggesting that processes common to all subjects could be used to explain them. Of course, some individuals diagnosed as agoraphobic avoid open *and* enclosed spaces (e.g. subject A, Chapter 4), and so the role of visuo-spatial cues is intriguing.

In the rest of this chapter I will discuss the main features of complaints of panic-anxiety which demand explanation. These are (1) the origins of the first episodes of panic, (2) the specificity of the eliciting cues for the first and subsequent panic episodes, (3) the maintenance of complaint and (4) fluctuations in complaint.

The use of the term *panic* begs a number of questions. Panic is a lay and not a scientific concept. I assume that panic belongs to a class of phenomena that involve a positive feedback relationship between the antecedents of reports of anxiety. As there are many possible antecedents (associated with different psychological processes), the class of panic-like phenomena is assumed to be larger than the range of complaints usually included under the term *panic*. Three other criteria define the broad phenomenon: (1) that the antecedents include self-produced stimuli, (2) that each episode is characterised by a rapid increment in distress and (3) that the panic-like episode is self-limiting (or can be terminated by withdrawal from an eliciting situation). The panics with which we are dealing include a large component of autonomic nervous system lability, flight, aversive somatic sensations and, commonly, vaguely expressed fears of the potential consequences of panic. However, other problem behaviours that involve more specific autonomic, motor or cognitive-verbal responses can also be included in the class of panic-like phenomena (e.g. motor 'paralyses' such as writers cramp; see also Hallam, 1976a).

ORIGINS OF THE FIRST EPISODES OF PANIC

Lacking empirical data, we have to speculate about the origins of the first panic. The events that initiate the first episode can be distinguished from life events (e.g. stressors) that may alter the person's responsivity in a general way. There is little evidence to suggest that panics are elicited directly and immediately by stressful interactions with the environment. However, some stressors may operate primarily by bringing about a change in the way that *other* events are evaluated. For example, I suggested in Chapter 3 that the frequently reported precipitating events—death of a relative, illness, or witnessed injury—may lead the individual to a changed evaluation of the probability of these events happening to himself or herself. This process can be compared with the illness worries that medical students develop in their early years of study (Mechanic, 1972).

The hypothesis that a positive feedback mechanism can account for the main features of panic requires that two assumptions are made: (1) that there are a number of antecedents of reports of anxiety and (2) that the antecedents are processes with system properties occurring in a temporal sequence. These essential ideas were contained in Lazarus' concept of emotions as response syndromes (Lazarus, 1966). In this systems view, even the response-produced feedback associated with the utterance 'I am anxious' may be seen as a stimulus for subsequent responses which are the antecedents of further reports of anxiety.

A positive feedback process might be initiated in the context of actual minor organic illness. The presence of illness may direct attention towards somatic sensations, and, if they are perceived as threatening, they may become the antecedents of reports of anxiety. Direction of attention towards somatic sensations may, in turn, make them more intense and/or salient so that fears of death/illness are reinforced. Somatic sensations associated with reports of anxiety can, of course, be mistaken for illness, for example, weakness, dizziness or difficulty in breathing.

Certain unfamiliar perceptual experiences have also been mentioned as initiating events by clinicians, for example, drug experiences and anaesthesia. The experience of depersonalisation and the possibly related phenomenon of 'break-off' in pilots have also been mentioned in accounts of the development of phobias (see Chapter 6). The kind of threat that these experiences present may be connected with fears of losing control, being judged insane or failing to perform normally. The feedback links are more difficult to understand, partly because the altered perceptual experiences which are assumed to initiate the chain of events are not themselves well understood.

Another possible feedback mechanism can be deduced from interruption theory (see Chapter 11). If flight (escape) is a common antecedent of reports of anxiety, and interruption of this response occurs, then the individual is also subjected to the consequence of interruption, which is assumed to be an increase in autonomic arousal. The possibility of a positive feedback interaction between these two antecedents (escape response/arousal) therefore arises. Many people with fears of public places report that their feelings of panic are exacerbated by the perception of barriers to escape, and even a commitment to a minor appointment seems to induce a sense of entrapment.

I have speculated about three other causes of an altered bodily state which may give rise to panic if other conditions for producing positive feedback are present. The first is the aftereffects of a long period of demanding or challenging circumstances, when the demand is lifted (see Chapter 11). It is possible that these effects arise acutely if the conditions of demand change rapidly. The second is a disinhibitory phenomenon produced in persons who have successfully handled threatening or potentially aversive events. I have assumed that the disinhibitory event alters the significance of the potential threat with the consequence that excitatory responses are suddenly released (see Chapter 10).

Finally, the possibility cannot be dismissed that the antecedents of panic are the same as the antecedents of reports of anxiety in general except that (1) the *perceived* source of panic does not relate to its actual determinants and (2) the causal attribution the subject makes (or another characteristic of the subject) leads to an exacerbation of the actual antecedents. This idea is embodied in Goldstein and Chambless' view that physiological arousal caused by interpersonal conflict is misattributed to external circumstances (Goldstein & Chambless, 1978). The real causes of the problem cannot therefore be dealt with.

The role of a variety of antecedent events, and the failure to make helpful causal attributions, are well illustrated in the interview with subject B (Chapter 4). The following section of the transcript is taken from a later point in the interview. It should be noted that subject B is an immigrant.

Q. What did your wife think about your problems?

Well, her attitude was that I wasn't getting enough rest, but whether that was so, I just do not know. That is where the big question sign comes in. Why, and how, did it happen? It's not as if you had any warning. I personally don't know what to say. I just go along with what other people say—a bit of everything put together.

I think in a way I wasn't observant enough of what was going on around me. I think that had something to do with it—it seemed that everyone else was aware of what could happen, apart from me. I could remember before this thing happened, I used to go to a party on Saturday night and leave straight from there for work. I didn't give it a thought, and my wife used to go on about me getting enough sleep, but I ignored it all.

Q. You were doing two jobs then?

Well, partly, yes. I got my cabbing badge in July, and I went home in September for a holiday. When I was sitting around on my holiday, relaxing, I was planning to give my notice in—I had been with my firm for quite a few years—and take up cabbing full-time. Try and get as much money as I can for the day when I could go home. But no sooner than I came back, I never had a chance to put any of it into practice.

Q. How soon after your return did you have your first panic?

About two weeks. I didn't get a chance to give my notice in.

Q. You had a very relaxing time in ____?

Yes. this is what I was saying. If my wife said I didn't get enough rest, how could that be if I was on four weeks holiday?

Q. Before you went away, about how many hours a week were you putting in?

Seven and a half per day and then I did the cabbing in the evening.

Q. What time did you come home?

Well, on a weekday, maybe nine o'clock, but on the weekend, sometimes it was quite late, on Friday and Saturday night. On Sunday I often had to do maintenance work in my regular job.

Q. You must have been doing 70–80 hours per week. Did you see this as a temporary phase?

Yes, it was my intention to give up my regular job and do cabbing full-time. But funnily enough, when I came back I never felt like doing the cabbing at all. After lying about for a month, I never felt up to it. I did feel I was wasting time, sort of thing, but I didn't have the urge to do it. I was caught up in two minds.

Q. What about going back to ____? Did you feel that you really wanted to go back?

Oh yes, that was the only thing that was on my mind.

Q. Do you still think about it now?

Well, it's gradually fading from my mind.

Q. So you had a quite a conflict here all the . . .

Yes, you know I've always said if I hadn't gone home for a holiday, this wouldn't have happened. This is my only belief.

Q. Why did you believe that?

When I came back I was in two minds, wishing I was home, but your family's here. Sometimes it was as if my body was here and my mind was there. When I went home, I felt all my years in England—I've wasted them. I could have made more of it. I would then be prepared for the day I was going home. So, although I wished I was home, I knew in my heart it was impossible. I felt that eventually the feeling would go. It's only now, 'alright, forget about it, it's just a dream'.

Subject B's story offers several possibilities for interpreting the origin of his initial panic. First, he appeared to adapt without signs of strain to the demands of two jobs over several months. However, after a rest period, and perhaps a loss of adaptation to the job stressors, the prospect of changing from secure employment to a more demanding and insecure means of making his living may have represented more of a challenge than he had anticipated. Second, he was placed in a position of acute conflict by his wish to return home, which he had nursed over many years, and the more practical alternative of staying in his adopted country. Lastly, a major life plan was interrupted when he was forced to realise that his family was unwilling to move and that he could never return home permanently. As the conflict was resolved by this realisation, his need to change employment dissolved. However, he was unable to articulate the meaning of his life situation (at that time) and remained doubtful, even during the interview, that his account of this complex chain of events was relevant to his psychological distress.

Several stressor events might be postulated as being relevant to the development of his initial panic episode: (1) a period of overwork, followed by a sudden removal of the need to continue this, (2) interruption of a major life-plan (i.e. loss of a cherished idea) and (3) fear of giving up his secure employment, and perhaps damage to his self-esteem because he was unable to do so.

The situation *specificity* of the first panic also requires explanation. Furthermore, his complaints of anxiety may have been *maintained* by different processes, including a fear of insanity (see Chapter 4).

SITUATION SPECIFICITY OF THE FIRST AND SUBSEQUENT PANICS

The development of a tendency to report panic is best conceptualised as an unfolding process of complementary environmental and organismic influences. When the individual is in a vulnerable (prepanic) state, the elicitation of panic by a particular set of circumstances may involve a chance element. However, once elicited it may be assumed that the stimulus circumstances associated with panic become important determinants of later reports of panic.

Although we have little evidence to go on, clinical experience suggests that the first panic does not occur just anywhere. Most occur in situations which could be described as presenting a surfeit of excitatory cues. Travel on public transportation is frequently mentioned. Travel may involve noise, crowds, enclosure, the absence of personal control over the means of transportation, possible dangers, choice, unfamiliarity and concern about meeting schedules. Situations that are reported as common fears in population surveys, such as high places, water, tunnels and darkness, are also common elements of travel.

Panic is by no means always first reported in public places. One of my clients awoke from sleep in a state she described as an intense fear of death by suffocation. Another, who had experienced the phenomenon of sleep paralysis on several occasions, reported that he panicked when this occurred. He developed a fear of closing his eyes and drifting into a state of relaxation.

The first panic undoubtedly comes as a surprising experience to many individuals. I have already noted that describing the first episode as

panic begs a number of causal questions (Chapter 9). That is, the occurrence of the phenomenon might depend on the subject's prior cognitive
characteristics and/or interpretation of the initial episode. Several authors have focussed their discussion on the subject's attribution of
causality to an internal or external source.

Goldstein and Chambless (1978) argued that arousal which follows
interpersonal conflict is interpreted as a fear of public places. There is
often an element of physical entrapment in public situations, and this is
assumed to elicit panic because there is semantic generalisation from the
experience of being trapped in a current life situation.

According to Mathews et al. (1981, p. 46), the two disorders of agoraphobia and anxiety neurosis have a similar developmental history, but
phobic avoidance, which marks off the former, is said to arise as the
joint product of a panic attack out-of-doors, an attribution to external
provoking stimuli, and an avoidant/dependent coping style. The external attribution is assumed to result from a general personality characteristic of external locus of control (Rotter, 1966). An external locus of
control refers to a tendency to describe the causes of events as due to
chance, fate, luck, and the like, rather than the result of one's own
voluntary initiation. In this sense, the client's belief that he or she is
mentally or physically ill can also be viewed as an example of an external
locus of control. Mathews et al. (1981) cited worry and stress as alternative attributions and suggested that the consequences of these beliefs
might not include avoidance of public places. However, these beliefs
could, perhaps, be examples of an internal or an external locus of
control.

The notion that Goldstein and Chambless (1978) seemed to be getting
at is an inability to perceive a connection between reports of feelings and
causal events, that is, a failure of comprehension. An external attribution occurs virtually by default.

Several different concepts are therefore contained within these observations of an external attribution. According to my own view, individuals with fears of public places are partly correct in attributing panic
to external circumstances. In fact, Mathews and his colleagues mentioned arousing environmental stimulation as one of the causes of panic.
However, as these authors rightly pointed out, intraindividual factors
are involved as well.

The role of an external attribution in the development of panic can be
questioned on the grounds that being afraid of X does not necessarily
imply attributing the cause of fear to X. When X is commonly accepted
as a reasonable cause of fear (e.g. a snake), the causal attribution is likely
to coincide with the object of fear. However, in the case of public places,

which are not commonly accepted sources of fear, this fear may be puzzling and attributed to other events such as stress or a medical condition. Moreover, if we wish to retain the definition of an attribution as an *articulated* belief, it would make little sense to explain a fear of public places as an unrecognised causal attribution. In other words, it is not clear that external attributions are actually made by persons with fears of external (public) situations. Goldstein and Chambless' (1978) concept of semantic generalisation is a feasible, if speculative, alternative account of the role of external cues in eliciting reports of fear.

It seems unlikely, in any case, that an external attribution is the primary explanation for the *avoidance* of public places. In a community survey of fears, Costello (1982) found that the degree of avoidance of public places was uncorrelated with reports of the severity of distress (psychological or somatic) in these situations. In all other fears he sampled, the amount of avoidance was significantly correlated with distress ratings. It seems, then, that acknowledging a fear of public places does not imply avoidance of public places. This is consistent with my general position that avoidance of public places is just one strategy (staying at home) for dealing with complaints of panic and anxiety and not the 'avoidance component' of a discrete phobia.

The events which are noticed during the first episode of panic, and their concomitant interpretation, may well set the pattern for stimulus generalisation and subsequent elicitation of panic. A woman described by Hallam (1976) was acutely aware of an urge to urinate and later developed a fear that she would do so in public places which lacked access to a toilet. Subject C's first episode (Chapter 4) occurred in an open space, and she later had difficulty crossing a room. It would appear that both interoceptive and exteroceptive cues become conditioned aversive stimuli.

The interpretation given to panic episodes can be extremely variable. Subject C said that, when she felt strongly that her experience was *not* reality, this meant that it would not matter what she *might* do and therefore that she *would* possibly do or say something embarrassing.

This chain of ideas seems no less fantastic than the beliefs about fear expressed in traditional societies. Rin and Lin (1962) observed four examples of 'acute fright reaction' in the course of an epidemiological survey of the aboriginal population of Taiwan. The reaction was described as an attack lasting a few hours to a week, consisting of a change of consciousness, excitement and hallucinations. The attacks occurred when the person was alone and rather fearful, for example, walking in the forest or hearing unusual sounds at night. The cause of the attacks was thought to be a mythical being who was seen or heard when the attack began. After the initial episode, the individual became sensitised to the situations in which it had occurred and even the thought of the mythical being could provoke them.

Hallowell (1938, p. 41) described a Salteaux Indian who 'could go nowhere unaccompanied by one or more companions. When alone he would always keep within sight of human habitation or people. This was the rule even when he had to urinate or defecate. If he had to relieve himself at night, his wife would always get up and go with him'. The man explained these fears by saying that 'he once dreamed that a jack-fish would swallow him, if this creature found him alone'.

These examples from hunting-and-gathering peoples suggest that some of the antecedents of fears of public places are common across very different cultures. (Hallowell also described a man who would not canoe across any extensive body of water and skirted the shore in his canoe.) However, causal attributions certainly differ between cultures, and we might speculate that these play a critical role in the processes leading to maintenance in the long term.

Why then do some individuals who report the panic-anxiety cluster of complaints show more situation-specific avoidance than others? These questions were discussed briefly elsewhere (Chapters 7, 9 and 12). It is worth noting that the subgroup who avoid public situations is mostly made up of women. I suggested that staying at home is a coping strategy that is consistent with sex-role expectations and pragmatic considerations. Further, staying in a safe place has other consequences such as an increase in the unfamiliarity of the public environment. Cues which predict the absence of panic may acquire the properties of safety signals which reinforce safety-seeking behaviour.

MAINTENANCE OF PANIC-ANXIETY

Anxiety is reported by most people in one situation or another, but there is no information on the frequency of anxiety which is reported as occurring suddenly for no apparent reason. It is not known how many individuals go on to complain of panic attacks and persisting complaints of anxiety.

There is a consensus that the subject's interpretation of the panic episode is of relevance to maintenance. Certain beliefs about the origins of panic (e.g. 'I am physically/mentally ill, likely to die during the panic') may act as cues for further physiological and behavioural effects which potentiate the existing antecedents of complaint. These 'catastrophic cognitions' as Goldstein called them, decline with successful behavioural therapy (Goldstein, 1982).

It has to be emphasised that panic is an aversive experience, and the sensations associated with it help to confirm the validity of catastrophic cognitions. The individual may not be able to think clearly, voluntary control of motor acts may be lost, the heart may beat dramatically fast, and so forth. As long as threatening beliefs are sustained, panic episodes may remain aversive, and the problem is likely to be maintained by a fear-of-fear mechanism.

Maintenance processes can be inferred from variables influencing the success or failure of exposure-based therapies (see Chapter 13). It is not yet known what makes these therapies effective, but long-duration exposure seems to be an important variable. Subtle attitudinal changes, and the nature of coping strategies during confrontation, are also likely to play a role. In essence, if a person is willing to confront the cues (imaginal or real) that elicit complaints of anxiety, there is a reasonable chance that the aversiveness of the experience will decline. Failure to confront a problem for a long period (and by implication, persistence of complaint) can be explained in at least four ways: (1) ignorance that this approach will have the desired effect, (2) a reluctance to tolerate aversive experiences, (3) failure to adopt a coping strategy that facilitates a reduction of complaint (see Chapter 13) and (4) positive benefits associated with the 'sick role' so that an acquired dependence on others is difficult to forgo (Mathews et al., 1981, p. 49).

A model of maintenance cannot be based entirely on the inferred mechanisms of exposure-based therapies. Exposure is not always successful when other factors seem favourable. The presence of enduring conflict or stressors may account for some cases of persisting complaint (e.g. marital conflict; see Chapter 12). Another factor worth mentioning again is the slow extinction of some forms of interoceptive conditioning. Furthermore, the interoceptive stimulus complex associated with the antecedents of panic may include somatic sensations caused by recurrent physiological dysfunctions. Vestibular dysfunction is a possible example. Faulty breathing habits leading to hyperventilation is another (see Chapter 5).

The long-term consequences of panic-anxiety may also produce vicious-cycle effects. The use of alcohol as a coping strategy (and possibly tranquillising medication) may lead to a feedback exacerbation of the problem (see Chapter 7). The long-term consequences include a loss of life satisfaction, restriction of activities, self-deprecation, potential interpersonal conflict and the effects of being labelled as having a neurotic disorder. These consequences may act as stressors or mood depressants and therefore maintain a vicious-cycle effect.

FLUCTUATION IN COMPLAINTS

Fluctuation is a noticeable feature of panic-anxiety complaints. Variation occurs from day to day and over longer periods as well. Weeks or months may pass without complaint. These fluctuations are often as puzzling to the client as to the clinical observer. Unlike other psychological problems such as depressed mood, complaints of anxiety respond more rapidly to changes in internal state brought about by provoking agents (e.g. sodium lactate) or pharmocological agents which have a calming effect.

The changeable nature of complaints of anxiety could be put forward as evidence in support of the main theme of this book that anxiety is a multireferential lay construct and that reports and complaints of anxiety have multiple antecedents. If we further assume that the antecedents are complex patterns of events occurring in temporal sequences and involving interactions between internal and external antecedent events, then the puzzling and 'irrational' nature of panic-anxiety might be expected. In other words, event relationships may be difficult to perceive.

Some variation in complaint is clearly related to day-to-day happenings such as the need to visit a dentist, attend a wedding or the temporary absence of a trusted companion. An interaction with depressed mood and hormonal variation have also been suggested. However, research on the determinants of fluctuations in complaint is sadly lacking.

This comment leads us back, in this concluding paragraph, to the question why it is that we know so little about the panic-anxiety cluster of complaints. The topic of anxiety has always been of central concern in twentieth-century psychology. There is no lack of experimental research and conceptual speculation. This book has argued that the concept of anxiety has been borrowed from a lay discourse about emotions and emotional distress—a discourse in which metaphorical allusions has lead to the creation of mental entities with an apparently timeless and objective nature. Lay discourse has so shaped our conceptualisations that we have looked for unique biological and psychological correlates of this putative fundamental emotion. I have suggested instead that anxiety is a multireferential lay construct so that our everyday usage of the term covers a number of different circumstances. The failure of reports of anxiety to correlate uniquely with behavioural and physiological processes is of no surprise and nonproblematic. The behaviour of reporting anxiety relates as much to the social practices that govern the expression of emotion as it does to measurable features of the individual. Originating as it does in a commonsense understanding, it is doubtful that a scientific concept of anxiety has a useful part to play in organising our thinking about the antecedents of reports of anxiety.

References

Abramson, L. Y., Garber, J., Seligman, M. E. P. Learned helplessness: An attribution analysis. In J. Garber & M. E. P. Seligman (Eds.), *Human helplessness*. New York: Academic Press, 1980.

Ackerman, S. H., & Sachar, E. J. The lactate theory of anxiety. *Psychosomatic Medicine*, 1974, *36*, 69–81.

Aitken, R. C. B., Lister, J. A., & Main, C. J. Identification of features associated with flying phobia in aircrew. *British Journal of Psychiatry*, 1981, *139*, 38–42.

Al-Issa, I. *The psychopathology of women*. Englewood Cliffs, N.J.: Prentice-Hall, 1980.

Altschule, M. D. *Bodily physiology in mental and emotional disorders*. New York: Grune & Stratton, 1953.

Ambrosino, S. V. Phobic Anxiety Depersonalisation Syndrome. *New York State Journal of Medicine*, 1973, *73*, 419–425.

American Psychiatric Association. *Diagnostic and Statistical Manual of Mental Disorders*, (3rd ed.). Washington, D.C.: The American Psychiatric Association, 1980.

Andrews, J. D. W. Psychotherapy of phobias. *Psychological Bulletin*, 1966, *66*, 455–480.

Anokhin, P. K. *Biology and neuropsychology of the conditioned reflex and its role in adaptive behaviour*. Oxford: Pergamon Press, 1974.

Appleby, I. L., Klein, D. F., Sachar, E. J., Levitt, M., Halpern, T. S. Biochemical indices of lactate-induced anxiety. In D. F. Klein, & J. G. Rabkin (Eds.), *Anxiety: New research and changing concepts*. New York: Raven Press, 1981.

Arrindell, W. A. Dimensional structure and psychopathology correlates of the fear survey schedule (FSS-III) in a phobic population: A factorial definition of agoraphobia. *Behaviour Research and Therapy*, 1980, *18*, 229–242.

Averill, J. R. A constructivist view of emotion. In R. Plutchik, & H. Kellerman (Eds.) *Emotion: Theory, research and experience* (Vol. 1). New York: Academic Press, 1980(a).

Averill, J. R. Emotion and anxiety: Sociocultural, biological, and psychological determinants. In A. O. Rorty (Ed.), *Explaining emotions*. Berkeley: University of California Press, 1980(b).

Baade, E., Ellertsen, B., Johnsen, T. B., & Ursin, H. Physiology, psychology and performance. In H. Ursin, E. Baade, & S. Levine (Eds.), *Psychology of stress: A study of coping men*. New York: Academic Press, 1978.

Baddeley, A. D. Selective attention and performance in dangerous environments. *British Journal of Psychology*, 1972, *63*, 537–546.

Bandura, A. *Principles of behavior modification*, New York: Holt, Rinehart and Winston, 1969.

Bandura, A. Self-efficacy: Toward a unifying theory of behavioral change. *Psychological Review*, 1977, *84*, 191–215.

Bandura, A. Self efficacy: Toward a unifying theory of behavioral change. *Advances in Behaviour Research and Therapy*, 1978, *1*, 139–162.

Bandura, A., Adams, N. E., & Beyer, J. Cognitive processes mediating behavioral change. *Journal of Personality and Social Psychology*, 1977, *35*, 125–139.

Barlow, D. H., Mavissakalian, M. R., & Schofield, L. D. Patterns of desynchrony in agoraphobia: A preliminary report. *Behaviour Research and Therapy*, 1980, *18*, 446–448.

Barron, F. An ego-strength scale which predicts response to psychotherapy. *Journal of Consulting and Clinical Psychology*, 1953, *17*, 327–333.

Basowitz, H., Persky, H., Korchin, S. J., & Grinker, R. R. *Anxiety and stress*. New York: McGraw-Hill, 1955.

Bates, H. D. Factorial structure and MMPI correlates of a fear survey schedule in a clinical population. *Behaviour Research and Therapy*, 1971, *9*, 355–360.

Beard, G. M. *A practical treatise on nervous exhaustion (neurasthenia)*. New York: William Wood, 1880.

Beck, A. T. *Cognitive therapy and the emotional disorders*. New York: International Universities Press, 1976.

Beck, A. T., Laude, R., & Bohnert, M. Ideational components of anxiety neurosis. *Archives of General Psychiatry*, 1974, *31*, 319–325.

Benedikt, V. Uber Platschwindel. *Algemeine Wiener Medizinische Zeitung*, 1870, *15*, 488.

Bianchi, G. N. The origins of disease phobia. *Australian and New Zealand Journal of Psychiatry*, 1971, *5*, 241–257.

Bianchi, G. N. Patterns of hypochondriasis: A principal components analysis. *British Journal of Psychiatry*, 1973, *122*, 541–548.

Biran, M., & Wilson, G. T. Treatment of phobic disorders using cognitive and exposure methods: A self-efficacy analysis. *Journal of Consulting and Clinical Psychology*, 1981, *49*, 886–899.

Bland, K., & Hallam, R. S. Relationship between response to graded exposure and marital satisfaction in agoraphobics. *Behaviour Research and Therapy*, 1981, *19*, 335–338.

Bonn, J. A., Harrison, J., & Rees, L. Lactate infusion as a treatment of 'free-floating' anxiety. *Canadian Psychiatric Association Journal*, 1971, *18*, 41–45.

Borkovec, T. Facilitation and inhibition of functional CS exposure in the treatment of phobias. In J. Boulougouris (Ed.), *Learning theory approaches to psychiatry*. New York: Wiley, 1982.

Borkovec, T. D., & Grayson, J. B. Consequences of increasing the functional impact of internal emotional stimuli. In K. Blankstein, P. Pliner, & L. H. Polivey, (Eds.), *Advances in the study of communication and affects* (Vol. 3). New York: Plenum, 1980.

Boulougouris, J. C., Marks, I. M., Marset, P. Superiority of flooding (implosion) to desensitisation for reducing pathological fear. *Behaviour Research and Therapy*, 1971, *9*, 7–16.

Bowen, R. C., & Kohout, J. The relationship between agoraphobia and primary affective disorders. *Canadian Journal of Psychiatry*, 1979, *24*, 317–322.

Bowlby, J. *Attachment and loss*. Vol. 2: *Separation, anxiety and anger*. London: Hogarth, 1973.

Breggin, P. R. The psychophysiology of anxiety. *Journal of Nervous and Mental Disease*, 1964, *139*, 558–568.

Brener, J. Visceral perception. In J. Beatty & H. Legewie (Eds.), *Biofeedback and behavior*. New York: Plenum, 1977.

Brewer, W. F. There is no convincing evidence for operant or classical conditioning in adult humans. In W. B. Weimer & D. S. Palermo (Eds.), *Cognition and the symbolic processes*. New York: Halsted Press, 1974.

Brewin, C., & Antaki, C. The role of attributions in psychological treatment. In C. Antaki & C. Brewin (Eds.), *Attributions and psychological change*. London: Academic Press, 1982.

Bridges, P. K. Recent physiological studies of stress and anxiety in man. *Biological Psychiatry*, 1974, *8*, 95–112.

Broadbent, D. E. Some relations between clinical and occupational psychology. Paper presented at the International Association of Applied Psychology 20th Annual Congress, Edinburgh, July, 1982.

Brown, G. W., & Harris, T. *Social origins of depression*. London: Tavistock Publications, 1978.

Buglass, D., Clarke, J., Henderson, A. S., Kreitman, N., & Presley, A. S. A study of agoraphobic housewives. *Psychological Medicine*, 1977, *7*, 73–86.

Burns, L. E., & Thorpe, G. L. Fears and clinical phobias: Epidemiological aspects and the national survey of agoraphobics. *Journal of International Medical Research*, 1977, *5*, Supplement (1), 132–139.

Butcher, J. N., & Pancheri, P. *A handbook of cross-national MMPI research*. Minneapolis: University of Minnesota Press, 1976.

Campbell, D., Sanderson, R. E., & Laverty, S. F. T. Characteristics of a CR in human subjects during extinction trials following a single traumatic conditioning trial. *Journal of Abnormal and Social Psychology*, 1964, *68*, 627–639.

Cappon, D. Orientational perception: III Orientational perception distortions in depersonalisation. *American Journal of Psychiatry*, 1969, *125*, 1048–1056.

Cappon, D., & Banks, R. Orientational perception: Review and preliminary study of distortions in orientational perception. *Archives of General Psychiatry*, 1961, *5*, 380–391.

Carey, G. Genetic influences on anxiety neurosis and agoraphobia. In R. J. Mathew (Ed.), *Biology of anxiety*. New York: Brunner Mazel, 1982.

Carruthers, M. Field studies: Emotion and b-blockade. In M. J. Christie & P. G. Mellett (Eds.) *Foundations of psychosomatics*. London: Wiley, 1981.

Cattell, R. B. Anxiety and motivation: Theory and crucial experiments. In C. D. Spielberger (Ed.), *Anxiety and behavior*. New York: Academic Press, 1966.

Chambless, D. L. Characteristics of agoraphobics. In D. L. Chambless, & A. J. Goldstein (Eds.), *Agoraphobia: Multiple perspectives on theory and treatment*. New York: Wiley, 1982(a).

Chambless, D. L. The measurement of fear-of-fear in agoraphobics, Part II. The revised agoraphobia cognitions questionnaire and the body sensations questionnaire. Paper presented at AABT, Los Angeles, November, 1982(b).

Chambless, D. L., & Goldstein, A. J. The treatment of agoraphobia. In A. J. Goldstein & E. Foa (Eds.), *The handbook of behavioral interventions: A clinical guide*. New York: Wiley, 1980.

Christie, R. V. Some types of respiration in the neuroses. *Quarterly Journal of Medicine*, 1935, *28*, 427.

Clancy, J., Vanderhoof, E., & Campbell, P. Evaluation of an aversion technique as a treatment for alcoholism. *Quarterly Journal of Studies on Alcoholism*, 1967, *28*, 476–485.

Clark, B., & Graybiel, A. The "break-off" phenomenon. *Journal of Aviation Medicine*, 1957, *28*, 171–176.

Cloninger, C. R., Martin, R. L., Clayton, P., & Guze, S. B. A blind follow-up and family study of anxiety neurosis: Preliminary analysis of the St. Louis 500. In D. F. Klein & J.

Rabkin (Eds.), *Anxiety: New research and changing concepts*. New York: Raven Press, 1981.

Cohen, M. E., Balal, D. W., Kilpatrick, A., Reed, E. W., & White, P. D. The high familial prevalence of neurocirculatory asthenia (anxiety neurosis, effort syndrome). *American Journal of Human Genetics*, 1951, *3*, 126.

Connolly, J., Hallam, R. S., & Marks, I. M. Selective association of fainting with blood-injury-illness fear. *Behavior Therapy*, 1976, *7*, 8–13.

Costello, C. G. Anxiety and the persisting novelty of input for the ANS. *Behavior Therapy*, 1971, *2*, 321–333.

Costello, C. G. Fears and phobias in women: A community study. *Journal of Abnormal Psychology*, 1982, *91*, 280–286.

Cox, D., Hallam, R., O'Connor, K., & Rachman, S. An experimental analysis of fearlessness and courage. *British Journal of Psychology*, 1983, *74*, 107–117.

Cox, D., & Rachman, S. Part II Performance under operational conditions. In S. Rachman (Ed.), Fear and courage among military bomb-disposal operators. *Advances in Behaviour Research And Therapy*, 1983, *4*, 127–152.

Coyne, J. C. & Lazarus, R. S. Cognitive style, stress perception, and coping. In I. L. Kutash & L. B. Schlesinger (Eds.), *Handbook on stress and anxiety*. San Francisco: Jossey-Bass, 1980.

Crowe, R. R., Pauls, D. L., Kerber, R. E., & Noyes, R. Panic disorder and mitral valve prolapse. In D. F. Klein & J. Rabkin (Eds.), *Anxiety: New research and changing concepts*. New York: Raven Press, 1981.

Crowe, R. R., Pauls, D. L., Slyman, D. J., & Noyes, R. A family study of anxiety neurosis. *Archives of General Psychiatry*, 1980, *37*, 77–79.

DaCosta, J. M. On irritable heart: A clinical study of a form of functional cardiac disorder and its consequences. *American Journal of Medical Science*, 1871, *61*, 17–52.

Davison, G. C. Systematic desensitisation as a counterconditioning process. *Journal of Abnormal Psychology*, 1968, *73*, 91–99.

Davison, K. Episodic depersonalisation. *British Journal of Psychiatry*, 1964, *110*, 505–513.

Delhees, K. H., & Cattell, R. B. *Manual for the clinical analysis questionnaire.* Champaigne, Ill.: Personality and Ability Testing, 1971.

Derogatis, L. R., & Cleary, P. A. Confirmation of the dimensional structure of the SCL-90. A study in construct validation. *Journal of Clinical Psychology*, 1977, *33*, 981–989.

Derogatis, L. R., Klerman, G. L., & Lipman, R. S. Anxiety states and depressive neurosis. *Journal of Nervous and Mental Disorder*, 1972, *155*, 392–403.

Derogatis, L. R., Lipman, R. S., Covi, L., & Rickels, K. Neurotic symptom dimensions as perceived by psychiatrists and patients of various social classes. *Archives of General Psychiatry*, 1971, *24*, 454–464.

Derogatis, L. R., Lipman, R. S., Covi, L., Rickels, K. Factorial invariance of symptom dimensions in anxious and depressive neuroses. *Archives of General Psychiatry*, 1972, *27*, 659–665.

Derogatis, L. R., Lipman, R. S., Rickels, K., Uhlenhuth, E. H., & Covi, L. The Hopkins Symptom Checklist—A self-report symptom inventory. *Behavioral Science*, 1974, *19*, 1–15.

Derogatis, L. R., Yevzeroff, H., & Wittelsberger, R. Psychological disorder and the nature of the psychopathological indicator. *Journal of Consulting and Clinical Psychology*, 1975, *43*, 183–191.

Dimsdale, J. E., & Moss, J. Plasma catecholamines in stress and exercise. *Journal of the American Medical Association*, 1980, *243*, 340–342.

Dixon, J. C. Depersonalisation phenomenon in a sample population of college students. *British Journal of Psychiatry*, 1963, *109*, 371–375.

Dixon, J. J., De Monchaux, C., & Sandler, J. Patterns of anxiety: The phobias. *British Journal of Medical Psychology*, 1957, *30*, 34–40.

Easterbrook, J. A. The effect of emotion on cue utilisation and the organisation of behavior. *Psychological Review*, 1959, *66*, 183–201.

Easton, J. D., & Sherman, D. G. Somatic anxiety attacks and propanolol. *Archives of Neurology*, 1976, *33*, 689–691.

Eastwood, M. R., & Trevelyan, M. H. The relationship between physical and psychiatric disorder. *Psychological Medicine*, 1972, *2*, 363–372.

Eelen, P. Conditioning and attribution. In J. Boulougouris (Ed.), *Learning theory approaches to psychiatry*. New York: John Wiley, 1982.

Eichman, W. J. Replicated factors in the MMPI with female neuropsychiatric patients. *Journal of Consulting Psychology*, 1961, *25*, 55–60.

Ellis, A. *Reason and emotion in psychotherapy*. New York: Lyle Stuart, 1962.

Ellis, A. A note on the treatment of agoraphobics with cognitive modification versus prolonged exposure in vivo. *Behaviour Research and Therapy*, 1979, *17*, 162–164.

Emmelkamp, P. M. G. The behavioral study of clinical phobias. In M. Hersen, R. M. Eisler, & P. M. Miller (Eds.), *Progress in behavior modification* (Vol. 8). New York: Academic Press, 1979.

Emmelkamp, P. M. G. In vivo treatment of agoraphobia. In D. L. Chambless & A. J. Goldstein (Eds.), *Agoraphobia: Multiple perspectives on theory and treatment*. New York: Wiley, 1982.

Emmelkamp, P. M. G., & Kuipers, A. C. M. Agoraphobia: A follow-up study four years after treatment. *British Journal of Psychiatry*, 1979, *134*, 352–355.

Emmelkamp, P. M. G., & Wessels, H. Flooding in imagination vs flooding in vivo: A comparison with agoraphobics. *Behaviour Research and Therapy*, 1975, *13*, 7–15.

Epstein, S. Toward a unified theory of anxiety. In B. A. Maher (Ed.), *Progress in experimental personality research* (Vol. 5). New York: Academic Press, 1967.

Epstein, S., & Fenz, W. D. Theory and experiment in the measurement of approach-avoidance conflict. *Journal of Abnormal and Social Psychology*, 1962, *64*, 97–112.

Epstein, S., & Fenz, W. P. Steepness of approach and avoidance gradients in humans as a function of experience: Theory and experiment. *Journal of Experimental Psychology*, 1965, *70*, 1–12.

Erdmann, G., & Janke, W. Interaction between physiological and cognitive determinants of emotions: Experimental studies on Schacter's theory of emotions. *Biological Psychology*, 1978, *6*, 61–74.

Erdmann, G., & van Lindern, B. The effects of beta-adrenergic stimulation and beta-adrenergic blockade on emotional reactions. *Psychophysiology*, 1980, *17*, 332–338.

Errera, P. Some historical aspects of the concept of phobia. *Psychiatric Quarterly*, 1962, *36*, 325–336.

Errera, P., & Coleman, J. V. A long term follow-up study of neurotic phobic patients in a psychiatric clinic. *Journal of Nervous and Mental Disorders*, 1963, *136*, 267–271.

Evans, I. M. A conditioning model of a common neurotic pattern: Fear of fear. *Psychotherapy: Theory, Research and Practice*, 1972, *9*, 238–241.

Evans, P. D., & White, D. G. Towards an empirical definition of courage. *Behaviour Research and Therapy*, 1981, *19*, 419–424.

Eysenck, H. J. The learning theory model of neurosis—New approach. *Behaviour Research and Therapy*, 1976, *14*, 251–267.

Eysenck, H. J., & Eysenck, S. B. G. *Manual of the Eysenck Personality Inventory*. London: University of London Press, 1964.

Eysenck, H. J., & Rachman, S. *Causes and cures of neurosis*. London: Routledge & Kegan Paul, 1965.

Farrar, C. H., Powell, B. J., & Martin, L. K. Punishment of alcohol consumption by apneic paralysis. *Behaviour Research & Therapy*, 1968, *6*, 13–16.

Feighner, J. P., Robins, E., Guze, S. B., Woodruff, R. A., Winokw, G., & Munoz, R. Diagnostic criteria for use in psychiatric research. *Archives of General Psychiatry*, 1972, *26*, 57–63.

Fenton, G. W. Hysterical alterations of consciousness. In A. Roy (Ed.), *Hysteria*. London: Wiley, 1982.

Fenz, W. D. Strategies for coping with stress. In I. G. Sarason & C. D. Spielberger (Eds.), *Stress and anxiety* (Vol. 2). New York: Wiley, 1975.

Fenz, W., & Epstein, S. Gradients of physiological arousal in parachutists as a function of an approaching jump. *Psychosomatic Medicine*, 1967, *29*, 33–51.

Fenz, W., & Epstein, S. Specific and general inhibitory reactions associated with mastery and stress. *Journal of Experimental Psychology*, 1968, *77*, 52–56.

Finlay-Jones, R., & Brown, G. W. Types of stressful life events and the onset of anxiety and depressive disorders. *Psychological Medicine*, 1981, *11*, 803–815.

Fisher, J. Some MMPI dimensions of physical and psychological illness. *Journal of Clinical Psychology*, 1964, *20*, 369–370.

Fleiss, J. L., Gurland, B. J., & Cooper, J. E. Some contributions to the measurement of psychopathology. *British Journal of Psychiatry*, 1971, *119*, 647–656.

Foa, E. B., & Kozak, M. J. Treatment of anxiety disorders: Implications for psychopathology. In A. H. Tuma & J. D. Maser (Eds.), *Anxiety and the anxiety disorders*. Hillside, N.J.: Lawrence Erlbaum, in press.

Foa, E. B., & Kozak, M. J. Emotional processing of fear: Exposure to corrective information. Unpublished manuscript, Temple University, Department of Psychiatry, 1983.

Fodor, I. G. The phobic syndrome in women. In V. Franks & V. Burtle (Eds.), *Women in therapy*. New York: Brunner/Mazel, 1974.

Frankenhauser, M. Experimental approaches to the study of catecholamines and emotions. In L. Levi (Ed.), *Emotions: Their parameters and measurement*. New York: Raven Press, 1975.

Freud, S. The justification for detaching from neurasthenia a particular syndrome: The anxiety neurosis. In J. Strachey (Ed.), The Complete Works of Sigmund Freud (Vol. 3). London: Hogarth Press and Institute of Psychoanalysis, 1964. (Originally published, 1894.)

Freud, S. New introductory lectures on psychoanalysis (lecture XXXII). In J. Strachey (Ed.), *The complete works of Sigmund Freud* (Vol. 22). London: Hogarth, 1964. (Originally published, 1932.)

Frohlich, E. D., Tarazi, R. C., & Dunstan, H. P. Hyperdynamic beta-adrenergic circulatory state. Increased beta-receptor responsiveness. *Archives of Internal Medicine*, 1969, *123*, 1.

Furer, M., & Hardy, J. D. The reaction to pain as determined by the galvanic skin response. *Association for Research in Nervous and Mental Diseases*, 1950, *29*, 72–89.

Garber, J., Miller, S. M., Abramson, L. Y. On the distinction between anxiety and depression: Perceived control, certainty and probability of goal attainment. In J. Garber & M. P. Seligman (Eds.), *Human helplessness*. New York: Academic Press, 1980.

Gelder, M. G., Marks, I. M., & Wolff, H. H. Desensitisation and psychotherapy in the treatment of phobic states; a controlled enquiry. *British Journal of Psychiatry*, 1967, *113*, 53–73.

Glaser, E. M. *The physiological basis of habituation.* London: Oxford University Press, 1966.

Goldfried, M. R., & Robins, C. On the facilitation of self-efficacy. *Cognitive Therapy and Research*, 1982, *6*, 361–380.

Goldfried, M. R., & Sobocinski, D. The effect of irrational beliefs on emotional arousal. *Journal of Consulting and Clinical Psychology*, 1975, *43*, 504–510.

Goldstein, A. J. Learning theory insufficiency in understanding agoraphobia—A plea for empiricism. *Proceedings of the European Association for Behaviour Therapy and Modification*, 1971, Munich: Urban and Schwarzenburg, 1973.

Goldstein, A. J. Agoraphobia: Treatment successes, treatment failures, and theoretical implications. In D. L. Chambless & A. J. Goldstein (Eds.), *Agoraphobia: Multiple perspectives on theory and treatment.* New York: John Wiley, 1982.

Goldstein, A. J., & Chambless, D. L. A reanalysis of agoraphobia. *Behavior Therapy*, 1978, *9*, 47–59.

Goorney, A. B., & O'Connor, P. J. Anxiety associated with flying; a retrospective survey of military aircrew psychiatric casualities. *British Journal of Psychiatry*, 1971, *119*, 159–166.

Granville-Grossman, K. L., & Turner, P. The effect of propanalol on anxiety. *Lancet*, 1966, *2*, 788.

Gray, J. A. *The psychology of fear and stress.* London: Weidenfeld & Nicholson, 1971.

Gray, J. A. *Elements of a two process theory of learning.* London: Academic Press, 1975.

Gray, J. A. Behavioural Inhibition System: A possible substrate for anxiety. In M. P. Feldman & A. Broadhurst (Eds.), *Theoretical and experimental bases for the behaviour therapies.* London: Wiley, 1976.

Gray, J. A. The neuropsychology of anxiety. *British Journal of Psychology*, 1978, *69*, 417–434.

Gray, J. A. *The neuropsychology of anxiety.* Oxford: Oxford University Press, 1982.

Gray, M. A., & McPherson, I. G. Agoraphobia: A critical review of methodology in behavioural treatment research. *Current Psychology Reviews*, 1982, *2*, 19–46.

Grings, W. W. Anticipatory and preparatory electrodermal behavior in paired stimulus situations. *Psychophysiology*, 1969, *5*, 597–611.

Grings, W. W. The role of consciousness and cognition in autonomic behavior change. In F. S. McGuigan & R. Schoonover (Eds.), *The psychophysiology of thinking.* New York: Academic Press, 1973.

Grings, W. W. Inhibition in autonomic conditioning. In D. Mostofsky (Ed.), *Behavioral control and modification of physiological activity.* New York: Prentice Hall, 1976.

Grinker, R. R., & Spiegel, J. P. *Men under stress.* London: Churchill, 1945.

Grosz, H. J. Pitts' and McClures' lactate anxiety study revisited. *British Journal of Psychiatry*, 1973, *122*, 116–117.

Grosz, H. J., & Farmer, B. B. Pitts' and McClures' lactate-anxiety study revisited. *British Journal of Psychiatry*, 1972, *120*, 415.

Hafner, R. J. The husbands of agoraphobic women and their influence on treatment outcome. *British Journal of Psychiatry*, 1977, *131*, 289–294.

Hafner, R. J. The marital context of the agoraphobic syndrome. In D. L. Chambless & A. J. Goldstein (Eds.), *Agoraphobia: Multiple perspectives on theory and treatment.* New York: Wiley, 1982.

Hallam, R. S. A complex view of simple phobias. In H. J. Eysenck (Ed.), *Case studies in behaviour therapy.* London: Routledge Kegan Paul, 1976(a).

Hallam, R. S. The Eysenck personality scales: Stability and change after therapy. *Behaviour Research and Therapy*, 1976(b), *14*, 369–372.

Hallam, R. S. Agoraphobia: A critical review of the concept. *British Journal of Psychiatry*, 1978, *133*, 314–319.

Hallam, R. S. Part II: Psychometric analyses. In S. Rachman (Ed.), *Fear and courage among military bomb-disposal operators*. *Advances in Behaviour Research and Therapy*, 1983, *4*, 105–120.

Hallam, R. S. Agoraphobia: Deconstructing a clinical syndrome. *Bulletin of the British Psychological Society*, 1983, *36*, 337–340.

Hallam, R. S., & Hafner, R. J. Fears of phobic patients: Factor analyses of self-report data. *Behaviour Research and Therapy*, 1978, *16*, 1–6.

Hallam, R. S., & Rachman, S. Theoretical problems of aversion therapy. *Behaviour Research & Therapy*, 1972, *10*, 341–363.

Hallam, R. S., & Rachman, S. Current status of aversion therapy. In M. Hersen, R. Eisler, & P. Miller (Eds.), *Progress in Behavior Modification* (Vol. 2). New York: Academic Press, 1976.

Hallam, R. S., & Rachman, S. Courageous acts or courageous actors? *Personality and Individual Differences*, 1980, *1*, 341–346.

Hallam, R. S., Rachman, S., & Hinchcliffe, R. Psychological aspects of tinnitus. In S. Rachman (Ed.), *Contributions to Medical Psychology* (Vol. 3). Oxford: Pergamon Press, 1984.

Hallowell, A. Fear and anxiety as cultural and individual variables in a primitive society. *Journal of Social Psychology*, 1938, *9*, 25–47.

Hamilton, V. Information processing aspects of neurotic anxiety and the schizophrenias. In V. Hamilton & D. M. Warburton (Eds.), *Human stress and cognition*. New York: Wiley, 1979.

Hand, I., & Lamontagne, Y. The exacerbation of interpersonal problems after rapid phobia removal. *Psychotherapy: Theory, Research and Practice*, 1976, *13*, 405–411.

Hand, I., Lamontagne, Y., & Marks, I. M. Group exposure (flooding) 'in vivo' for agoraphobics. *British Journal of Psychiatry*, 1974, *124*, 588–602.

Hastings, D., Wright, D., & Glueck, B. *Psychiatric experiences of the 8th Air Force*. New York: Josiah Macy Foundation, 1944.

Heide, F. J., & Borkovec, T. D. Relaxation-induced anxiety: Paradoxical anxiety enhancement due to relaxation training. *Journal of Consulting and Clinical Psychology*, 1983, *51*, 171–182.

Helgason, T. Epidemiology of mental disorders in Iceland. *Acta Psychiatrica Scandinavica*, Supplement 173, 1964.

Henderson, R. W., Forgetting of conditioned fear inhibition. *Learning and Motivation*, 1978, *9*, 16–30.

Henderson, S., Byrne, D. G., & Duncan-Jones, P. *Neurosis and the social environment*. Sydney: Academic Press, 1982.

Hersen, M. Self-assessment of fear. *Behavior Therapy*, 1973, *4*, 241–257.

Hodgson, R., & Rachman, S. II Desynchrony in measures of fear. *Behaviour Research and Therapy*, 1974, *12*, 319–326.

Hodgson, R. J., Stockwell, T. R., & Rankin, H. J. Can alcohol reduce tension? *Behaviour Research and Therapy*, 1979, *17*, 459–466.

Hollon, S. D., & Bemis, K. M. Self-report and the assessment of cognitive functions. In M. Hersen & A. S. Bellack (Eds.), *Behavioral assessment: A practical handbook* (2nd ed.). Oxford: Pergamon, 1982.

Houston, B. K., Bloom, L. J., Burish, T. G., & Cummings, E. M. Positive evaluation of stressful experiences. *Journal of Personality*, 1978, *46*, 205–214.

Ingham, J. G. Change in MPI scores in neurotic patients; A three year follow-up. *British Journal of Psychiatry*, 1966, *112*, 931–939.

James, W. What is an emotion. *Mind*, 1884, *9*, 188–205.

James, I. M., Pearson, R. M., Griffiths, D. N. W., & Newbury, P. Effect of oxprenolol on stage fright in musicians. *Lancet*, 1977, *2*, 952–954.

Janis, I. L. Decision making under stress. In L. Goldberger & S. Breznitz (Eds.), *Handbook of stress: Theoretical and clinical aspects.* New York: Free Press, 1982.

Jannoun, L., Munby, M., Catalan, J., & Gelder, M. A home-based treatment programme for agoraphobia: Replication and controlled evaluation. *Behavior Therapy*, 1980, *11*, 294–305.

Jansson, L. & Ost, L. Behavioral treatment for agoraphobia: An evaluative review. *Clinical Psychology Review*, 1982, *2*, 311–336.

Jaynes, J. *The origin of consciousness in the breakdown of the bicameral mind.* Boston: Houghton Mifflin Co., 1976.

Jones, M., & Mellersh, V. A comparison of the exercise response in anxiety states and normal controls. *Psychosomatic Medicine*, 1946, *8*, 180.

Kassebaum, G. C., Couch, A. S., & Slater, P. E. The factorial dimensions of the MMPI. *Journal of Consulting and Clinical Psychology*, 1959, *23*, 226–236.

Kelly, D. *Anxiety and emotion.* Springfield, Ill.: C. C. Thomas, 1980.

Kelly, D., & Walter, C. J. S. The relationship between clinical diagnosis and anxiety, assessed by forearm blood flow. *British Journal of Psychiatry*, 1968, *114*, 611–626.

Kelly, D., Mitchell-Higgs, N., & Sherman, D. Anxiety effects of sodium lactate assessed clinically and physiologically. *British Journal of Psychiatry*, 1971, *119*, 129–141.

Kelly, G. A. *The psychology of personal constructs.* New York: W. W. Norton, 1955.

Kelvin, R. P., Lucas, C. J., & Ojha, A. B. The relationship between personality, mental health, and academic performance in university students. *British Journal of Social and Clinical Psychology*, 1965, *4*, 244–253.

Kerr, T. A., Roth, M., Schapira, K., & Gurney, C. The assessment and prediction of outcome in affective disorders. *British Journal of Psychiatry*, 1972, *121*, 167–174.

Kiesler, D. J. Experimental designs in psychotherapy research. In A. E. Bergin & S. L. Garfield (Eds.), *Psychotherapy and behavior change: An empirical analysis.* New York: Wiley, 1971.

Kilpatrick, D. G., Sutker, P. B., & Smith, A. D. Deviant drug and alcohol use: The role of anxiety, sensation seeking and other variables. In M. Zuckerman & C. D. Spielberger (Eds.), *Emotions and Anxiety.* Hillsdale, N.J.: Lawrence Erlbaum, 1976.

Kimmel, H. D. Instrumental inhibitory factors in classical conditioning. In W. F. Prokasey (Ed.), *Classical conditioning.* New York: Appleton Century Croft, 1965.

Kimmel, H. D., & Burns, R. A. Adaptational aspects of conditioning. In W. K. Estes (Ed.), *Handbook of learning and cognitive processes.* Vol. 2: *Conditioning and behavior theory.* Hillsdale, N.J.: Lawrence Erlbaum, 1975.

Klein, D. F. Delineation of two drug-responsive anxiety syndromes. *Psychopharmacologia (Berlin)*, 1964, *5*, 397–408.

Klein, D. F. The importance of psychiatric diagnosis in prediction of clinical drug effects. *Archives of General Psychiatry*, 1967, *16*, 118–126.

Klein, D. F. Anxiety reconceptualised. In D. F. Klein & J. Rabkin (Eds.), *Anxiety: New research and changing concepts.* New York: Raven Press, 1981.

Klerman, G. L. Anxiety and depression. In G. D. Burrows & B. Davies (Eds.), *Handbook of studies on anxiety.* Elsevier: North Holland Medical Press, 1980.

Lacey, J. I., and Lacey, B. C. Verification and extension of the principle of autonomic response stereotypy. *American Journal of Psychology*, 1958, *71*, 50–73.

Lader, M. H. *The psychophysiology of mental illness.* London: Routledge Kegan, Paul, 1975.

Lader, M. H. Benzodiazepine dependence. In R. Murray, A. H. Ghodse, C. Harris, D. Williams, & P. Williams (Eds.), *The misuse of psychotropic drugs.* London: Gaskell, 1981.

Lader, M. H. Biological differentiation of anxiety, arousal, and stress. In R. J. Mathews (Ed.), *The biology of anxiety.* New York: Brunner Mazel, 1982.

Lader, M. H., & Mathews, A. M. Physiological changes during spontaneous panic attacks. *Journal of Psychosomatic Research,* 1970, *14,* 377–382.

Lader, M. H., & Mathews, A. M. A physiological model of phobic anxiety and desensitisation. *Behaviour Research and Therapy,* 1968, *6,* 411–421.

Lader, M. H., & Wing, L. Physiological measures, sedative drugs and morbid anxiety. Maudsley Monograph No. 14. London: Oxford University Press, 1966.

Lang, P. J. The mechanism of desensitisation and the laboratory study of fear. In C. M. Franks (Ed.), *Behavior therapy: Appraisal and status.* New York: McGraw-Hill, 1969.

Lang, P. The application of psychophysiological methods to the study of psychotherapy and behavior modification. In A. E. Bergin & S. L. Garfield (Eds.), *Handbook of psychotherapy and behavior change: An empirical analysis.* New York: Wiley, 1971.

Lang, P. J. Imagery in therapy: An information processing analysis of fear. *Behavior Therapy,* 1977, *8,* 862–886.

Lang, P. J. A bioinformational theory of emotional imagery. *Psychophysiology,* 1979, *16,* 495–512.

Lang, P. J. The cognitive psychophysiology of emotion: Fear and anxiety. Paper prepared for the NIMH conference on anxiety and anxiety disorders, Tuxedo, N.Y., Sept. 1983.

Lang, P. J., Kozak, M. J., Miller, G. A., Levin, G. N., & McClean, A. Emotional imagery: Conceptual structure and pattern of somatic-visceral response. *Psychophysiology,* 1980, *17,* 179–192.

Lang, P. J., Melamed, B., & Hart, J. A psychophysiological analysis of fear modification using an automated desensitisation technique. *Journal of Abnormal Psychology,* 1970, *76,* 220–234.

Lange, C. G. *The emotions (1885),* English translation. Baltimore: Williams and Wilkins, 1922.

Lautch, H. Dental phobia. *British Journal of Psychiatry,* 1971, *119,* 151–158.

Laverty, S. G. Aversion therapies in the treatment of alcoholism. *Psychosomatic Medicine,* 1966, *28,* 651–666.

Lawlis, G. F. Response styles of a patient population on the fear survey schedule. *Behaviour Research and Therapy,* 1971, *9,* 95–102.

Lazarus, H. R., & Kostan, J. J. Psychogenic hyperventilation and death anxiety. *Psychosomatics,* 1969, *10,* 14.

Lazarus, R. S. *Psychological stress and the coping process.* New York: McGraw-Hill, 1966.

Lazarus, R. S. Thoughts on the relation between emotion and cognition. *American Psychologist,* 1982, *37,* 1019–1024.

Lazarus, R. S., & Averill, J. R. Emotion and cognition with special reference to anxiety. In C. D. Spielberger (Ed.), *Anxiety: Current trends in theory and research* (Vol. 2). New York: Academic Press, 1972.

Lazarus, R. S., & Launier, R. Stress related transactions between person and environment. In L. A. Pervin & M. Lewis (Eds.), *Perspectives in interactional psychology.* New York: Plenum, 1978.

Leff, J. *Psychiatry around the globe: A transcultural view.* New York: Marcel Dekker, Inc., 1981.

Leshner, A. I. *An introduction to behavioral endocrinology.* Oxford: Oxford University Press, 1978.

Levi, L. Parameters of emotion. In L. Levi (Ed.), *Emotions: Their parameters and measurement*. New York: Raven Press, 1975.

Liebowitz, M. R., & Klein, D. F. Agoraphobia: Clinical features, pathophysiology and treatment. In D. L. Chambless & A. J. Goldstein (Eds.), *Agoraphobia: Multiple perspectives on theory and treatment*. New York: Wiley, 1982.

Lindsay, S. The fear of dental treatment. In S. Rachman (Ed.), *Contributions to medical psychology* (Vol. 3). Oxford: Pergamon, 1984.

Lipman, R. S., Covi, L., & Shapiro, A. K. The Hopkins Symptom Checklist (HSCL). *Journal of Affective Disorders*, 1979, *1*, 9–24.

Lipman, R. S., Rickels, K., Covi, L., Derogatis, L. R., & Uhlenhuth, E. H. Factors of symptom distress—doctor ratings of anxious neurotic patients. *Archives of General Psychiatry*, 1968, *21*, 328–338.

Lipowski, Z. J. Psychiatry of somatic diseases: Epidemiology, pathogenesis, classification. *Comprehensive Psychiatry*, 1975, *16*, 105–123.

Lum, L. C. The syndrome of chronic habitual hyperventilation. In O. W. Hill (Ed.), *Modern trends in psychosomatic medicine*. London: Butterworth, 1976.

Lum, L. C. Hyperventilation and anxiety state. *Journal of the Royal Society of Medicine*, 1981, *74*, 1–4.

Lykken, D. J., Macindoe, I., & Tellegen, A. Perception: Autonomic response to shock as a function of predictability in time and locus. *Psychophysiology*, 1972, *9*, 318–333.

McClure, J. L. An assessment of the prevalence of depersonalisation experiences in the general population with special reference to age and sex variation. Diploma in Psychological Medicine, London University, 1964.

McCubbin, J. A., Richardson, J. E., Langer, A. W., Kizer, J. S., & Obrist, P. A. Sympathetic neuronal function and left ventricular performance during behavioral stress in humans: The relationship between plasma catecholamines and systolic time intervals. *Psychophysiology*, 1983, *20*, 102–110.

MacNab, B. I. E., Nieuwenhuijse, B. Jansweyer, W. N. H., & Kuiper, A. Height/distance ratio as a predictor of perceived openness-enclosure of space and emotional responses in normal and phobic subjects. *Nederlands Tijdschrift voor de Psychologie*, 1978, *33*, 375–388.

McNair, D. M., & Kahn, R. J. Imipramine compared with a benzodiazepine for agoraphobia. In D. F. Klein & J. Rabkin (Eds.), *Anxiety: New research and changing concepts*. New York: Raven Press, 1981.

McReynolds, P. Assimilation and anxiety. In M. Zuckerman & C. D. Spielberger (Eds.), *Emotion and anxiety: New concepts, methods and applications*. Hillsdale, N.J.: Lawrence Erlbaum, 1976.

Magarian, G. J. Hyperventilation Syndromes: Infrequently recognised common expressions of anxiety and stress. *Medicine*, 1982, *61*, 219–237.

Malmo, R. B. Anxiety and behavioral arousal. *Psychological Review*, 1957, *64*, 276–287.

Malmo, R. B. Studies of anxiety: Some clinical origins of the activation concept. In C. Spielberger (Ed.), *Anxiety and Behavior*. New York: Academic Press, 1966.

Malpass, R. S. Theory and method in cross-cultural psychology. *American Psychologist*, 1977, *32*, 1069–1079.

Mandler, G. *Mind and emotion*. New York: Wiley, 1975.

Mandler, G. Thought processes, consciousness and stress. In V. Hamilton & D. M. Warburton (Eds.), *Human stress and cognition*. New York: John Wiley, 1979.

Mandler, G. Stress and thought process. In L. Goldberger & L. Breznitz (Eds.), *Handbook of stress: Theoretical and clinical aspects*. New York: Free Press, 1982.

Marañon, G. Contribution à l'étude de l'action emotive de l'adrenaline. *Revue Française d'Endocrinologie*, 1924, 2, 301–325.

Marks, I. M. Components and correlates of psychiatric questionnaires. *British Journal of Medical Psychology*, 1967, 40, 261–271.

Marks, I. M. Agoraphobic syndrome (phobic anxiety state). *Archives of General Psychiatry*, 1970, 23, 538–553.

Marks, I. M. Behavioral psychotherapy of adult neurosis. In S. L. Garfield & A. E. Bergin (Eds.), *Handbook of psychotherapy and behavior change*. New York: Wiley, 1978.

Marks, I. M., Gray, S., Cohen, D., Hill, R., Mawson, D., Ramm, E., & Stern, R. S. Imipramine and brief therapist-aided exposure in agoraphobics having self-exposure homework. *Archives of General Psychiatry*, 1983, 40, 153–162.

Marks, I. M., Hallam, R. S., Connolly, J. C., & Philpott, R. *Nursing in behavioural psychotherapy: An advanced clinical role for nurses*. London: Royal College of Nursing, 1977.

Marks, I. M., & Herst, E. R. A survey of 1,200 agoraphobics in Britain. *Social Psychiatry*, 1970, 5, 16–24.

Marks, I. M., & Lader, M. H. Anxiety states (anxiety neurosis): A review. *Journal of Nervous and Mental Disorder*, 1973, 156, 3–18.

Marshall, G., & Zimbardo, P. G. Affective consequences of inadequately explained physiological arousal. *Journal of Personality and Social Psychology*, 1979, 37, 970–998.

Marshall, W. L., Gauthier, J., & Gordon, A. The current status of flooding therapy. In M. Hersen, R. M. Eisler & P. M. Miller (Eds.), *Progress in behavior modification* (Vol. 7). New York: Academic Press, 1979.

Maslach, C. Negative emotional biasing of unexplained arousal. *Journal of Personality and Social Psychology*, 1979, 37, 953–969.

Mathews, A., Gelder, M. G., & Johnston, D. W. *Agoraphobia: nature and treatment*. London: Tavistock, 1981.

Mathews, A. M., Johnston, D. W., Shaw, P. M., & Gelder, M. G. Process variables and the prediction of outcome in behaviour therapy. *British Journal of Psychiatry*, 1974, 125, 256–264.

Mathews, A. M., Johnston, D. W., Lancashire, M., Munby, M., Shaw, P. M., & Gelder, M. G. Imaginal flooding and exposure to real phobic situations: Treatment outcome with agoraphobic patients. *British Journal of Psychiatry*, 1976, 129, 362–371.

Mathews, A. M., Teasdale, J., Munby, M., Johnston, D., & Shaw, P. A home-based treatment program for agoraphobia. *Behavior Therapy*, 1977, 8, 915–924.

Mathews, R. J., Ho, B. T., Francis, D. J., Taylor, D. L., & Weinman, M. L. Catecholamines and anxiety. *Acta Psychiatrica Scandinavica*, 1982, 65, 142–147.

Mavissakalian, M., & Michelson, L. Patterns of psychophysiological change in the treatment of agoraphobia. *Behaviour Research and Therapy*, 1982, 20, 349–356.

Mavissakalian, M., & Michelson, L. Self-directed in vivo exposure practice in behavioral and pharmacological treatments of agoraphobia. *Behavior Therapy*, 1983, 14, 506–519.

Mavissakalian, M., Michelson, L., & Dealy, R. S. Pharmacological treatment of agoraphobia: Imipramine versus imipramine with programmed practice. *British Journal of Psychiatry*, 1983, 143, 348–355.

Mavissakalian, M., Michelson, L., Greenwald, D., Kornblith, S., & Greenwald, M. Cognitive-behavioral treatment of agoraphobia: Paradoxical intention vs self-statement training. *Behaviour Research and Therapy*, 1983, 21, 75–86.

Mechanic, D. Social psychological factors affecting the presentation of bodily complaints. *New England Journal of Medicine*, 1972, 286, 1132–1139.

Meyers, D. H., & Grant, G. A study of depersonalisation in students. *British Journal of Psychiatry*, 1972, 121, 59–65.

Miller, S. M. Controllability and human stress: Method evidence and theory. *Behaviour Research and Therapy*, 1979, *17*, 287–304.

Milton, F., & Hafner, J. The outcome of behaviour therapy for agoraphobia in relation to marital adjustment. *Archives of General Psychiatry*, 1979, *36*, 807–811.

Mineka, S. Animal models of anxiety-based disorders: Their usefulness and limitations. Paper read at NIMH conference on anxiety and the anxiety disorders, Tuxedo, New York, September, 1983.

Misch, W. The syndrome of neurotic anxiety: The somatic and psychic components of its genesis and therapy. *Journal of Mental Science*, 1935, *81*, 389–414.

Monteiro, W., Marks, I. M., & Ramm, E. Marital adjustment and treatment outcome in agoraphobia, *British Journal of Psychiatry* (in press).

Mullaney, J. A., & Trippett, C. J. Alcohol dependence and phobias. *British Journal of Psychiatry*, 1979, *135*, 565–573.

Munby, M., & Johnston, D. W. Agoraphobia: The long-term follow-up of behavioural treatment. *British Journal of Psychiatry*, 1980, *137*, 418–427.

Munjack, D. J., & Moss, H. B. Affective disorder and alcoholism in families of agoraphobics. *Archives of General Psychiatry*, 1981, *38*, 869–871.

Murphy, J. M. Psychiatric labelling in cross-cultural perspective. *Science*, 1976, *191*, 1019–1028.

Neftel, K. A., Adler, R. H., Kappeli, L., Rossi, M., Dolder, M., Kaser, H., Bruggesser, H., & Vorkauf, H. Stage-fright in musicians: A model illustrating the effect of beta-blockers. *Psychosomatic Medicine*, 1982, *44*, 461–470.

Nemiah, J. C. Anxiety: Signal, symptom, syndrome. In S. Arieti (Ed.), *American Handbook of Psychiatry* (2nd ed., Vol. 3). New York: Basic Books, 1974.

Noyes, R., & Clancy, J. Anxiety neurosis: A five year follow-up. *Journal of Nervous and Mental Disorder*, 1976, *162*, 200–205.

Noyes, R., Clancy, J., Hoenk, P. R., & Slymen, D. J. The prognosis of anxiety neurosis. *Archives of General Psychiatry*, 1980, *37*, 173–178.

Noyes, R., Hoenk, P. P., Kuperman, S., & Slymen, D. J. Depersonalisation in accident victims and psychiatric patients. *Journal of Nervous and Mental Disorder*, 1977, *164*, 401–407.

Ohman, A., Erixon, G., & Lofberg, I. Phobias and preparedness: Phobic versus neutral pictures as conditioned stimuli for human autonomic responses. *Journal of Abnormal Psychology*, 1975, *84*, 41–45.

Ohman, A., Fredrikson, M., Hugdahl, K. Toward an experimental model for simple phobic reactions. *Behavioural Analysis and Modification*, 1978, *2*, 97–114.

Parker, G. Reported parental characteristics of agoraphobics and social phobics. *British Journal of Psychiatry*, 1979, *135*, 555–560.

Paul, G. *Insight versus desensitisation in psychotherapy*. Stanford: Stanford University Press, 1966.

Pavlov, I. P. *Psychopathology and psychiatry: Selected works*. Moscow: Foreign Languages Publishing House, 1961.

Pennebaker, J. W. *The psychology of physical symptoms*. New York: Springer-Verlag, 1982.

Peterson, C. Learned helplessness and attributional interventions in depression. In C. Antaki & C. Brewin (Eds.), *Attributions and psychological change*. London: Academic Press, 1982.

Peyser, H. Stress and alcohol. In L. Goldberger & S. Breznitz (Eds.), *Handbook of stress: Theoretical and clinical aspects*. New York: Free Press, 1982.

Pilowsky, I. Dimensions of hypochondriasis. *British Journal of Psychiatry*, 1967, *113*, 89–93.

Pilowsky, I., & Spence, N. D. Patterns of illness behaviour in patients with intractable pain. *Journal of Psychosomatic Research*, 1976, *19*, 279–287.

Pitts, F. N., & Allen, P. E. Biochemical induction of anxiety. In A. D. Pokorny & R. L. Williams (Eds.), *Phenomenology and treatment of anxiety*. New York: Spectrum, 1979.

Pitts, F. N., & McClure, J. N. Lactate metabolism in anxiety neurosis. *New England Journal of Medicine*, 1967, 277, 1329.

Plutchik, R., & Ax, A. F. A critique of "determinants of emotional state" by Schacter and Singer (1962). *Psychophysiology*, 1967, 4, 79–82.

Pratt, R. T. C., & McKenzie, W. Anxiety states following vestibular disorders, *Lancet*, 1958, 2, 347–349.

Presley, A. S. A semantic differential study of agoraphobic housewives: Aspects of self-perception and perception of others. Unpublished manuscript, Royal Dundee Liff Hospital, Scotland, 1976.

Quitkin, F. M., Rifkin, A., Kaplan, J., & Klein, D. F. Phobic anxiety syndrome complicated by drug dependence and addiction, a treatable form of drug abuse. *Archives of General Psychiatry*, 1972, 27, 159–162.

Rachman, S. The conditioning theory of fear acquisition: A critical examination. *Behaviour Research and Therapy*, 1977, 15, 375–387.

Rachman, S. *Fear and courage*. San Francisco: Freeman, 1978.

Rachman, S. Emotional processing. *Behaviour Research and Therapy*, 1980, 18, 51–60.

Rachman, S., & Hodgson, R. I Synchrony and desynchrony in fear and avoidance. *Behaviour Research and Therapy*, 1974, 12, 311–318.

Ramsay, I., Greer, S., & Bagly, C. Propanalol in neurotic and thyrotoxic anxiety. *British Journal of Psychiatry*, 1973, 122, 555–559.

Reiss, S. Pavlovian conditioning and human fear: An expectancy model. *Behavior Therapy*, 1980, 11, 380–396.

Rescorla, R. A. Pavlovian conditioned inhibition. *Psychological Bulletin*, 1969, 72, 77–94.

Rescorla, R. A., & Cunningham, C. L. The erasure of reinstated fear. *Animal Learning and Behavior*, 1977, 5, 386–394.

Reveley, A., & Murray, R. Genetic studies of anxiety neurosis. *Journal of Drug Research*, 1982, 7, 35–42.

Rickels, K. Psychopharmacological approaches to treatment of anxiety. In W. E. Fann, I. Karacan, A. D. Pokorny & R. L. Williams (Eds.), *Phenomenonology and treatment of anxiety*. New York: Spectrum, 1979.

Rin, H., & Lin, T. Mental illness among Formosan aborigines as compared with the Chinese in Taiwan. *Journal of Mental Science*, 1962, 108, 134–146.

Roberts, A. H. Housebound housewives: A follow-up study of a phobic anxiety state. *British Journal of Psychiatry*, 1964, 110, 191–197.

Ross, L., Rodin, J., & Zimbardo, P. G. Toward an attribution therapy: The reduction of fear through induced cognitive emotional misattribution. *Journal of Personal and Social Psychology*, 1969, 12, 279–288.

Roth, M. The phobic anxiety depersonalisation syndrome. *Proceedings of the Royal Society of Medicine*, 1959, 52, 587–595.

Roth, M. The phobic-anxiety-depersonalisation syndrome and some general aetiological problems in psychiatry. *Journal of Neuropsychiatry*, 1960, 1, 292–306.

Roth, M., Garside, R. F., & Gurney, C. Clinical and statistical enquiries into the classification of anxiety states and depressive disorders, In *Proceedings of Leeds Symposium on Behavioural Disorders*. London: May and Baker, 1965.

Roth, M., & Mountjoy, C. Q. The distinction between anxiety states and depressive disorders. In E. S. Paykel (Ed.), *Handbook of affective disorders*. Edinburgh: Churchill Livingstone, 1982.

Rothstein, W., Holmes, G. R., & Boblett, W. E. A factor analysis of the fear survey schedule with a psychiatric population. *Journal of Clinical Psychology*, 1972, 28, 78–80.

Rotter, J. B. Generalised expectancies for internal versus external control of reinforcement. *Psychological Monographs,* 1966, *80* (Whole No. 609).

Roy, A. Hysterical neurosis. In A. Roy (Ed.), *Hysteria.* London: Wiley, 1982.

Ryle, G. *The concept of mind.* New York: Barnes and Noble, 1949.

Sampson, E. E. Cognitive psychology as ideology. *American Psychologist,* 1981, *36,* 730–743.

Sanderson, R. E., Campbell, D., & Laverty, S. G. An investigation of a new aversive conditioning treatment for alcoholism. *Quarterly Journal of Studies on Alcohol,* 1963, *24,* 261.

Saperstein, J. C. On the phenomenon of depersonalisation. *Journal of Nervous and Mental Disorder,* 1949, *110,* 236–251.

Sarbin, T. R. Anxiety: Reification of a metaphor. *Archives of General Psychiatry,* 1964, *10,* 630–638.

Sarbin, T. R. Ontology recapitulates philology: The mythic nature of anxiety. *American Pychologist,* 1968, *23,* 411–418.

Sartory, G. Benzodiazepines and behavioural treatment of phobic anxiety. *Behavioural Psychotherapy,* 1983, *11,* 204–217.

Schacter, S., & Singer, J. Cognitive, social and physiological determinants of emotional state. *Psychological Review,* 1962, *69,* 379–399.

Schalling, D., Cronholm, B., & Asberg, N. Components of state and trait anxiety as related to personality and arousal. In L. Levi (Ed.), *Emotions: Their parameters and measurement.* New York: Raven Press, 1975.

Schapira, K., Kerr, T. A., & Roth, M. Phobias and affective illness. *British Journal of Psychiatry,* 1970, *117,* 25–32.

Schapira, K., Roth, M., Kerr, T. A., & Gurney, C. The prognosis of affective disorders: The differentiation of anxiety states from depressive illness. *British Journal of Psychiatry,* 1972, *121,* 175–181.

Schwartz, R. M. Cognitive-behavior modification: A conceptual review. *Clinical Psychology Review,* 1982, *2,* 267–293.

Schweitzer, L., & Adams, G. The diagnosis and management of anxiety for primary care physicians. In W. E. Fann, I. Karacan, A. D. Pokorny, & R. L. Williams, (Eds.), *Phenomenology and treatment of anxiety.* New York: Spectrum, 1979.

Sedman, G. Theories of depersonalisation. *British Journal of Psychiatry,* 1970, *117,* 1–14.

Seligman, M. E. P. Phobias and preparedness. *Behavior Therapy,* 1971, *2,* 307–321.

Seligman, M. E. P. *Helplessness: On depression, development and death.* San Francisco: W. H. Freeman, 1975.

Sergeant, A. G. S., & Yorkston, N. J. Some implications of using methohexitone to relax anxious patients. *Lancet,* 1968, *2,* 653–655.

Sheehan, D. V., Ballenger, J., & Jacobsen, G. Treatment of endogenous anxiety with phobic, hysterical, and hypochondriacal symptoms. *Archives of General Psychiatry,* 1980, *37,* 51–59.

Sim, M., & Houghton, H. Phobic anxiety and its treatment. *Journal of Nervous and Mental Disease,* 1966, *143,* 484–491.

Skinner, B. F. *Science and human behavior.* New York: McMillan, 1953.

Skoog, G. Onset of anancastic conditions. *Acta Psychiatrica Neurologica Scandinavica,* Supplement 184, *41,* 1965.

Smail, P., Stockwell, T., Canter, S., & Hodgson, R. Alcohol dependence and phobic anxiety states. I: A prevalence study. *British Journal of Psychiatry,* 1984, *144,* 53–57.

Snaith, R. A clinical investigation of phobias. *British Journal of Psychiatry,* 1968, *114,* 673–697.

Solyom, L., Beck, P., Solyom, C., & Hugel, R. Some etiological factors in phobic neurosis. *Canadian Psychiatric Association Journal,* 1974, *19,* 69–77.

Solyom, L., Silberfeld, M., & Solyom, C. Maternal overprotection in the etiology of agoraphobia. *Canadian Psychiatric Association Journal*, 1976, *21*, 109–113.

Solyom, C., Solyom, L., LaPierre, Y., Pecknold, J., & Morton, L. Phenelzine and exposure in the treatment of phobias. *Biological Psychiatry*, 1981, *16*, 239–247.

Sours, J. L. The "break-off" phenomenon. *Archives of General Psychiatry*, 1965, *13*, 447–456.

Stampler, F. M. Panic disorder: Description, conceptualisation, and implications for treatment. *Clinical Psychology Review*, 1982, *2*, 469–486.

Steinman, A. Cultural values, female role expectancies and therapeutic goals: Research and interpretation. In V. Franks and V. Burtle (Eds.), *Women in therapy*. New York: Brunner Mazel, 1974.

Stockwell, T., Hodgson, R., & Rankin, H. Tension reduction and the effects of prolonged alcohol consumption. *British Journal of Addiction*, 1982, *77*, 65–73.

Stockwell, T., Smail, P., Hodgson, R., & Canter, S. Alcohol dependence and phobic anxiety states II: A retrospective study. *British Journal of Psychiatry*, 1983, *144*, 58–63.

Storms, M. D., & McCaul, K. D. Attribution processes and the emotional exacerbation of dysfunctional behavior. In J. H. Harvey, W. J. Ickes, & R. F. Kidd (Eds.), *New directions in attribution research* (Vol. 1). Hillsdale, New Jersey: Lawrence Erlbaum, 1976.

Storms, M. D., & Nisbett, R. E. Insomnia and the attribution process. *Journal of Personality and Social Psychology*, 1970, *16*, 319–328.

Stricklund, B. R., Internal and external expectancies and health-related behaviors. *Journal of Consulting and Clinical Psychology*, 1978, *46*, 1192–1211.

Sutton-Simon, K., & Goldfried, M. R. Faulty thinking patterns in two types of anxiety. *Cognitive Research and Therapy*, 1979, 193–203.

Suzman, M. Effect of beta-blockade on the anxiety of electrocardiogram. *Post-graduate Medical Journal*, 1971, *47*, (supplement 104).

Tennant, C., Bebbington, P., & Hurry, J. The role of life events in depressive illness: Is there a substantial causal relation. *Psychological Medicine*, 1981, *11*, 379–389.

Terhune, W. The phobic syndrome: A study of 86 patients with phobic reactions. *Archives of Neurology and Psychiatry*, 1949, *62*, 162–172.

Thomas, G., & O'Callaghan, M. Pavlovian principles and behaviour therapy. In G. Davey (Ed.), *Applications of conditioning theory*. London: Methuen, 1981.

Thorpe, G. L., & Burns, L. E. The agoraphobic syndrome: *Behavioural approaches to evaluation and treatment*. Chichester: John Wiley, 1983.

Torgerson, S. The nature and origin of common phobic fears. *British Journal of Psychiatry*, 1979, *134*, 343–351.

Tyrer, P., & Lader, M. H. Response to propanalol and diazepam in somatic and psychic anxiety. *British Medical Journal*, 1974, *2*, 14–16.

Tyrer, P. *The role of bodily symptoms in anxiety* (Maudsley Monograph No. 23). Oxford: Oxford University Press, 1976.

Valins, S. The perception and labelling of bodily changes as determinants of emotional behavior. In P. Black (Ed.), *Physiological correlates of emotion*. New York: Academic Press, 1970.

Walford, R. E. People who hear a continuous hum. *Science Chelsea*, 1979, *8*(3), 7–9.

Watson, J. P., & Marks, I. M. Relevant and irrelevent fear in flooding—A crossover study of phobic patients. *Behavior Therapy*, 1971, *2*, 275–283.

Watts, F. N. Attributional aspects of medicine. In C. Antaki, & C. Brewin (Eds.), *Attributions and psychological change*. London: Academic Press, 1982.

Weekes, C. *Simple effective treatment of agoraphobia*. New York: Bantam Books, 1976.

Weissman, M. M. The epidemiology of anxiety disorders. Paper read at NIMH conference, Anxiety and anxiety disorders, Tuxedo, New York, September, 1983.

Westphal, C. Die Agoraphobie: Eine neuropathische Erscheinung. *Archiv fur Psychiatrie und Nervenkrankheiten,* 1871, *3,* 138–161.

Wheeler, E. O., White, P. D., Reed, E. W., & Cohen, M. E. Neurocirculatory asthenia (anxiety neurosis, effort syndrome, neurasthenia) 20 year follow-up study of 173 patients. *Journal of the American Medical Association,* 1950, *142,* 878–889.

Wiggins, J. S. Content dimensions in the MMPI. In J. N. Butcher (Ed.), *MMPI: Research developments and clinical application.* New York: McGraw Hill, 1969.

Williams, S. L., Dooseman, G., & Kleifield, E. Comparative effectiveness of guided mastery and exposure treatments for intractable phobias. *Journal of Consulting and Clinical Psychology,* 1984, *52,* 505–518.

Williams, S. L., & Rappoport, A. Cognitive treatment in the natural environment for agoraphobics. *Behavior Therapy,* 1983, *14,* 299–313.

Wolpe, J. *Psychotherapy by reciprocal inhibition.* Stanford: Stanford University Press, 1958.

Wolpe, J. The dichotomy between classically conditioned and cognitively learned anxiety. *Journal of Behavior Therapy and Experimental Psychiatry,* 1981, *12,* 15–42.

Woodruff, R. H., Guze, S. B., & Clayton, P. J. Anxiety neurosis among psychiatric outpatients. *Comprehensive Psychiatry,* 1972, *13,* 165–170.

Yorkston, N. J., Sergeant, H. G. S., & Rachman, S. Methohexitone relaxation for desensitising agoraphobic patients. *Lancet,* 1968, *2,* 651–653.

Zillman, D. Attribution and misattribution of excitatory reactions. In J. H. Harvey, W. Ickes, & W. F. Kidd (Eds.), *New directions in attribution research* (Vol. 2). Hillsdale, New Jersey: Lawrence Erlbaum, 1978.

Zillman, D. Treatment of excitation in emotional behaviour. In J. T. Cacioppo, & R. E. Petty (Eds.) *Social Psychophysiology.* New York: Guilford Press, 1983.

Zitrin, C. M., Klein, D. F., Woerner, M. G., & Ross, D. C. Treatment of phobias I: Comparison of imipramine hydrochloride and placebo. *Archives of General Psychiatry,* 1983, *40,* 125–138.

Zung, W. W. K. A rating instrument for anxiety disorders. *Psychosomatics,* 1971, *12,* 271–379.

Index

31